Rethinking Age in Africa

RETHINKING AGE IN AFRICA

◇◇◇◇◇◇◇◇◇◇◇◇◇◇◇◇◇◇◇◇◇◇◇◇◇◇◇◇◇◇◇

Colonial, Post-Colonial and Contemporary Interpretations of Cultural Representations

Edited by
Mario I. Aguilar

Africa World Press, Inc.

P.O. Box 1892   P.O. Box 48

Trenton, NJ 08607   Asmara, ERITREA

Africa World Press, Inc.

P.O. Box 1892
Trenton, NJ 08607

P.O. Box 48
Asmara, ERITREA

Copyright © 2007 Mario I. Aguilar
First Printing 2007

Book design: Saverance Publishing Services (SPS)
Cover design: Ashraful Haque and SPS
Cover photos: WHO/P. Virot

Library of Congress Cataloging-in-Publication Data

Rethinking age in Africa : colonial, post-colonial, and contemporary interpretations of cultural representations / edited By Mario I. Aguilar.
   p. cm.
   Includes bibliographical references and index.
   ISBN 1-59221-494-0 (hard cover) -- ISBN 1-59221-495-9 (pbk.)
   1. Age groups--Africa. 2. Aging--Social aspects--Africa. 3. Older
   people--Africa--Social conditions.   4. Intergenerational relations--
Africa.
   5. Social change--Africa. 6. Africa--Social conditions--1960-   .
   I. Aguilar, Mario I.
   GN645.R48 2006
   305.2096--dc22

                              2006014904

To Paul Baxter
[A *gadamoji* for all those who study age]
Nagaat!

To the memory of Fr. Brendan O'Reilly SVD +2000
[A wise elder who believed in the young and helped them in
their rebellions]
Ubi caritas et amor, Ubi caritas Deus ibi est!

Table of Contents

PROLEGOMENA

It was in September 1998 at the biennial meeting of the African Studies Association of the United Kingdom (School of Oriental and African Studies, London) that *The Politics of Age and Gerontocracy in Africa: Ethnographies of the Past and Memories of the Present* (Africa World Press, 1998) was presented to Paul Spencer.

At that meeting, Kassahun Checole, President and Publisher of the Red Sea Press and the Africa World Press reiterated his interest in the topic of age in relation to Africa. My gratitude to him and the staff at the AWP for encouraging the preparation of this second volume on age in Africa.

This volume is dedicated to Paul Baxter, who conducted studies on age among Boorana in northern Kenya and further studies on the Arssi and Oromo peoples in general. Paul and Pat Baxter have over the years encouraged all those working on age and particularly those working on the study of the Oromo. Thus, their home in Bramhall, Cheshire (England), has been a true home for many of us. Without such encouragement many younger scholars would not have persevered in their own studies. To Paul and Pat, greetings and Peace! - From all contributors and also from young Sara.

As I was toiling through the editing of the manuscript I received the sad news of the death of Brendan O'Reilly. Brendan was a remarkable man in that he had the gift of encouraging others to try to understand and live more committed lives in Africa. He welcomed me when I arrived in Kenya in 1987 and 1992 and he showed enormous enthusiasm about issues of age among Boorana. He very reluctantly returned to his home country Ireland, but with Africa in his heart. He died of a sudden heart attack in June of 2000. Brendan, Nagaat! Rest in Peace.

Other volumes on age are in preparation and hopefully they will be of interest to Africans and western scholars. The volumes will continue bringing in new scholarship and contemporary research on Africa, and issues related to history and anthropology, religion and politics, the old and the young in the dynamic scenarios of African nations, cities, towns, villages and societies.

Mario I. Aguilar
St. Andrews, Scotland, September 2005

Introduction

THE PRESENT AND THE PAST OF AGE NOTIONS: THE *STATUS QUAESTIONIS* WITHIN HISTORICAL ANTHROPOLOGY

Mario I. Aguilar

The cultural idea of age is certainly central for African societies. The old, the 'elders', the ancestors, and those with knowledge occupy a central place in most African societies. Notions of age, therefore, are defined and limited by their local construction, and the way in which narratives and stories about those notions are produced and contested by members of a particular society. As in the case of the Tuareg, 'cultural elaborations of age conform to observations about power, personal destiny, notions of personal agency, and reproductive symbolism over the life course that are widespread in African rituals and cosmologies' (Rasmussen 1997:viii, cf. Aguilar 1999).

Therefore, it is the life course that embodies the possibility of any ongoing representation, understanding, and social construction of age. The life course defines identities and perceptions, in the individual and the social realm. Through ritual and social celebrations of the life course individuals are not only made into social beings, but they are also taught how to behave (or misbehave) within certain social patterns. Thus, classical monographs on African societies constructed notions of sociability and personhood within a localized understanding, and self-contained societies. Works by Victor Turner, for example, expressed the social beauty of a 'symbolic forest', through which the Ndembu of Zambia, became every year renewed in their social and their individual identity (Turner 1967). Rites of passage, as suggested by Van Gennep, had certain characteristics and social moments, however they expressed change and continuity, life and death, youthfulness as well as elderhood, the sociability of the living as well as of the dead (the ancestors).

THE PROBLEM OF HISTORY AND CHANGE

Such rich ethnographic work became associated with the geographically and culturally bounded-societies that could be studied in isolation. Changes within Africa that were already present in colonial times brought other elements to the study of age. Conversion as change provided symbolic and religious elements from other traditions that were not existent before in those 'isolated societies'. Notions of age remained culturally constructed, however within a rational choice of belonging that could separate issues of language, ethnicity, social and religious practices (Aguilar 1995).

Within past bounded-societies, the study of age-systems was associated with the actual study of age within Africa, as a response to the need to know, to organize and to classify on the part of clearly defined ethnic groups. Those systems were very complex and required linear and mathematical explanations. They, nevertheless accounted, in the eyes of the anthropologist, for clear changes and progressions, marked by communal and individual rituals. The fact that all other possibilities of understanding age within Africa were not considered crucial within anthropology speaks as much of a certain colonial attitude as a difficulty by Europeans to cope with change and the uncertainty of variation and difference. One must remember that the colonial enterprise could be defined as a science, of ordering, that required colonial functionaries in order to be carried through (Mudimbe 1988). However, as a result of such colonial enterprise notions of age, as well as many others, were contested and significant changes within the social structures of African societies were also manipulated and implemented.

For example, the challenges posed by Christian missionaries to African rites of passage expressed the clash between cultures as well as the clash between different symbolic systems (Hinga 1998). Such diversity of classificatory systems in constant interaction with each other needed to be studied with tools such as those provided by the history of culture and the history of religion. Thus, anthropological perceptions of age-notions had to be complemented with a thorough investigation on how those notions and the systems that expressed those notions evolved, changed and in some cases became obsolete in the past.

The past and the present textualization of such notions remain as the current aim of the study of age within the contemporary world of Africa, within the continent and in the diaspora. While the study of past notions of age constitute an interpretative project, the study of contemporary developments in the understanding of particular African notions of age relates to an inter-disciplinary project which encompasses the work of anthropologists and historians of culture and/or historians of religion.

THE ESSAYS IN THIS VOLUME

This collection of essays builds upon the theoretical parameters already suggested in the 'Introduction' to *The Politics of Age and Gerontocracy in Africa* (Aguilar 1998b), and in the different chapters within that volume. This is the sequel, the second volume of such investigation and hopefully the second of several to come. In such volumes contributors provide an overview of a particular notion of age in a particular context within Africa so as to enrich our further understanding of contemporary African life.

It is clear that the Status Quaestionis of an anthropology of age, of a historical study of age and of a socio-religious understanding of symbolic classifications of the old and of the young rests within the challenge of understanding such change today and in the years to come. It is not possible to answer the central question 'Is the concept of age culturally constructed or is it a biological typology related to human development?' in a few essays. New contributions in the psychology of aging (Stuart-Hamilton 2000), and on the cross-cultural study of aging (Sokolovsky 1997) have made important complementary contributions to the contemporary debate on aging in general. However, the question, the answers and the subject itself keep changing. The *mutatio societatis* creates already a conflict.

Therefore the question of age is rethought within these essays in a multi-cultural and poli-semantic manner. However, such poli-semantic axiom continues to be located within Africa and its peoples. If the study of age and its cultural construction requires a political act of self-assertion and cultural richness, as suggested in the previous volume, in this collection of essays authors try to rethink ethnographic materials through fieldwork, historical archival research, aesthetic interpretations and social contradictions.

Some readers will feel that this collection offers essays on particular aspects of age, it does not provide a final answer to our question and certainly that the authors do not share the same argument. Indeed, this volume reflects the social process of aging in itself. It is unpredictable, contradictory, intense and articulated in many different ways. However, as life has to be lived, age as a social process has to be explored. Thus, if history and anthropology, text and fieldwork seem to be central in order to understand African societies, the old and the young in Africa as individuals start to appear on the research agenda.

For example, two chapters (L. Aguilar and Law) deal with a meta-narrative of individuality in which African artists describe reality through art, and at the same time they describe changes in themselves and their historical experiences. In fact, they both bring the complexity of the individual and that of art into the contemporary debate on age and its notion's creation. Other essays show the diversity of changes in the perception of particular notions of age.

In chapter one Kathleen Smythe explores the history of the Fipa of Tanzania and their encounter with Christian missionaries. For the Fipa patterns of sleeping and changes in those patterns were associated with growing up and becoming older. Such notions were challenged by Christian missionaries. They stressed an individual's initiation into the Church and the reception of the sacraments of initiation. Thus, notions of age changed and became diversified rather than culturally unified.

In chapter two Thomas Burges explores the same cultural and colonial encounter within Tanganyika and Zanzibar. Within such colonial discourse, effective measures were taken in order to control the possible laziness and rebelliousness of the youth.

Football clubs and youth groups were effectively used by the colonial administrator in order to challenge youth 'idleness' associated by the colonial administration with nationalism. This historical exploration suggests clearly that the presence of the youth in urban centers created similar problems as those experienced by the young themselves in contemporary Africa. Those youth were out of the cultural control that would have been exercised by the old in the past.

In chapter three Julianne Freeman describes the ritual roles assigned to senior Bamana women in the Beledugu region of Mali. As different modes of knowledge are present among contemporary Bamana, senior women continue their work of passing knowledge to younger women, within moments of central importance to any community, such as birth or death.

In chapter four Maria Cattell explores issues of power and kinship and their implications for development in the context of Abaluyia women of Kenya. It is clear that older women are less powerful now than in the past and that there is lots of poverty among them. Thus, the old have less contact with the young, who aspire to go to school and who spend most of their time in school related activities. Cattell makes the case that processes of development should include older women and their indigenous views of society and its running.

In chapter five Bahira Sherif describes changes in family life and the role of parents and older members of the family in Cairo, Egypt. She suggests that enormous changes have taken place, and that changes over the life course have had profound effects on the lives of men and women in terms of status, access to resources and opportunities, and potential problems and disadvantages.

In chapter six Seyoum Hameso explores the problems and advantages of the Sidama age-system in Ethiopia. Hameso's view as a Sidama himself is that changes in administrative policy that resulted in economic crisis and oppression by the Abyssinians did not allow the Sidama age-system to continue. However, he challenges views that suggest that older systems do not have solutions for contemporary problems by suggesting that in times of crisis older men should be allowed to guide others, restoring them the privileges they had in the past through an organized age-system.

In chapter seven Stella Herzog explores changes among the old within the Nnewi Igbo of Nigeria. In a society that has had enormous mobility in migration and had access to education she suggests that the power of the elders should remain as the central point of cohesion for an ever-changing society.

In chapter eight Theophilos Rifiotis undertakes a comparative and analytical exercise on rituals of initiation among the Makonde (Mozambique), Mbala (Democratic Republic of Congo), Tumbuka-Kamanga (Malawi), Tshokwe (Angola) and Luba (Democratic Republic of Congo). Through the analysis of stories and myths Rifiotis suggests that the inherent conflict between groups of different ages is resolved by a common oral understanding of proper sociability. The tension, however, does exist and needs to be explored further.

In chapter nine Jennifer Law explores the life and work of a South African artist, Penny Siopis. In doing so, Law suggests that there is a creative force that comes out of the biographical and the autobiographical. Thus, she sets an agenda of aesthetic interpretation trying to elucidate the personal and the aging process within the social and the political of a particular present.

In chapter ten Laurel Birch de Aguilar explores some of the multiple biographical and aesthetical changes of Cuthy Mede, a Malawian artist. Rendering the object into text, as well as the spoken and written words about art in general, she explores several paintings of Mede and links those paintings with aspects of his life. This analysis strongly suggests the changing perceptions of aging as well as the influences on the maturation process of Mede as a member of society and Mede as a creative artist.

In chapter eleven M. Aguilar explores the ways in which to be old is mirrored by the cultural constructions of the young among the Boorana of Kenya. Within a traditional setting of Kenya pastoralists the young have to find new ways by which to re-invent themselves within traditional cultural categories. However, their life outside their place of birth and outside the influence of their parents and relatives becomes strongly related to economic and symbolic resources that keep a continuity with the cultural ways of the old.

It is such description of the young and their perception of reality that complements the study of older members of society. Thus, such notion provides a bridge between studies of gerontocracy and the recipients of gerontocratic systems, the young in Africa today. It is clear that more studies of the young need to be undertaken if the notion of age associated solely with the old is to be fully understood.

References

Aguilar, Mario I. 1995. 'African Conversion from a World Religion: Religious Diversification by the Waso Boorana in Kenya', *Africa: Journal of the International African Institute* 65 (4): 525-544.

Aguilar, Mario I. 1998a. *Being Oromo in Kenya*. Trenton, N.J.: Africa World Press.

Aguilar, Mario I. 1998b. Ed.. *The Politics of Age and Gerontocracy in Africa: Ethnographies of the Past and Memories of the Present*. Trenton, N.J.: Africa World Press.

Aguilar, Mario I. 1999. Review of Susan J. Rasmussen, *The Poetics and Politics of Tuareg Aging: Life Course and Personal Destiny in Niger*, *Journal of the Royal Anthropological Institute* 5 (1): 130-131.

Hinga, T.M. 1998. 'Christianity and Female Puverty Rites in Africa: The Agikuyu Case', in *Rites of Passage in Contemporary Africa*, ed. James L. Cox. Cardiff: Cardiff Academic Press, 168-197.

Mudimbe, V.Y. 1988.*The Invention of Africa: Gnosis, Philosophy, and the Order of Knowledge*. Bloomington and Indianapolis: Indiana University Press and London: James Currey.

Rasmussen, Susan J. 1997. *The Poetics and Politics of Tuareg Aging: Life Course and Personal Destiny in Niger*. Dekaln, IL: Northern Illinois University Press.

Sokolovsky, Jay. 1997. Ed. *The Cultural Context of Aging: Worldwide Perspectives*. 2nd Edition. Westport, Connecticut and London: Bergin & Garvey.

Stuart-Hamilton, Ian. 2000. *The Psychology of Ageing: An Introduction*. 3rd. Edition. London: Jessica Kingsley Publishers.

Turner, Victor. 1967. *The Forest of Symbols: Aspects of Ndembu Ritual*. Ithaca and London: Cornell University Press.

Chapter 1

WHERE ONE SLEPT MATTERED: FIPA SOCIALIZATION AND CULTURAL PERCEPTIONS OF GROWTH IN NKANSI, UFIPAA[1]

Kathleen R. Smythe

Initiation has received much more scholarly attention than any other facet of African childhood (Beidelman 1997, Richards 1956, Spencer 1988, Swantz 1970). While researchers of African societies have rightly observed that initiation and accompanying circumcision ceremonies are an important rite within an individual's childhood, technically in most societies initiation is the endpoint of childhood, the critical liminal phase during which a child 'died' and an adult individual was 'born' (Droogers 1980). An emphasis on initiation alone, though perhaps encapsulating cultural values in an intense way is not enough. If we want to fully understand how a boy grows to be an adult or, as in the case here, how a girl or boy grows to be a Nkansi adult woman or man, we also need to look towards processes outside initiation. There is much that a child learns about her culture in the 'comings and goings in everyday routine' (Beidelman 1997: 26) that 'speak to the same issues as initiation rites and even foreshadow initiation patterns' (Ottenberg 1989: xiii). During Kaguru initiation in Tanzania, for example, boys were removed from the village and their natal families to live in the bush. The significance of receiving initiation lessons in the bush, 'a realm of dangerous disorder' but also 'a source of enormous, potentially useful force', however, only has meaning to the initiate if he has already learned about the power and danger of the bush earlier in his childhood. Initiation can only be potent if the boy already has an understanding of his culture and his place in society.

Initiation, then, is but one of many ways in which African societies have socialized their young. Initiation not only marks a child's physical and mental maturation, but also aids in his/her socialization. It is the same with other markers and measures of a child's intellectual, social and physiological development. In most African societies, including the one where this study takes place, these other markers tell us important things about what it means to be a child in that particular culture. By looking beyond initiation, we learn more about the fundamental relationships and experiences through which a child learns about himself and his culture over a number of years than we ever could by examining particular rites of initiation which, though often intense, are of a relatively short duration.

In this chapter, I will address the ways in which Fipa recalled their own growth and socialization as they matured in the early and mid-twentieth century and some of the ways in which socialization changed in subsequent years. By charting and exploring Fipa cultural perceptions of development, I seek to answer two questions: (1) how did Fipa children learn to be Fipa adults in the early and mid-twentieth century? And, (2) how did the presence of Catholic missionaries affect not only the way Fipa children were socialized but their perceptions of a child's development.

THEORETICAL BACKGROUND

This study of socialization and African childhood in Nkansi draws on the foundations laid by numerous scholars in several fields. In varied ways, Sigmund Freud, Erik Erikson, and Jean Piaget developed models for human development in their own cultures that have been very influential in academic circles (Erikson 1950, Jacobs 1992, Piaget 1963). Freud and Piaget in particular assumed that human development is primarily determined by our biology and conceived of models to help us understand growth universally without much concern for other social or cultural influences. We must 'start with a recognition of the biologically given, ... [with] what all human beings have in common' (Mead and Wolfenstein 1955: 6). However, we must also recognize the fundamental role culture plays in determining how a people recognize, respond to and incorporate the intellectual, social and physiological transitions of childhood into their culture. As we shall see below, changes in sleeping location in Ufipa were driven by concerns derived from human sexuality and, in this way, were biologically driven. Yet, decisions about where and with whom children should sleep at different ages were cultural responses to problems presented by biology. From these responses, we learn much about Fipa cultural values and important relationships for Fipa children.

Starting with Margaret Mead (1930), anthropologists have stressed the vital importance of culture on a child's development (Mead and Wolfenstein 1955). In the 1960s six pairs of scholars from Harvard chose six different cultures and, armed with an identical research design and questions, went to the field to study children in cross-cultural perspective (Whiting 1963). They hoped to find out how much of childhood was culturally determined. I follow in Mead's footsteps. I take the cultural context to be of crucial importance but differ from Mead in that I wish to understand childhood in Ufipa for its own sake rather than in an effort to compare it to childhood or models of childhood in another society.

Ethno-pediatrics is the latest field to emerge from this school of thought and is concerned with how child-rearing techniques, such as approaches to sleeping and crying, are not only determined by biology but also by cultural influences. The !Kung, a hunter-gathering society in southern Africa, emphasize development of motor skills more than American parents who emphasize early independence of their children. Japanese parents, on the other hand, work at integrating children into their families and, in particular, in cultivating a mother-child bond (Small 1998). How have Fipa farmers constructed Fipa children? What do they emphasize in the maturation of their future generations?

Other scholars have examined childhood within a particular cultural context. O. F. Raum was one of the first to do so in Africa and wrote a detailed study of Chaga childhood (Raum 1940). Simon Ottenberg described and analyzed Igbo boys' lives from birth through initiation, maintaining that a boy's early separation from his mother is essential in order to create a mature male in Afikpo society. This early separation is reinforced at the time of initiation. Ottenberg argues, and I would agree, that even though the years before and after initiation are often neglected, they are fundamental to the maturation process and to an individual's socialization and enculturation (Ottenberg 1989: xv).

In Jean Davison's historical study of Kikuyu women, we can see quite clearly how one developmental stage or rite builds on another. One of the Kikuyu women with whom Jean Davison worked, Wanjiku, described different pre-initiation rites in her childhood as painful but not as painful as circumcision. With each rite, Wanjiku declared, she was 'buying maturity with pain' (Davison 1994: 59). In this life narrative, then, one can see the progressive way in which Kikuyu adults socialized and instructed their female children in what it meant to be a woman in Kikuyu society. This study is intended to focus on how Fipa themselves talk about their development. If Wanjiku 'bought her maturity with pain', how did Fipa view their stages of childhood?

THE FIPA BACKGROUND

The area today known as Ufipa in Tanzania lies between Lakes Rukwa and Tanganyika in the southwestern corner of the country. The term Fipa homogenizes a dozen or so smaller groups who speak different, but often mutually intelligible, languages. The eponym is also the result of several historical processes. The identity of the inhabitants of this region was formed over the last two hundred years as members of two large kingdoms - Nkansi and Lyangalile. Fipa identity was further solidified during German colonial rule when the area was known as the Ufipa district. The data here represent information collected from a sub-area of Ufipa, the modern-day district of Nkansi (with close historical parallels to the kingdom of Nkansi). The Fipa language, as recorded here, is the particular language, *iciKandaasi*, spoken by the people in and around Chala, the base for my fieldwork.[2] However, I will use Fipa to refer to the people and Kifipa to refer to the language presented here because that is most often how people of Chala and Nkansi describe themselves and their language to outsiders today.

Fipa villages, before Ujamaa villagization in the 1970s, were generally small and divided from other settlements by bush or cultivated land or both. Many older Fipa described living in settlements of 10-50 houses as they grew up. Membership was largely, though not exclusively, determined by kinship ties. By the 1940s and 1950s villages were growing larger and often contained 100 or more houses. The changes in sleeping location described below occurred within this village or extended family setting. As colonial economic change impacted Ufipa, some men and women were drawn to earn wages in other parts of the colony and extended Fipa families began to splinter, but the majority of Fipa, until quite recently, grew up in the geographical space of a village area.

In Nkansi, children experienced their own maturation as a process of successive sleeping arrangements that reflected and facilitated increasing social integration and responsibility. There was neither initiation nor circumcision of boys or girls and no elaborate rites of passage for either sex, individually or as a group.[3] Where a child slept, with parents, grandparents, or peers, was part of the growth process and a significant part of his cultural training. Changes in sleeping location were closely related to cultural perceptions of the stages of development. Significant points of transition are described in Kifipa by the verb *ukuchenjela* (to become intelligent/aware) and echoed in three stages of childhood, *umwanche uncheche* (small child), *umwanche* (child), and *unsungu* (girl) or *unumendo* (boy). Elderly Fipa used those terms to describe their own process of growth. They also used those terms in order to mark a child's increasing awareness of the world around her.[4] There were, then, three ways of noting a child's development in Nkansi. Firstly, by gaining awareness (primarily attuned to intellectual growth but also concerned with social growth). Secondly, by observing stages of childhood (which were reflections of physical and intellectual growth). Thirdly, by the implementation of changes in their sleeping location (which were driven by a need to control sexuality within the family but facilitated social and intellectual growth as well). Each one of those notions assumed distinct periods or stages in their social life. At the same time, however, each stage was flexible enough to meet the challenges presented by Fipa of varying backgrounds and abilities as well as those presented by Catholic missionaries (except in the case of sleeping location as we shall see later).

FIPA CULTURAL PERCEPTIONS OF GROWTH

Sleeping with Mother. A Fipa infant, *umwanche uncheche*, first slept with her mother at least until she was weaned. How long a child breast-fed and remained sleeping in her parents' home depended on individual circumstances. Although two or three years were the norm, two elderly Fipa, who were the last born, recalled breast-feeding until the age of five. Last-born children often breast-fed many years because there was no reason to wean them. While five years was long for the early part of this century, it reflects generally longer periods of breast-feeding than in the present-day. As the century progressed and women had more children, the period of breast-feeding diminished.[5] Though most children remembered little of this stage, one of the elderly Fipa who nursed until the age of five did remember it.

> D: I was nursing, even in the night I was nursing at the age of five.
> K: Until the age of five?
> D: Yes.... Five years I nursed. I went to herd goats, and when I returned sweating I went to my mother, 'Sit

so that I may nurse'. She said, 'You, sir!' My mother's breasts were full and I nursed *choot* [mimicking the sound], I nursed a lot until it was spilling. Until she said, 'Go away and play'. Until I was five years old (DC, 15 May 1995, Chala).[6]

Even if children remembered little of this stage, the importance of nursing at one's mother's breast was central to a child's sense of self and belonging. When I visited the village of Majengo, a diminutive man entered the house where I was sitting with my hosts, resting between interviews, and insisted on telling me his story that I recorded in brief. He told me that his mother had died when he was very young, so he missed suckling at his mother's breast and never stayed with one relative a very long time. The way he told the story and insisted on being heard indicated that he carried this loss around with him still. Another man in his sixties believed that many of his problems stemmed from his unfortunate childhood. He believed that he still had to work so hard because he had grown up without his biological mother and was instead raised by his grandparents (JS, 14 January 1995, Chala). Fipa's reverence for their mothers indicates that what a child remembers and learns from childhood on is important. However, it is also important what the child is told and less distinctly remembers about his early years alongside his mother (as it should be) or a substitute (in other cases).

Sleeping with Grandparents. A four to five year old that was not constantly watched was called *umwanche*, a child, whether male or female. This stage was associated with becoming increasingly aware of the wider world and understanding one's relationship to other people and one's responsibilities. It was also usually linked to a change in sleeping location, often to a grandparent's house or at least to a room separate from the parents', and by beginning to learn to work around the house, field, and farm.

Ukuchenjela[7] was closely associated with the years of *uumwanche*, childhood. It is most literally translated as 'to become intelligent'. It was often used interchangeably with *kupata amano*, *kupata amalango*, or *kupata akili*, 'to get intelligence' in Kifipa and in Kiswahili. A better translation might be, 'to obtain the capacity for intelligence' because they rarely meant that suddenly one became intelligent but that one now had the capacity to become so. But such a translation misses some of its' meaning, for when Fipa used it in telling the stories of their childhood, they also meant, 'when I became aware of the world around me'. As we will see in the bits of recollections that follow, in their discourse, Fipa often pinpoint *ukuchenjela* as occurring at a specific point in their early years. This reflects the fact that in their memory, the process of gaining intelligence or the capacity for intelligence has been captured at a certain moment.

Ukuchenjela was so closely tied to childhood and not later points in a child's development because Fipa link *ukuchenjela* with memory. When a child began to understand events, he or she also began to remember them as well and thus started 'becoming aware/intelligent'. It is these early memories that constitute the beginning of *uumwanche*, childhood. Several people I interviewed described themselves as becoming aware while engaging in a certain task or living with a relative other than their birth mother, confirming the associations between awareness, learning of tasks, and sleeping with a relative other than one's mother. For example, MC and several others began their narratives talking about herding cows as small children. When I asked MC how old she was when she started herding, she said that she did not know but it was after she became intelligent (MC, 14 October 1995, Chala: EK, 18 February 1996, Msilihofu). Another man associated becoming intelligent with living at his aunt's. He began his narrative in this way:

> *Mzee*: When I began to be intelligent [*napata amano, nachenjela*], they gave me, they took me to my [paternal] aunt.... When I awoke she started to teach me how to work, to farm with strength, and ... to carry a load of firewood. So I worked and was growing up [*nankula*] at the same time. When I became intelligent [*nduchenjela*], they took me to school.

A bit later he continued:

K: Why did your mother take you to live with your aunt?

Mzee: Because my aunt did not have a child. They said, 'Let's give her a child to help her with the work'.

K: How many years did you live with your aunt?

Mzee: I woke up at her place. They took me from the time when I did not have much intelligence [*amano*] (KM, 21 January 1996, Chala).

Mzee clearly shows the importance of intelligence (in all its various stages) in the growth of a Fipa child. He contradicts himself as to when he began gaining intelligence because in these early years it is a way of marking the significant points of childhood. He first noted that it occurred after his move, then while he learned to work, and finally when he went to school. The association of becoming intelligent with school is a more contemporary use of the term. Even though becoming intelligent is a gradual process for all children, in Fipa discourse it is closely tied to the period of childhood, *uumwanche*. In particular, when a child began to remember events was when she began to be aware of the world around her and her place in it.

One of the components of *uumwanche* is sleeping at one's grandparents. Similar to other places in Africa, many Fipa children did not remain sleeping in their parents' home until marriage. Young children, after being weaned, went to stay with their grandmother in the evening. Christine Obbo noted that Baganda children were often sent to stay with grandparents or some other relatives so often that people who stayed with other relatives were known by the name *Bakirerese* (Obbo 1988: 107, Smythe 1997b). Raum noted a similar practice in Chagaland whereby grandparents had rights in their grandchildren. Customarily, the first-born child was given to the paternal grandfather and the second child went to stay with the maternal grandparents for as little as a year or, perhaps, until she married (Raum 1940: 157-158).

Similarly, elder Fipa explained that it was their custom to send children, particularly first-born children, to live with grandparents, often for an unspecified period of time. Until quite recently, it was fairly common for parents and paternal grandparents (and sometimes maternal grandparents) to all live in the same village so that a move did not necessitate moving too far from one's natal home. Though not all children, like *Mzee* above, slept with their grandparents, it was considered the norm by those with whom I spoke and almost half of older Fipa I met had spent time living at their grandparents'. Some children ended up living with grandparents on the death of their mother. In my interviews, grandmothers more than any other female members, such as aunts, became the caretakers of orphans. This suggests that culturally Fipa grandmothers were seen as natural caretakers of their grandchildren.

Many Fipa, like *Mzee* above and Sr. Priscila below, made the move to another relative's before becoming aware.

> P: When I was a child [*mtoto*, Swahili], I stayed at my mother's. But when my mother got a second child, I went to stay with my grandmother because I was the first child and my mother needed to care for the [second] child.
>
> K: How old were you when the second child was born? Do you know? Just to estimate?
>
> P: ... maybe I was two years old....
>
> K: Yes, and what especially do you remember about staying at your grandmother's?
>
> P: ... The time I went to her place, grandmother was pregnant so she did not carry me a lot.... But I ate well. I slept on the floor on a goatskin or cow hide .... When I began to be intelligent [*kupata akili*, Swahili] I knew that my grandmother slept on a bed and we were lying on the floor with her children.... I was the lone grandchild at that time because my mother was my grandmother's first-born.
>
> K: So did you grow up [*ulikulia*, Swahili] at your mother's or at your grandmother's?
>
> P: I grew up [*nilikulia*] at grandmother's (Sr. Priscila Ndegeya, 2 March 1996, Sumbawanga).

As an *umwanche* the custom was to stay with a grandparent in the evening, but sometimes circumstances made this impractical. If a child's grandparents did not live nearby, she might move to a friend's grandparents or at least to another room or dwelling in the family compound that she would share with other similarly aged children. Or a girl might sleep at her grandmother's and then return to her parents very early in the morning in order to do the necessary work at home, as did one woman who was the eldest daughter in her family (EK, 4 September 1995, Chala). If grandparents lived far away, it was possible to go and stay with them for a relatively brief period of time rather than for the duration of one's childhood. A sixty-five year old man recalled going 'to greet' his grandfather for a year on Lake Tanganyika. There he herded his father's and grandfather's cows (EK, 18 February 1996, Msilihofu).

At this stage in childhood, though, it was important to move away from one's parents' bedroom and to begin learning about one's culture and relatives. The best way to achieve both these objectives was to live with grandparents who were moral and cultural educators. Moving to one's grandparents widened the social arena in which a child lived as he then had more contact with the older members of the village. Evenings were usually spent around a fire listening to riddles, stories, or songs that were meant to educate as well as entertain.

For Fipa, like many other Africans, grandparents, as members of an alternate generation, had especially close relationships with their grandchildren (Smythe 1997b, Raum 1940: 159). It was particularly important in some cases for first-born children to have the opportunity to live with grandparents if they could offer them more love and nurture than their parents whose energies were often divided, between work and other small children. Many Fipa had very fond memories of their grandparents with whom they were more willing to share problems such as illness, difficult relationships and menstruation (VC, 18 February 1996, Msilihofu; EK, 4 April 1996, Chala).

Though the most important benefits of living with grandparents, as far as this study is concerned, were in terms of education and socialization, this arrangement endured because it met other needs as well. As children became aware and could begin to question their parents' activities at night or as children grew and the potential for incest increased, children needed a separate place to sleep. Because Fipa houses in the first half of the century were small dome-shaped houses with only one living space, children were forced to sleep elsewhere. Clearly, however, as in the case of Sr. Priscila above, grandparents could still be sexually active. It is likely that the intimacy achieved by members of alternate generations made such an arrangement more acceptable than children sleeping near sexually active parents.

Parents also benefited from grandparents' assistance in child rearing. For example, Sr. Priscila went to live with her maternal grandmother when her mother had a second child, even though her grandmother was still bearing children herself. One woman explained that grandmothers, who were more experienced at raising children, could help ease the transition to a second child for their daughters.

> M: If a woman has married and given birth, she sits and nurses him. When she becomes pregnant again, that small child [*mtoto mdogo*, Kiswahili]... is taken to her grandmother's....
> K: Ahh. And they do this with every child or just the first child?
> M: Especially the first child.
> K: Because?
> M: Because they know she does not yet know how to care for that infant [*mtoto mdogo*] and he will disturb her. She does not yet have the experience of caring for a family (MC, 14 April 1996, Chala).

In addition, Sr. Priscila and others noted that they ate well at their grandparents suggesting that older families were more established and often had a larger quantity and a greater variety of food because of their status in the community (EK, 19 July 1995, Chala).[8] Finally, for grandparents there was an emotional and physical benefit because grandchildren helped with work such as herding cows, collecting firewood, or hauling water and kept their grandparents' company as they grew older.

Beginning to work and learning to perform simple tasks is the third characteristic of *uumwanche* to be considered. While work was associated with this stage of childhood, what was most significant in the eyes of elders was that the child, boy or girl learn to work and be obedient than that he or she learn to perform only certain gendered tasks. A more rigid reinforcement of gendered work roles came in the next stage of childhood.

The lack of distinction between male and female in the term *umwanche* reflects a general lack of concern for gender distinctions until a child reached the age of puberty. Boys and girls played together and tasks, though nominally gender-divided, were usually done by the child who was available regardless of gender. This differs greatly from the situation reported at Afikpo by Ottenberg, where Igbo are particularly attentive to the gender of a child from birth and boys separated increasingly from females from the age of five on (Ottenberg 1988).

According to Fipa cultural norms, females cooked, grounded flour, fetched water, took care of younger siblings, swept and worked on the farm. Males collected firewood, herded cows and other stock and worked on the farm. But, circumstances often required individuals to trespass on these norms. An older woman, born in 1925, for example, told me that her first children were all boys so she taught them to carry water and to perform other tasks normally reserved for female children (VK, 15 January 1995, Chala). A man in his seventies related how the coincidence of a house full of boys and a sickly mother necessitated his learning and performing all the tasks that girls usually did.

> I: ... we were all boys.... Therefore because Mom was not well, what could we do? We had to fetch water and cook on the fire and I even had to grind flour.
> K: To grind flour? (laughs!)
> I: Yes.
> K: And you swept?
> I: Of course.

> K: How was it if your friends came and found you
> cooking, sweeping or grinding, what did they say?
> I: There was nothing to say because if I was sweeping
> and they saw mother, it was a normal thing (IL, 18
> February 1996).

Tasks, like grinding or herding, were more closely associated with gender than most of the others and yet even these, as we saw above, were not rigidly adhered to. Two of the women I talked with had herded cattle for a number of years. One of them was recruited by her parents because she had no male siblings, the other because her brothers were much younger than she. One of the women remembered missionary priests disapproving of the girls' herding because they feared the girls would fail to learn the work of the home. The missionaries asked Fipa parents to put an end to such practices. But MC told me that not only did she herd but that she was expected to perform the more feminine tasks as well. She fetched water, ground millet, cooked and swept in the afternoon after she had finished caring for the stock (MC, 14 October 1995, Chala; PS, 8 September 1995, Chala). Such insistence that these tasks be performed by children, no matter what their gender is, suggests that Fipa (unlike the European missionaries) were much more concerned with utilizing children's labor and training children to be obedient helpmates around the home, than socializing them to narrow channels of behavior. Furthermore, such crossover of roles, particularly during the period of childhood, reinforces the notion that gender distinctions at this point in time were not significant.[9]

By the end of *uumwanche*, a child was ten or twelve years old. *Wachenjela*, she had become fully aware or intelligent, in the eyes of the community, and was now able to function as an independent figure in the society, both socially and physically. She had often spent a year, half a dozen years, or more living with her grandparents and heard their stories and wisdom. She carried out tasks without supervision and could be sent on errands successfully (Sr. Oliva Nyaronga, 9 June 1995, Sumbawanga). From now on, work and age-mates played a much more important part in her life.

Sleeping with Peers. As Fipa physically matured beyond *uum-wanche*, they reached a new stage of girlhood, *uunsungu_*or boyhood, *uunumendo*. At this stage, boys and girls were gendered beings. Boys and girls moved to sleep with their peers, often in a separate building. If the previous years were marked by learning tasks, education and socialization at the hands of grandparents and other relatives, this period was marked by peer socialization and regularly performing adult tasks.

One woman noted that it was work that separated a child from a girl.

> Really, a child [*umwanche*] has no work, because she is still a child [*umwanche*]. She sleeps and does not wake early. She plays, performs a task and she goes to sleep right away.... She does not bathe.... But if you are a girl [*unsungu*], you awake and the first job is to go to the river to draw water for drinking and ... for cooking. And then to sweep the house, and heat the water for mother and father, especially father... Then you cook something and eat and go to the farm. A child [*umwanche*] has no work (Sr. Oliva Nyaronga, 29 September 1995, Sumbawanga).

Sr. Oliva, who differentiated the work of a child and girl above, also noted a difference between the work of a boy and a girl.

> K: [And] the work of a boy [*unumendo*]?
> O: To cut firewood, to make sure there is enough firewood. And they sleep over there. They don't sleep in the house they sleep in an *intuli*. When he wakes up, he knows the first task is to cut firewood. After that he sits at home or at his friend's. Other than that, a boy doesn't have any work around the house.... Boys [*alumendo*] don't stay at home. They roam about and wait for food to get hot. But a girl [*unsungu*], you are around the house, you cook, they eat, you wash the dishes and other things (Sr. Oliva Nyaronga, 29 September 1995).

Whereas before girls and boys were expected to do their part to help out at home, at this point, boys were less likely to perform feminine tasks and so tended to have more leisure time.

Girls' work in particular was associated with the work of adulthood. Sometimes older Fipa associated this last stage with being a full person, *untu umpuma*, because he or she performed labor equal to that of his/her elders and was beginning to participate more fully in society, but full inclusion in society as an adult did not occur until marriage. One woman put it this way:

> E: The work of an adult [*uikolo*] is difficult and the work of a child [*umwanche*] is light.
> K: And the work of a girl [*unsungu*]?
> E: The work of a girl [*unsungu*] is the work of an adult [*uikolo*] (EK, 16 October 1995, Chala)

For the first time, Fipa were expected to behave at all times as gendered beings. One woman recalled her entrance into *uunsungu* in this way:

> I went to Father and I told him, 'Father, why do I have these things [breasts] coming out here and I don't see them on my older brother?' 'What did Father say?' He said, 'Wait and he, too, will get them.' He did not want to tell me anything...
>
> But then the next day when we were playing with dirt behind the house, Father told Mother inside the house.... 'Anna, don't you see that this child has grown [*amekua*, Swahili]. Why have you not explained to her the things pertinent to older children? She is a girl [*msichana*, Swahili], this one. She should stop playing with the boys and even her older brother'. From this day, Mother was harsh. If I told my older brother, 'Let's go draw water' or 'Let's go play', I saw that mother was forbidding it. She said, 'Come back. Come inside or I'll beat you' (Sr. Irena Sokoni, 17 Jan 1996, Chala).

Girls were expected to sit appropriately, to associate more formally with boys and men, and to take seriously the tasks that would be required of them as mothers and wives. The assumption was that girls in particular could almost take care of themselves.

Fipa girls and boys, upon being able to perform adult tasks and reaching puberty, usually moved into a separate building that was used exclusively for sleeping and socializing by boys and girls. These buildings were called *intuli*. *Intuli* were built near the parents' or grandparents' compounds. Frequently, these two compounds were in close proximity. Grandparents' influence, therefore, often continued to be important at this stage as well. They still spent time in the evening with their grandchildren, particularly their granddaughters, who sometimes slept in a separate room at their grandmothers' instead of an *intuli*. Fipa youth did not eat or cook in their *intuli* but continued to rely on their mothers' for food and continued to work in their parents' fields. Occasionally girls cooked in their *intuli* on holidays, as will be explored below, but the norm was to treat the *intuli* as dwelling space and not a home. Boys and girls stayed in such an arrangement until marriage.

Fipa were not unique in separating adolescents' living quarters from those of married adults. The Maasai in northern Tanzania and southern Kenya did so until quite recently in the form of warrior villages where boys were responsible for protecting the herds (Spencer 1993: 140-156). Nyakyusa adolescent boys in southern Tanzania used to live in separate villages from their parents in order to facilitate cooperation and political allegiance among age-mates as well as to avoid incest. The Wilsons, who did anthropological work among the Nyakyusa, found that girls also had at one time slept in communal homes, but no longer did so by the 1930s (Wilson 1951: 35, 86, 158-162). Such arrangements are not limited to Tanzania either. Nongenile Zenani in her autobiography mentions a 'young people's house' used among the Xhosa in South Africa (Scheub 1988: 26) and at Afikpo in the 1950s, young Igbo boys in Nigeria, from the age of five until marriage, lived in *ulote* (Ottenberg 1989: 47-50).

The practical reason offered by Fipa for moving into *intuli* was avoidance of incest. Small, dome-shaped Fipa houses provided little space and privacy for parents and thus necessitated that young children move from them to their grandparents' house. As children matured, separation from their parents' sleeping quarters provided protection against incest as well as respect for all involved.

> K: Do you remember why you began to sleep in an *intuli*? ...
> A: First, I wanted to be with ... my friends because ... my mother was a widow, and following our customs, it is not good to sleep near one's parents when you reach a certain age... there was a living room and kitchen in the same space and your parents were sleeping right there. You had no place to sleep so you must go where your peers were (AS, 10 March 1996, Kate).

Here the absence of the boy's father increased the potential for incest. One eighty-year-old woman replied sharply, 'If you are a girl with breasts, would you sleep with your father? (AC, 17 February 1996, Isale)

Intuli also recognized a Fipa adolescent's increasing need for his own space and freedom, while at the same time offering a chance for peer group socialization. One man told me that *intuli* offered *alumendo* (boys) and *asungu* (girls) the chance to stay out late in the evening.

> N: ... when you are old enough you want to play at all hours. So it becomes difficult to go and ask your parents at ten or eleven o'clock at night.
> K: Yes.
> N: So the person himself decides [to sleep in an *intuli*] because of his own condition.
> K: So the youth saw that it gave them more freedom?
> N: Yes, there was more freedom and respect because you cannot sleep at your parent's house when you are older (NC, 25 February 1996, Chala).

Yet, fundamentally this freedom was experienced within a peer group. An older woman, born in 1929, stated that as a girl she slept in an *intuli* with other girls and on Christian holidays they would buy their own food - rice, chicken, meat and plantains - and cook and eat it separately from their parents (HF, 11 March 1996, Kate).

Intuli were also a crucible place for learning as a peer group about sexuality and engagement. Several men and women alluded to the fact that discussion in the evening in the *intuli* centered on members of the opposite sex and other adolescent concerns (BM, 16 February 1996, Isale). *Intuli* were favored locations for night dances and marriage proposals earlier in the century, both of which were done in groups (Smythe 1997a: chapter 7). Note the way in which this man, born in 1949, described his experience looking for a wife.

> V: We went in a group to look for girls [*asungu*]. We... washed our clothes and ironed them, and then we went to the villages looking for girls [*asungu*].
>
> K: Uh-hmm. And what did you do? When you entered a village where did you go?
>
> V: When we went to a village we went to the boys [*alumendo*], our peers, of that village.... 'Show us where the girls [*asungu*] are.' And the girls [*asungu*], many of them slept in one *intuli*. So maybe you found ten of them together. We boys [*alumendo*] went to the doorway and stood outside.
>
> K: In the evening?
>
> V: In the evening. [They said] 'There are boys [*alumendo*].' So we sat and the girls [*asungu*] looked at us. And we also looked at them. And then we began to choose them and to speak with them. [A boy and a girl] left the group and spoke to teach other (VC, 18 February 1996, Msilihofu).

For boys and girls, the process of engagement usually occurred in the company of friends, often *intuli* mates.

For boys, *intuli* were critical in the transition from boyhood to adulthood. It used to be that a boy without an *intuli* was ineligible for marriage. A boy's *intuli* became the first house he shared with his wife after they married. The fact that she began cooking in it distinguished it from an *intuli*. An elderly Fipa man recalled the importance of *intuli*.

> V: When I was a boy I had my own house, an *intuli*....
> In the old days you could not get married without an *intuli*. You had an *intuli* and a field... Then, when you got married and your wife came [to live with you], she would stay... and cook at her in-laws and then you would hand over your kitchen to her, your *intuli*, and she would begin to cook and make beer. This was when it ceased being an *intuli* and it became a house. You could not get married until you had an *intuli*. It was forbidden... until you had a place for your wife to come, an *intuli* and a field.
> K: When you had your *intuli* were you alone or with your friends?
> V: I built my *intuli*, but my friends came to sleep in it (VD, 1 April 1996, Chala).

By day, Fipa girls and boys worked hard at the tasks they would have to perform as adults. By night, they slept with their age mates, often in an *intuli*. *Intuli* mark the third stage of Fipa childhood and offered freedom for youth, reduced the chances of incest, gave boys the chance to practice the art of house-building, and provided a dancing ground for meeting peers of the opposite sex.

Before the mid-twentieth century, Fipa children moved through three successive sleeping arrangements as they intellectually, physically, and socially matured. By gaining intelligence, learning to work, and sleeping with parents, grandparents and peers, they gained the necessary skills to operate in the adult Fipa world. But the world of Fipa adults and children changed considerably in the twentieth century and Fipa socialization did not escape the effects of European presence.

MISSIONARY IMPACT ON FIPA SOCIALIZATION

Sleeping Location. Catholic missionaries who worked in Ufipa from the 1880s on reacted strongly to many aspects of Fipa behavior and morality that they thought were anti-Christian. They were especially concerned about what they saw as a lack of parental supervision over children and youth. Through their moral teachings and example of rectangular house construction, missionaries encouraged children to stay in the same house as their parents until marriage. White Fathers' missionaries introduced more nuclear ideas of family that greatly affected socialization patterns.

In their teachings, missionaries stressed that many girls' and boys' behavior was immoral because they slept with their grandmothers or other older women instead of with their immediate family. Children's relationships with grandparents were deemed particularly troublesome. 'There are children in the faith living in a pagan environment because the old men and old women are still pagans and their influence, especially that of the old women which is always great, reacts against the Christian influence' (RA 1922-23, Kirando report, WFRH). Missionaries assumed that more time spent with parents, Christian or not, would mean better conduct and morality.[10] A woman born in 1939, who was a Catholic Sister for several years said that when she was growing up, the missionaries forbid children to sleep at their grandparents' because that way, 'a parent is not able to control them'. She told me that the missionaries enforced this to the point that they refused to give sacraments to children who were sleeping at their grandparents (MC, 12 November 1995, Chala). Missionaries, then, were aware of the important educational role that grandparents played in Fipa society and hoped that by reducing grandparent-grandchild contact, they would reduce their influence.

One of the factors that made it possible for Fipa to consider changing the way in which their children moved from one sleeping location to another was the construction of rectangular houses. These houses had multiple rooms so that youth did not have to leave their parents' abode upon becoming aware of their parents' sexual relations. Instead, they could move to a separate room that they often shared with their siblings. One of the elders in the village of Chala who spent twelve years on the coast as a driver recalled that when he left Ufipa in 1938 people still slept in dome-shaped houses (*intutu* or *insimba*). However, when he returned in 1950 these types of houses had almost disappeared in favor of rectangular houses that were modeled on those of the missionaries (VD, 1 April 1996, Chala; NC, 25 February 1996, Chala; PM, 19 January 1996, Milundikwa). As we will see below, the missionaries actively encouraged Fipa to build rectangular houses instead of dome-shaped ones.

Through preaching, threats, and new house architecture, missionaries did manage to reduce grandparents' educational role in Nkansi and with it their association with the *uumwanche* stage of childhood. They were not so successful, however, in eliminating grandparents' homes as an optional dwelling. Fipa children continue to spend time with their grandparents, though they now live with their grandparents more out of necessity than before. Grandparents now raise orphaned grandchildren, grandchildren from economically deprived families, or grand-children who attend primary school far from their natal home. My adopted family cared for an ever-changing number of their grandchildren during my stay, most of these children had lost one or both parents. Both of my female research assistants lived with their grandparents out of personal preference, one for three or four years and one for ten years. These particular granddaughters spent evenings with their grandparents hearing stories and learning about their family and the past so they benefited from the cultural wisdom of their grandparents as well but such cultural education has become more the exception than the rule. One research assistant noted that she lived with her paternal grandfather while she was attending school because he paid her school fees, bought her uniform, and sometimes gave her treats such as tea and candy (EK, 19 July 1995, Chala). Some pupils lived with their grandparents while they attended school because their grandparents lived close to the school, while their parents had moved out of the village to live on their farms at least half of the year.

Missionaries also disapproved of children sleeping together in *intuli* from the beginning. It was not the idea of communal dormitories that was so repugnant to the missionaries but the illicit sexual activity that such arrangements potentially encouraged. In addition, missionaries were concerned that youth in *intuli* and at their grandmothers' homes suffered in moral instruction because they were not under their parents' watchful eye.

As early as 1897, missionaries in Kirando declared that girls should abandon their communal homes and live with their parents (Kirando Council Book, 28 November 1897, WFRH). The reporter of the weekly staff meetings in Karema recorded in 1917:

> We discussed the measures to take in order to discourage the bad habits principally among the girls. We will warn the parents that they have the serious work of keeping an eye on their children. Those who by Assumption have not built in their compound a small house for their daughters will be exposed and refused the sacraments (Karema Council Book, 27 February 1917, WFRH).

In this entry, the missionaries want the girls to be closer to their parents. A year later, the missionary priests wanted to ensure that girls were supervised at night by an adult, presumably a parent: 'We decide in view of the danger in which the girls put themselves, we cannot admit the older girls who sleep alone in a house to the sacraments. The boys who are in the same situation risk not being admitted as well' (Karema Council Book, April 1918, WFRH).

It was not until the late 1940s, however, that Bishop Holmes-Siedle launched a diocese-wide campaign to suppress the communal dorms.

> The surveillance of the parents is rendered even more difficult in the parts of the high plateau because of the detestable custom of the *nsalo*. The *nsalo* is the communal dormitory of the girls. There is also a communal dormitory for the boys; children and young men sleep there, far from their parents, a custom which is the cause of many sins; also we have made a cam-

paign for their suppression (RA 1947-1948, Karema
report, WFRH).[11]

The Bishop 'preached on the subject in no uncertain manner in
all the missions...' (*The Link* 2 Nov. 1947, 14, WFRH) and the
missionaries encouraged Fipa to build bigger houses so that the
whole family could sleep in one house (Fr. Lukewille, 21 March
1996, Sumbawanga). By 1958 the White Sisters in Chala noted
that the creation of the *l'Oeuvre de l'Action Catholique* had suc-
ceeded in suppressing the communal dorms in the village where
the priests had not been able to (White Sisters' Annual Reports
1957-58, WSA). Catholic Action was a group of lay leaders in
the church who pressured their peers into destroying this custom.
The lay leaders met periodically with the missionaries to discuss
matters of the church and thus acted as a liaison between missionaries and villagers.

The missionaries also carried out a rosary campaign in the
1950s in which they encouraged families to pray together in the
evening. Several people mentioned that this campaign coincided
with the priests' desire for bigger houses. Thus, they advocated
building houses with three bedrooms, one for the parents, one
for the boys, one for girls and a sitting room in between where the
family could gather in the evening to pray together (*Petit Echo*,
No. 453, Aug.-Sept. 1955, 403-404, WFRH; DC, 24 November
1995, Chala). Missionaries were fairly successful at reducing the
influence of grandparents and the number of *intuli* so that today
Fipa maturation is not so clearly tied to building relationships
with other relatives and with peers as they mature.

UKUCHENJELA AND STAGES OF GROWTH

In addition to reforming family life and sleeping arrangements, missionaries introduced Catholic rites of baptism and first
communion that were incorporated into Fipa notions of age and
maturity. Some Fipa spoke of becoming intelligent at about the
same time that they received the sacrament of first communion
indicating that by mid-century, Fipa society had integrated one
of the rites of the Catholic Church into their concept of maturity, *ukuchenjela*. One woman said, 'I was baptized when I was

still suckling at my mother's breast. Do you hear? ... And when
I became intelligent [*nachenjela*] then I took communion' (MK,
5 July 1995, Chala; also OM, 15 October 1996, Miyombo). Sr.
Oliva recalled:

> K: When did you become a grown-up person [*untu
> umpuma*]?
> O: To begin to be a grown-up person? ... About 13
> or 14 years old. Yes. Because if we reached the age of
> eight or nine we got first communion. That is when
> you began to know things, when you gained intelli-
> gence [*akili*] and you remembered things completely,
> then you got first communion and confirmation. At
> the age of eight, nine or ten that is when you began
> to be a grown-up person [*mtu mzima*, Kiswahili] (Sr.
> Oliva Nyaronga, 9 June 1995, Sumbawanga).

Another woman echoed this last sentiment, remembering that
when she received first communion, there was quite a celebration, women ululating and adults telling her *wakula*, you have
grown up! (NF, 11 February 1996, Lyele). In this adaptation to
Western institutions of childhood, we see a cultural recognition
and acceptance of the Catholic Church and Western schools
as important means for socializing Fipa children and preparing
them for adulthood.

Increasingly, Western institutions were assimilated into local
ideas of development. Instead of associating 'becoming aware'
with learning a task such as herding or living with another relative, more and more children equate their moment of awareness
with full membership in the Catholic Church (i.e. first communion) and school attendance. An old man began his narrative
thus: 'When I came to get intelligence [*amano*] and I came to
know things, then my father took me to school here at home,
here at Chala' (TS, 22-23 April 1996, Chala). A young man born
in 1970 began his narrative by stating that when he reached the
age of nine, he got intelligence and was registered to start school,
illustrating how the two events were linked in his mind (CK, 2
April 1996, Chala). Gaining intelligence, then, has become less

associated with memory and more associated with acceptance into the Catholic Church and elementary school.

While Fipa were finding that their notions of childhood development could assimilate foreign institutions, French missionaries probably saw how similar were the two cultures' divisions of childhood. White Fathers deemed the obtaining of intelligence as important as Fipa themselves. In nineteenth-century French society, the second stage of childhood, the age of discernment, began at the age of six or seven 'when the child was ready to leave the comforting environment of the home and family' (Heywood 1988:14) and would roughly correspond to *uumwanche* in Ufipa. Fr. Robert differentiated three stages in Fipa childhood: birth to the age of reason, the age of reason to puberty, and puberty to marriage (*Table d'enquete*, 115-180). It is difficult to know whether Fr. Robert is applying French markers of growth to Ufipa or describing Fipa stages with French terminology. If he is applying French markers of growth this constitutes more evidence to suggest that the two cultures' stages were similar. If he was using French terminology in order to describe Fipa stages of maturation, then Fipa cultural notions of growth were not the only ones adapting to new situations.

There is one significant difference, however, between the way missionaries and Fipa employed the notion of gaining intelligence. Fipa, as the previous examples show, tended to see it as an enabling factor in allowing them to learn and become proficient at new tasks. Missionaries and teachers, though, tended to focus on screening out those who did not have sufficient intelligence for first communion or entrance to school. Missionary priests expected that children who received first communion would be sufficiently mature to understand the rite. One man explained how he received first communion in the 1920s:

> I took first communion in 1926.... When I began to study it was 1920... In 1927 they said, '...They do not yet have intelligence [*amalango*]. When they come up here to take first communion, they laugh'. [So] they forbid us [because] we were not yet aware [*yachile yachenjile*].... [In] 1928 they said we were intelligent enough [*yachenjela*] and that was when

we took first communion. That same year of 1928 they gave us confirmation (KM, 21 January 1996, Chala).

A younger man recalled being sent away from school because he was not yet intellectually mature. 'I went to standard one in 1970... they sent me away. They said that my intelligence [*akili*] had not yet matured...' (GL, 8 July 1995, Chala). Fipa used to associate *ukuchenjela* with memory and an increasing ability to participate in the world of adults. Now it is tied to specific rites and Western notions of intelligence required for participation in the Eucharistic and in elementary school.

CONCLUSION

Traditionally, Fipa had multiple ways of marking the growth and development of their children and ensuring their proper socialization. Each stage of growth was equated with a child's awareness of the world around her, interaction with the wider community, and an increasing ability to contribute to the family economy. Living with and learning from parents, grandparents, and then peers, Fipa children, boys and girls, learned how to work and play in appropriate ways.

European Catholic missionaries, however, came to Ufipa in the late 19th century intent on creating a Christian society in which Christian parents played the most important role in socializing their children. They achieved this by preaching, withholding sacraments, and introducing multi-roomed rect-angular houses to replace single-roomed dome-shaped houses. The only change in sleeping location now to mark the transition from *uumwanche uncheche* to *uumwanche* or from *uumwanche* to *uunsungu* or *uunumendo* is now to move to another room in the parents' house where Fipa children now stay until marriage. In the past, Fipa socialization used to include moral lessons given by a grandmother and the performance of night dances at *intuli*. Today, Fipa maturation is shaped by lessons on Christianity, geog-raphy, and maths. While Fipa used to recognize that coming to the end point of becoming aware and reaching puberty ushered in an intense period of peer interaction and work for girls, now these developments more often are marked by participation in first communion and admission to elementary school.

Perhaps the most intriguing aspect of Fipa childhood development was the association between memory and awareness/intelligence. The beginning of childhood, *uumwanche*, and the first steps toward being an individual in the social and economic spheres, occurred at the point when a child began to remember. Now, however, after almost a century of European missionary influence, *ukuchenjela* is not so much related to memory as it is to admittance to the Catholic Church and elementary school. The notion of 'becoming aware' or 'gaining intelligence' is still very important in Fipa society. Such notion has found relevance in the new Catholic and Western context that prevails in Ufipa in the late twentieth century, while a change in sleeping location was believed to be antithetical to Catholic membership and has faded in significance.

Notes

1. This chapter is a revised version of chapter five in my dissertation, 'Fipa Childhood'. Dissertation research was conducted in Nkansi District, Ufipa from 1994-1996. It was also presented at the 1998 Oral History Association meeting in Buffalo, New York and at the 1998 African Studies Association meeting in Chicago. Research was supported by funding from the Wenner-Gren Foundation, Johann Jacobs Foundation, a Fulbright-Hays Doctoral Dissertation Fellowship and University of Wisconsin-Madison travel grant. Writing was supported in part by a grant from the American Association of University Women. I also appreciate the cooperation of the Tanzanian Commission on Science and Technology and National Archives in facilitating my research. I wish to thank Iris Berger, Andor Skotnes, Jan Shetler, and Thomas Spear for reading previous drafts of this chapter and offering valuable critical comments.

2. For a more detailed explanation of Fipa languages or dialects, as Willis calls them, see Willis 1981: 4-9.

3. In other areas of Ufipa, there were initiation rites for girls. In Umambwe, along the present-day Zambia border, girls were initiated at the time of their menstruation at least into the 1950s

(Anonymous, 14 November 1995, Sumbawanga; Willis, 1966: 51).

4. Spelling of Fipa words is made difficult by the fact that often words have long vowels, transliterated by Roy Willis, a scholar of Fipa society, using double vowels. I checked some of the spellings used here with Fipa elders and others with written sources available in the United States. For more on the verb *ukuchenjela*, see the Bemba's multivariate use of it as cited in Serpell 1993. Struck defines *ukukula* as to build. But elders in Nkansi also used it as I indicate here (Struck 1908).

5. See Sr. Oliva Nyaronga, 2 June 1995, Sumbawanga. White Fathers in Kate noted that the average number of children per family was two to three in 1912 but that it was not rare for a monogamous family to have seven or more children (RA 1912-1913). In 1948 the Bishop of Karema Vicariat wrote in his annual report, 'Another characteristic of Karema Vicariat, at least for Ufipa, is its prodigious birth rate. The villages swarm with children....' (RA 1947-1948). Several years later Fr. Robert noted that families of five to seven children were the rule, *Table d'enquete*, 295. Statistics collected in the 1980s indicated that the fertility rate in Rukwa was nine children per woman compared to seven in the rest of the country. Taken from a poster in the District Office, Namanyere entitled, *Takwimu za Mkoa Rukwa na Taifa* (Statistics of Rukwa Region and the Nation) printed by RUDEP.

6. I have chosen to use the initials of Fipa with whom I spoke since a few expressed a reluctance to have their words associated with them as individuals. Catholic Sisters and priests did not object to my using their full names, so I do. When I use the term *mzee* (in Kiswahili a respectful term for an old man), I do so to avoid confusion because the individual's first name begins with a 'K' as does mine.

7. In Kifipa, *ukuchenjela* would be conjugated in the following manner in the first person singular. Present tense: *nduchenjela* (I am becoming aware, I am aware). Perfect tense: *nachenjela* (I became aware sometime in the past). Past tense: *nachenjile* (I became aware at a specific point in time). Future tense: *nankula* (I will become aware). This information is drawn from Kifipa grammar lessons with Angelo Mbalamwezi, May 1995, Sumbawanga.

8. Kristen Hawkes and her colleagues recently suggested that the reason human females live far beyond their reproductive years is

to provision their grandchildren with food when their mothers are too busy feeding their other children. This research is based on a study of 300 Hadza hunter-gatherers in northern Tanzania (Gibbons 1997: 536).

9. While a relative lack of gender distinction in this phase of Fipa growth is reflected in the data I have collected thus far, I do realize that in many other places gender distinctions in terms of labor were important earlier. In the future, I wish to explore more carefully the impact missionaries had on reinforcing gendered divisions of labor, particularly in light of arguments I have made earlier that some of the most obvious fault lines in Fipa society were not those of gender, but of age. Oyeronke Oyewumi makes a similar argument in her recent book, *The Invention of Women: Making an African Sense of Western Gender Discourses*. Oyewumi argues that Western scholars and discourses have created a modern Yoruba society in which gender is a much more salient social division than it was before the colonial period.

10. Obviously missionaries preferred parents to be Christian. Pagan parents 'give permission to their children to follow the religion, but unhappily train them still in certain pagan practices which are hardly compatible with the promises of their baptism' (RA 1923-1924, Chala report).

11. No Fipa used the term *nsalo* in conversation with me. After I left the field and began writing, I wrote to one of the men I had interviewed and asked him what the difference between the terms was and he said that *nsalo* were for boys who had not yet reached puberty and *intuli* for boys who had. This will be something I will have to explore further in my next research trip (Pius Mwanakulya, personal communication, 4 November 1998).

References

Archival Sources
White Fathers Archives, Rome
Chala Mission Diary, 1912-1928
Kate Mission Diary, 1909-1956
White Sisters Archives, Rome
White Sisters Annual Reports, Sumbawanga, 1959-1960
White Sisters Annual Reports, Kate, 1928-1966
White Sisters Chala Diary, 1951-1969

White Sisters Kate Diary, 1922-1926, 1963-1967
White Fathers Regional House, Nyegezi, Tanzania
Rapports Annuels, 1908-1957
Chronique Trimestrielle, 1897-1909
Petit Echo, 1913, 146-1971
Karema Council Books, 1895-1970
Ujiji Council Notes, 1930-1950
Kate Council Books, 1906-1951
Kirando Council Diary, 1895-1913
Karema Mission Diary, 1919-1938
The Link (Karema Diocese), 1947-1970
La Mission de Karema: 1885-1935 (Ujiji: CM Press, n.d.)

UCLA Library, Special Collections

Table d'enquête sur les moeurs et les coutumes indigenes, Diocese de Karema,
Tribu des Wafipa by Fr. Robert

Books, Articles, and Theses

Aries, P. 1962. *Centuries of Childhood*. Translated by Robert Baldick. New York: Vintage.

Beidelman, T. O. 1997. *The Cool Knife: Images of Gender, Sexuality, and Moral Education in Kaguru Initiation Ritual*. Washington, DC : Smithsonian Institution Press.

Bertsch, F. 1964. *Notes on the History of Karema Diocese*.

Blakely, T., van Beek, W.E.A., and Thomson, D. L., eds. 1994. *Religion in Africa: Experience and Expression*. Portsmouth: Heinemann.

Bouniol, J. 1929. *The White Fathers and Their Missions*. London: Sands and Co.

Brusco, E. and L. F. Klein. 1994. *The Message in the Missionary: Local Interpretations of Religious Ideology and Missionary Personality*. Williamsburg: Studies in Third World Society.

Buchert, L. 1995. *Education in the Development of Tanzania, 1919-1990*. Athens: Ohio University Press.

Bury, B. 1983. 'The Human Ecology and Political Economy of Agricultural Production on the Ufipa Plateau, Tanzania, 1945-1981'. Ph.D., Columbia University.

Castle, E.B. 1966. *Growing Up in East Africa*. London: Oxford University Press.

Centner, Th. H. 1963. *L'Enfant Africain et ses Jeux dans le Cadre de la Vie Traditionelle au Katanga.* Elisabethville: CEPSI.

Cohen, D.W., and E.S. Atieno-Odhiambo. 1989. *Siaya: The Historical Anthropology of an African Landscape.* Athens: Ohio University Press.

Comaroff, J. and J. Comaroff. 1985. 'Christianity and Colonialism in South Africa', *American Ethnologist* 13 (1): 1-22.

D'Almeida-Topor, H., C. Coquery-Vidrovitch, O. Goerg, and F. Guitart, eds. 1992. *Les Jeunes en Afrique.* Paris: L'Harmattan.

Davison, J. 1996. *Voices from Mutira: Change in the lives of rural Gikuyu women 1910-1995.* Boulder: Lynne Rienner Press.

DeMause, L. 1974. *The History of Childhood.* New York: Psychohistory Press.

Droogers, A. 1980. *The Dangerous Journey: Symbolic Aspects of Boys' Initiation among the Wagenia of Kisangani, Zaire.* The Hague: Afrika-Studiecentrum.

Erikson, E. 1950. *Childhood and Society.* New York: Horton.

Erny, P. 1981. *The Child and His Environment in Black Africa.* Translated by G.J. Wanjohi. Nairobi: Oxford University Press.

Fox, L. K. 1967. *East African Childhood: Three Versions.* Nairobi: Oxford University Press.

Garvey, B. 1974. 'The Development of the White Fathers' Mission Among the Bemba-Speaking Peoples, 1891-1964'. Ph.D., University of London.

———. 1994. *Bembaland Church: Religious and Social Change in South Central Africa, 1891-1964.* New York: E.J. Brill.

Gatheru, R. M. 1964. *Child of Two Worlds.* London: Routledge and Paul.

Gibbons, A. 1997. 'Why Life After Menopause?', *Science* 276: 536.

Goody, E. 1966. 'The Fostering of Children in Ghana: A Preliminary Report', *Ghana Journal of Sociology* 2 (1): 26-33.

Gray, R. 1990. *Black Christians and White Missionaries.* New Haven: Yale University Press.

Grindal, B. 1972. *Growing Up in Two Worlds: Education and Transition Among the Sisala of Northern Ghana.* New York: Holt, Rinehart and Winston.

Harkness, S. and C.M. Super. 1991. 'East Africa' , in J.M. Hawes and N.R. Hiner ed., *Children in Historical and Comparative Perspec-*

tive: An International Handbook and Research Guide. New York: Greenwood Press.

Hastings, Adrian. *The Church in Africa, 1450-1950*. Oxford: Clarendon Press, 1994.

Heremans, R. 1966. *Les Établissements de l'Association Internationale Africaine au Lac Tanganika et Les Pères Blancs, Mpala et Karema, 1877-1885*. Tervuren: Musée Royal de l'Afrique Centrale.

———. 1983. *L'Education dans les Missions des Pères Blancs en Afrique Centrale (1879-1914): Objectifs et Réalisations*. Brussels: Editions Nauwelaerts.

Heywood, C. 1988. *Childhood in Nineteenth Century France: Work, Health, and Education among the 'Classes Populaires'*. Cambridge: Cambridge University Press.

Hiner, N. R. and J. M. Hawes, Joseph M. eds. 1985. *Growing Up in America: Children in Historical Perspective*. Urbana and Chicago: University of Illinois Press.

Hoehler-Fatton, C. 1996. *Women of Fire and Spirit: History, Faith and Gender in Roho Religion in Western Kenya*. New York: Oxford University Press.

Hollos, M. and P.E. Leis. 1989. *Becoming Nigerian in an Ijo Society*. New Brunswick: Rutgers University Press.

Iliffe, J. 1979. *A Modern History of Tanganyika*. Cambridge: Cambridge University Press.

Jacobs, M. 1992. *Sigmund Freud*. London: Sage Publications.

Kaye, B. 1962. *Bringing Up Children in Ghana: An Impressionistic Survey*. London: George Allen and Unwin, Ltd.

Kimambo, I. 1991. *Penetration and Protest in Tanzania*. Athens: Ohio University Press.

Koponen, J. 1994. *Development for Exploitation: German Colonial Policies in Mainland Tanzania, 1884-1914*. Helsinki: Raamattutalo Pieksamaki.

Lechaptois, Mgr. 1932. *Aux Rives du Tanganyika*. Alger: Imprimerie des Pères Blancs.

Lemba, Fr. P. 1975. 'The Underdevelopment of Sumbawanga District (Rukwa Region)'. M.A. Thesis, University of Dar es Salaam.

LeVine, R. A. and B.B. LeVine. 1966. *Nyansongo: A Gusii Community in Kenya*. New York: John Wiley and Sons.

Linden, I. 1977. *Church and Revolution in Rwanda*. Manchester: Manchester University Press.

Luke, C. 1989. *Pedagogy, Printing and Protestantism: The Discourse on Childhood.* Albany: State University of New York Press.

Mascerenhas, A. 1977. *Participation of Children in Socio-Economic Activities: The Case of Rukwa Region.* University of Dar es Salaam: Bureau of Resource Assessment and Land Use Planning.

Masemann, V. 1974. 'The "Hidden Curriculum" of a West African Girls' Boarding School', *Canadian Journal of African Studies* 8: 479-494.

Mead, M. 1930. *Growing Up in New Guinea.* New York: William Morris and Co.

Mead, M. and M. Wolfenstein, Martha eds.1955. *Childhood in Contemporary Cultures.* Chicago: University of Chicago Press.

Obbo, C. 1988. 'Bitu: Facilitator of Women's Educational Opportunities' in P. Romero, ed., *Life Histories of African Women*, pp. 99-112. Atlantic Highlands, N.J.: Ashland Press.

Oppong, C. 1973. *Growing Up in Dogban.* Ghana: Ghana Publishing Corporation.

———. 1983. *Female and Male in West Africa.* London: Allen and Unwin.

Ottenberg, S. 1989. *Boyhood Rituals in an African Society: An Interpretation.* Seattle: University of Washington Press.

Pels, P. 1993. *Critical Matters: Interactions Between Missionaries and Waluguru in Colonial Tanganyika, 1930-1961.* Amsterdam: Amsterdam School of Social Research.

Peshkin, A. 1972. *Kanuri Schoolchildren: Education and Social Mobilization in Nigeria.* New York: Holt, Rinehart and Winston.

Piaget, J. 1963. *The Origins of Intelligence in Children.* Trans. Margaret Cook. New York: W.W. Norton and Co., Inc.

Popplewell, G.D. 1937 'Notes on the Fipa', *Tanganyika Notes and Records* 3: 95-105.

Raum, O.F. 1940. *Chaga Childhood: A Description of Indigenous Education in an East African Tribe.* London: Oxford University Press, 1940.

Read, M. 1960. *Children of their Fathers: Growing Up Among the Ngoni of Nyasaland.* New Haven: Yale University Press.

Reynolds, P. 1986. *Growing Up in a Divided Society: The Contexts of Childhood in South Africa.* Cape Town: D. Philip, 1986.

———. 1989. *Childhood in Crossroads: Cognition and Society in South Africa.* Cape Town: D. Philip.

————. 1991. *Dance, Civet Cat: Child Labour in the Zambezi Valley*. Athens: Ohio University Press.

————. 1996. *Traditional Healers and Childhood in Zimbabwe*. Athens: Ohio University Press.

Richards, A. 1956. *Chisungu: A Girls' Initiation Ceremony among the Bemba of Northern Rhodesia*. London: Faber and Faber Ltd.

Riesman, P. 1986. 'The Person and the Life Cycle in African Social Life and Thought', *African Studies Review* 29: 71-138.

————. 1992. *First Find Yourself A Good Mother: The Construction of Self in Two African Communities*. New Brunswick: Rutgers University Press.

Robert, R.P.J.M. 1949. *Croyances et Coutumes Magico-Religeuses de Wafipa Païens*. Tabora: Tanganyika Mission Press.

Scheub, H. 1988. 'And So I Grew Up: The Autobiography of Nongenile Masithathu Zenani' in P. Romero, ed., *Life Histories of African Women*, pp.7-46. Atlantic Heights, N.J.: Ashfield Press.

Schildkrout, E. 1978. 'Changing Economic Roles of Children in Comparative Perspective', in C. Oppong, ed, *Marriage, Fertility and Parenthood in West Africa*, pp. 289-305. Canberra: Australian National University.

Serpell, R. 1993. *The Significance of Schooling: Life and Journeys in an African Society*. Cambridge: Cambridge University Press.

Small, M. 1998. *Our Babies, Ourselves: How Biology and Culture Shape the Way We Parent*. New York: Anchor Books, 1998.

Soyinka, W. 1981. *Ake: The Years of Childhood*. New York: Random House.

Spear, T. and I. Kimambo, forthcoming. *Through African Eyes: African Expressions of Christianity in East Africa*.

Spencer, P. 1988. *The Maasai of Matapato: A Study of Rituals or Rebellion*. Manchester: Manchester University Press.

Spencer, P. 1993. 'Becoming Maasai, Being in Time' in T. Spear and R. Waller eds., *Being Maasai*, pp. 140-156. London: James Currey.

Stewart, C. C. 1992. 'When Youth Concludes: Changes in Marriage and the Production of Youth since 1890 (in Mauritania)' in H. d'Almeida-Topor ed., *Les Jeunes en Afrique*, pp. 103-115. Paris: L'Harmattan.

Sumbawanga Diocese. 1985. *History of Sumbawanga Diocese, 1885-1985*. Peramiho: Peramiho Printing Press.

Swantz, M-L. 1986. *Ritual and Symbol in Transitional Zaramo Society*. Uppsala: Scandanavian Institute of African Studies.

Tambila, A. 1981. 'A History of the Rukwa Region (Tanzania) c. 1870-1940: Aspects of Economic and Social Change from Pre-Colonial to Colonial Times'. Ph.D. Dissertation, University of Hamburg.

Thomas, L. 1996. "" *Ngaitana* (I will circumcise myself)": The Gender and Generational Politics of the 1956 Ban on Clitoridectomy in Meru, Kenya', *Gender and History* 8 (3): 338-363.

UNICEF. 1973, 1975. *The Young Child Study in Tanzania.* Dar es Salaam: UNICEF.

Vorkevisser, C. M. 1973. *Socialization in a Changing Society: Sukuma Childhood in Rural and Urban Mwanza, Tanzania.* The Hague: CFSO.

Wessenlingh, F. 1972. *Historia ya Jimbo la Sumbawanga.* Kantandala, Tanzania.

Whiting, B., ed. 1963. *Six Cultures: Studies of Child-Rearing.* New York: John Wiley and Sons, Inc.

Willis, R. 1964.'Traditional History and Social Structure in Ufipa', *Africa* 34: 340-352.

———. 1966. *The Fipa and Related Peoples of South-West Tanzania and North-East Zambia.* London: International African Institute.

———. 1967. 'The Head and the Loins: Levi-Strauss and Beyond', *Man* 2 (4): 519-534.

———. 1968. 'Changes in Mystical Concepts and Practices among the Fipa', *Ethnology* 7: 139-157.

———. 1970. 'Kaswa: Oral Tradition of a Fipa Prophet', *Africa* 40: 248-256.

———. 1972.'Pollution and Paradigms', Man 7 (3): 369-378.

———. 1973. 'The Indigenous Critique of Colonialism: A Case Study', in T. Asad ed., *Anthropology and the Colonial Encounter*, pp. 245-256. London: Ithaca Press.

———. 1974. *Man and Beast.* London: Hart-Davis, MacGibbon.

———. 1980. 'Executive Women and the Emergence of Female Class Consciousness: The Case of the Fipa', *Anthropology* 4: 1-10.

———. 1981. *A State in the Making: Myth, History and Social Transformation in Pre-Colonial Ufipa.* Bloomington: Indiana University Press.

———. 1985. 'Do the Fipa have a Word for it?', in D. Parkin ed., *The Anthropology of Evil*, pp. 209-223. Oxford: Basil Blackwell.

———. 1989. 'The "Peace Puzzle" in Ufipa', in S. Howell and R. Willis eds., *Societies at Peace: Anthropological Perspectives*, pp. 133-145. London: Routledge.

————. 1989. 'Power Begins At Home: The Symbolism of Male-Female Commensality in Ufipa', in W. Arens and I. Karp eds., *Creativity of Power*, pp. 113-128. Washington: Smithsonian Institution Press.

Wilson, M. 1951. *Good Company: A Study of Nyakyusa Age-Villages.* New York: Oxford University Press.

————. 1977. *For Men and Elders: Change in the Relations of Generations and of Men and Women among the Nyakyusa-Ngonde People, 1875-1971.* New York: Africana Publishing Company.

Wright, M. 1971. *German Missions in Tanganyika 1891-1941.* Oxford: Clarendon Press.

————. 1985. 'Iron and Regional History: Report on a Research Project in Southwestern Tanzania', *African Economic History* 14: 147-164.

Chapter 2

MOBILITY AND DISCIPLINE: COLONIAL AGE DISCOURSE IN TANZANIA

Thomas Burgess

For most of the colonial period Britain demonstrated little interest in African youth in Tanganyika as a distinct social identity, lacking any sort of policy on youth 'development'. Colonial agents were satisfied to leave the work of forming and influencing younger Africans mostly to Christian missionaries, introducing only a few schemes such as football leagues and the Boy Scouts to young men in towns. If colonial agents took a direct interest in youth, it was in the context of their worries over the accelerating growth of colonial towns, and the related phenomena of 'de-tribalization'. However, after World War II other worries appeared.

With the simultaneous rise in youth mobility and nationalism, colonial agents not only expressed doubts and suspicions about the younger generation but also made concerted efforts to restrict their movements, and to resist their aspirations to obtain access to the wages, education, and consumption items only available in the towns. As young Africans, particularly males, seemed after the war to have the potential of disrupting or undermining the colonial order, 'youth' appeared in colonial vision as a more distinct identity. How colonials discussed and acted on their concerns over the perceived problem of youth indiscipline is the subject of this chapter. This chapter looks firstly at Tanganyikan colonial discourses on youth, and secondly it focuses more specifically on Zanzibar.

The study of particular remarks by colonial researchers, police officers, District and Provincial Commissioners, sports administrators, intelligence officers, labor and social welfare agents reveals interesting insights. 'Idleness' and nationalism were in the colonial mind frequently considered to be synonymous, and young men of insecure status, the most recent arrivals to the town, were thought to be predisposed towards both. They were also perceived to be examples of the deterioration of the social control exerted over youth by their elders and the 'tribe'. A primary colonial assumption on age was that, the erosion, through greater youth mobility, of ties between the youth and their parents or elders created a corresponding disrespect for the laws and institutions of the colonial state. Thus, the moral order of the villages was defined as superior to that emerging in the towns. For these reasons, the colonial state in the nationalist period began to take an active interest in either expelling unemployed, 'undesirable' and 'disorderly' youth from the towns, or in organizing the regulation of their leisure hours. By the 1950s colonial officials, particularly in Zanzibar, began to consider the task of controlling the young to be of paramount state concern.

INTER-WAR COLONIAL DISCOURSE

Prior to World War II colonial servants in Tanganyika said little about particular generations. What they did say about age was said in the context of growing worries over 'detribalization', urbanization, and its related social ill: unemployment. In Tanganyika in the 1920s and 1930s, for example, a small group of colonial officials began to apply the latest British social theories to these apparent trends. Research that resulted from these efforts was often collected in colonial District Books, and in issues of journals such as the *Tanganyika Notes and Records*. David Anthony writes, regarding such a circle of scholars in Dar es Salaam, that,

> Many of these social scientists shared a view of African society as one which left to itself in its 'correct', preferably rural habitat would serve African needs in ways and to a degree impossible in an urban area. By contrast, the urban centers were considered to have the repositories of every possible evil imaginable, from

prostitution, to unemployment, high crime rates and social degeneracy.[1]

Probably labor conditions in Dar es Salaam provoked this interest, where unemployment noticeably worsened during the world depression of the 1930s. One-third of the adult African male population of Dar es Salaam was unemployed, amounting to 3,308 African men, according to the Native Census of 1931. Many of these were laid off from jobs in the service industry, or in government offices. Despite the scarcity of employment, according to Anthony, Africans continued to arrive in the capital, seeking to escape the taxes and insecurities of the countryside.[2]

Such mobility and 'idleness' was alarming and uncomfortable to colonials. The writings of E.C. Baker, a scholar employed by the Tanganyikan government in the 1930s to study 'de-tribalization', reflect these concerns. Baker wrote that with the improvement of communications and the new chance for young people 'to roam', generational conflict was increasing in the countryside; parents were losing control of their children. The movement of youth to the towns in pursuit of wage employment undermined village ethics. He claimed that the numbers of 'detribalized' youth in the towns needed to be contained, because they lacked respect towards, parents, elders and the state.[3]

For example, Baker remarked that the missionary suppression of the initiation ceremonies for junior males among the Wapare in Tanga Province in the 1920s might in the long run prove to be a mistake, because,

> The sudden emancipation of the young men from a sanction which made all conform to a social type must have far-reaching effects on the future development of the tribe, and if great care is not taken by missionaries and administrative officers to maintain a tribal consciousness, an independence of thought and action which is inimical to ordered tribal society may result.[4]

Baker's primary concern was clearly maintaining colonial order. He perceived 'tribal conservatism', or the controlling influence of senior males on rural life, to be the foundation for the colonial status quo, which might be undermined by the release of youth from 'traditional' obligations and deference towards the older generation. These young non-conformists, 'restless' in the monotony of village conditions, finding rural life 'gave them little scope for individuality', and 'impatient of parental advice', migrated to the towns, where,

> The young African throws himself into an atmosphere that is entirely divorced from all his tribal conceptions. The standard at which he aims is that of a town where living conditions are conducive to detribalization and a high degree of immorality.[5]

The immature morality of the towns was caused, according to Baker, by the too sudden transition from 'rigid tribalism to one of *complete freedom of movement*' [*my emphasis*].[6] Parental authority must also be more 'enlightened' and 'consistent'. Standards of living in the countryside must be raised above the subsistence level. The towns, with their 'confusion' of races and tribes,

> Present a problem to which it is difficult to find a satisfactory solution. The problem is of considerable importance ... because the rural population that, as is the case in Europe, is too apt to consider that an urban mode of living is the standard at which it should aim. Most young men of today visit the towns at some time during their adolescence and model their ideas on the social conditions that they find in them.[7]

Baker thus articulated many of the primary worries and fears of colonial officials: that traditional African social bonds were beginning to unravel due to the influence of the towns, the cash economy, and youth mobility. The new correspondence between age and travel produced young dissenters free from rural restraints on behavior, contaminated by the iniquities of town life.

Established African townspeople for their own reasons in the 1930s also sometimes deplored some of the effects of urban growth. In the pages of *Kwetu*, the sole independent African newspaper in Dar es Salaam from 1937 to 1951, the complaints of educated Christian clerks and wage-earning migrants from the interior were heard. They were concerned about crime, taxes, housing, drunkenness, the color bar, and the colonial court system.[8] An average *Kwetu* reader, however, was concerned with the breakdown of rural morals in the disorderly urban atmosphere of the town.[9]

Erica Fiah, the Ugandan-born, mission-educated editor of *Kwetu*, amplified these sentiments, claiming that for most Africans the countryside offered more discipline than the town. In February 1939, for example, Fiah urged the government 'to check the demoralizing influences of a steadily growing band of juvenile delinquents, found among the already existing hooligans in all our big towns'. These were mostly, according to Fiah, school leavers, or the 'underprivileged' that could be encountered 'loafing in the bazaars and hotels, walking out late at night, and sleeping in obscure nooks'. These youth 'were born of narrow-minded parents or were protégés of indifferent guardians ... in such circumstances children, boys especially, will go adrift in the broader world outside and do what they can to sustain life'. These boys evolve into criminals, thieves, tax dodgers, claimed Fiah, who 'rob our children whom we send on errands... Their bad influence in our towns is too well known to require retelling, and just now it might be reasonable to put our heads together and ask ourselves whether we should not devise remedial measures'.[10]

In the 1930s colonial officials and literate towns men were uncomfortable with some of the perceived effects which unrestricted mobility had on junior males. The indiscipline of town living disrupted parental authority, and weakened 'tribal' codes of behavior, and encouraged a dangerous and growing individualism among the young. Commentary on 'de-tribalization' demonstrated a temporary alliance between established African townsmen and colonial agents. Both were suspicious of migrant laborers who didn't seem to fit into or occupy a respected position either in the image of an Europeanizing urban community or a stable village patriarchal society. Such marginal people were thought to lack a certain 'moral fiber' the general definition of which was a common ground for Christian, capitalist and African discourses, shared and repeated by African elders and colonial agents.

STAY ON THE LAND

After World War II colonial servants were less content to just report and worry about these undesirable young men, but made efforts to control their movements and to force them to stay in the rural areas. They also, however, began to recognize that *some* migrant laborers *did* occupy a necessary and permanent role in the growing economies of the towns. Recognizing by the 1950s the value of a stable work force, officials conceded that a controlled number of African males needed to be treated as regular urban wage earners and residents.[11] For this reason colonial agents began to more seriously differentiate between desirable urban youth and criminal idlers. According to Frederick Cooper, a selected amount of young men were to be considered 'industrial men', as 'predictable, known being[s]' necessary for a productive, orderly state. In other words, they were to 'separate an identifiable group of people from the backwardness of rural Africa'. Steven Feierman also suggests that 'employers and administrators' in the 1950s 'wanted a carefully modulated proletarianization' of African labor.[12]

Officials adjusted to the realities of accelerating post-war urbanization in a period of general prosperity in Tanganyika by encouraging the replacement of low-wage migrant laborers with a relatively higher-paid, permanent work force. Opportunities for casual labor declined in many ports, plantations, and factories as employers and colonial agents found in this period that granting higher wages might also encourage a more efficient, manageable and stable workforce. African workers organized trade unions which demanded better wages, encouraging their own proletarianization.[13] This meant that the overall numbers of Africans working for wages rose sharply in the last years of colonial rule. Nevertheless, the dividing line between casual and steady labor was observed in more and more industries and workshops, encouraging increasingly distinct colonial images of both disciplined youth and their loafing counterparts.

One reason for more rapid urbanization was a major expansion of education in the post-war era, increasing the numbers of young Africans hitting the roads, expecting their primary schooling would earn them wage employment in the towns. Although in Tanganyika only one quarter or less of the total migration of wage labor was rural to urban the British in the 1950s were especially concerned with the new travel habits of primary school leavers. They feared the emergence of a class of young men without jobs but with some education who would constitute an urban crowd, who would focus their discontent on the colonial state itself, rather than on the chiefs, and on national instead of local issues. The distance between colonial subjects and their masters was lessened in towns like Dar es Salaam; there simply were fewer intermediaries between alien government agents and Africans. Colonial authority was therefore more exposed to resistance, more vulnerable to the derision and complaints of frustrated young townsmen. These were relatively difficult for the colonial state to dismiss or ignore with the emergence of nationalist and trade union movements in the 1940s and 1950s, which expressed urban antagonisms unlike any movements ever witnessed. Colonials wanted to avoid the creation of a dangerous jobless class as much as they wanted to create an urban working class.

In his close scrutiny of the recent arrivals to Dar es Salaam J.A.K. Leslie (see below) identified this new working class as the 'new men' of the capital, who set new standards of achievement for African townsmen. They possessed both literacy and disciplined work habits, and were rapidly securing an advance in their generational status. Those unable to find employment, according to the police, colonial scholars, District Commissioners, and the Governor, became 'spivs' and 'hooligans.' These young men, lacking opportunities for further education, unable to find work, and unwilling to return to the rural areas, were, according to the British, only interested in leisure and theft. Delayed in their generational mobility, 'hooligans' attached themselves to the dangerous 'social complex of idleness' in the towns[14] considered one of the most serious ills of the late colonial order.

These two categories formed an 'historical dialectic' during the 1950s, and were largely projections of the anxieties and hopes of colonialists attempting to control the process of 'modernization', and to either resolve or ignore its contradictions.[15] One of these was youth mobility. Colonial agents could only deplore the flight of youth to the towns. Read the following excerpt from the Bagamoyo District Annual Report of 1953:

> The young, energetic and forceful, move off to Dar es Salaam, whose golden pavements are now so near. The affairs of the town have tended to remain in the hands of the elderly, the cautious and the conservative. It is not surprising therefore, if in this town of ghosts and memories, of half-forgotten splendor and ruined palaces, it should be difficult to find much desire to look forward, and plan for the future, and if the ferment of new ideas is slow in coming.[16]

Here, the symbol of the older generation is a ruined palace. Bagamoyo, abandoned by the young, is a place of decay and idleness, of forgotten splendor.

And yet even when young men stayed in the rural areas they sometimes aroused the fears of colonial agents, particularly as the nationalist movement intensified. In Masasi District of Tanganyika the District Commissioner noted in 1954 an emerging problem of disorderly youth. These were primary or middle school graduates no longer interested in farming. The idleness of these, the DC wrote, 'may well become a problem here' unless 'a large number of them can be persuaded to return to the land'. Only this kind of heavy labor would absorb their 'mental, physical and moral energies'.[17]

As if in confirmation of the warnings of 1954 of the dangers of youth having too much freedom to move, the DC wrote in 1957 about,

> The horde of young 'spivs' who consider that four years at a primary school should give them exemption from all manual labor. *These youngsters roam the district like packs of jackals,* stealing, scrounging, drinking, and generally making a thorough nuisance of themselves. All that could be done in 1957 was to keep them on the move and prevent them 'packing' at their favorite haunts – Masasi, Lulindi and Nangoo – by frequent 'spiv raids' on these places. In 1958 it is hoped that the Native Authorities will face up to *the task of keeping these youngsters on the land and of*

> *instilling in them a discipline* which the schools and
> the families have been unable to impose [emphasis
> added].[18]

The DC deplored unrestricted movement of youth unhinged
from rural life, and advocated the full force of the law to control
the roaming 'packs of jackals' dismissing manual work as intoler-
able. Such youth had, according to the DC, a dissipating influence in rural life, enervating the discipline of the progressive
peasants working for a better life.[19]

In the following year, the DC reported 'a deterioration in
the general tone in the district caused by the irresponsible local
leadership of TANU [Tanganyika African National Union]'. The
Provincial Commissioner's report of the same year echoes that of
the DC, reporting a decline in respect for established authority,
resulting from 'the emotional ferment of politics and [sic] is most
marked among the young men'. This political fervor had not as
yet reached a 'crisis' stage, but accounted in 1958 for 'isolated
instances of resisting arrest, threatening tax collectors and other
illegal acts which have led to prosecutions'.[20]

The DC of Masasi did record a promising new development in 1958 in the effort to keep youth on the land, that of the
apparently thriving Young Farmer's Clubs of the district. These
associations of young men, established in the previous year, collectively cultivated showcase *shamba* of usually two acres. These
shamba 'act as demonstration plots showing the advantages of tie
ridging. In the dry season, those clubs that clear and level a football pitch are rewarded with a free first issue of goal posts and a
football....'. Of the seven Young Farmer's Clubs founded in 1957,
five remained in 1958, and a further five were being established.
The DC wrote:

> It is too early to say how successful these clubs are
> in their objects of keeping the young men in their
> villages or driving them into useful employment, of
> serving as demonstration plots and of brightening up
> life in the villages. Unfortunately but not unnaturally
> they have the least appeal in places where the 'spiv'
> problem is the greatest.[21]

Here the distinction is apparent between 'useful' and disorderly youth, so central to colonial age discourse. Young Farmer's Clubs represented the future as conceived by the British, the rationalization of economic relations and the rising productivity of African farms. The Young Farmers' Clubs encouraged young men to *stay in the villages* and to not become 'detribalized', or in other words, undisciplined. The registration of the Mwanza Federation of Young Farmers Clubs (1957) claimed that the purpose of their association was,

> To bring together the young people of the district with a view to developing individual capacity and ability to serve the community. To encourage amongst members an interest in country life and farming ... To form a means of continued education not only in the art and science of farming but also in the art and science of living.[22]

After his prosaic account in 1957 of delinquency and the complete disinterest on the part of the 'spiv' element to remain in the villages, the DC's reports by 1959 are laconic and straightforward. The District Commissioner merely notes a further deterioration of law and order in the district, and another year of poor tax collection. Of the Young Farmer's Clubs, the DC writes that they 'have not taken root except in the Nanyumbu Liwaliate where there are six of them, with membership of between 10 and 24 young farmers. Most of them hold weekly dances and are now at work on their communal *shamba*'.

Finally, in summary the DC reported that,

> For most of the year there was considerable ill-feeling between the Administration and the people of the District, and in October the District Commissioner was roughly handled in an incident at a TANU Youth League meeting. By the end of the year the atmosphere had improved.[23]

This rough handling happened at the end of October, when the TANU Youth League organized a Province-wide gathering of youth at Masasi to sing, dance, perform dramas, and give reports on local youth activities from as far away as Mtwara and Songea.

'It was like a Boy Scout camp', remembered John Nzunda, then TANU's Provincial Secretary and principal organizer of the event. During these evening nationalist celebrations, the DC, named Geoffrey Thirtle, arrived in his land rover and began to 'abuse' the Youth League members present, calling them hooligans. Thirtle said also that all TANU party leaders were 'thieves', except Nyerere, and that their brains were buried under a cashew tree.

Nzunda, who had obtained a government permit for the gathering, wanted to avoid a potentially violent confrontation. He also thought it necessary to defend the dignity of the event, and of its participants. He ordered female youth to tear their *kanga* for material with which to bind the arms and legs of the DC. This accomplished, Nzunda commandeered his vehicle, and he and some other youths delivered the incapacitated DC to the nearest police station. After being released the DC in a rage attempted to have his young captors locked up, without results. Instead, after an official investigation by the Provincial Commissioner, and a court case, the DC was dismissed from his post. Thus colonial prejudices against African youth precipitated a highly embarrassing situation for colonial authorities.[24] In this incident the colonial discourse on generation was exposed for its false portrayal of youth as hooligans; indeed, the only person found to be breaking the law was the DC himself.

THE SPIV RAID

The developments in Masasi District in the 1950s were not isolated, but repeated in other rural areas touched by 'politics'. In 1951 the PC of Mwanza Province noted 'a progressive lessening in tribal discipline' alongside a growing political consciousness among many Africans.[25] The greatest problems with youth were reported not from the rural areas, however, but from the growing towns. The towns were important arenas for youth to explore new ways of securing advances in their generational status independent of village sanctions and the domination of the elders. They were also more closely supervised by colonials, interested in imprinting the functional and orderly patterns of streets and buildings of the towns onto the very movements and habits of their young arrivals. Idleness in a realm of visible discipline would not be tolerated. The urban development officer for Ukerewe reported in 1958 that 'The problem of *wahuni* [hooligans] and young boys without occupation in the town is considerable...'[26] From Mwanza the District Commissioner reported in 1957 that,

> A regrettable feature in Mwanza, as in other large towns, is the bad manners and lack of respect for law and order displayed by many Africans, particularly those of the younger generation.[27]

The DC identified those with a few years or less of formal education as the most 'objectionable'.[28]

The survey of Dar es Salaam undertaken in 1956 by J.A.K. Leslie, a British sociologist under the commission of the Tanganyikan government, illustrates officials' working assumptions as they worried about underemployment, and reacted to a situation of growing political activity. His account is of a capital city going through rapid transformation, with its population increasing in the decade after 1943 from 37,000 to 72,300. The mobility of a populace in which two-thirds were born outside the town gave nationalism enormous influence in the 1950s, despite every British attempt to stabilize the 'working' population.[29]

According to Leslie, youth were drawn to Dar es Salaam in 'the search for an un-contributing anonymity in town; and by the glamour of the town's reputation'. This anonymity allowed young Africans to forget kinship and ethnic bonds, and to 'soar away in a new and freer orbit, vying with the other bright stars in the firmament, of whom he sees pictures and hears accounts even in his country quiet'.[30] The towns provided, according to Leslie, a new opportunity for young people, 'while remaining invisible to the authorities, to shine among his fellows, as it were to jump the long queue of promotion in the esteem of the community'.[31]

Thus, we see town life for the young conceived by Leslie as a new world of the private, isolated individual, avoiding taxes and pursuing the consumer luxury items unavailable in the villages, symbolic of urban status. At the top of this 'new-world' were the 'new men' who through employment were guaranteed generational mobility outside of the assistance of their elders. These 'new men', so wrote Leslie, were 'almost exclusively Christian, and many are educated; they attack the power of the elders and advocate the equality of young and old'.[32] The social impact of 'new men' was so great in Dar es Salaam they produced a counter-movement. In opposition to the 'new men' were Islamic elders, who defended their privileged position in society. These 'accorded no recognition to the claims of the "new man", the brash, the bustling, the man who wanted to get on and impose himself on the world'. Leslie wrote that '.... in a world where the traditional rural standards of living are now discovered to be poverty', adherence to Muslim traditions gave dignity to people suddenly thought of as poor and uneducated.[33]

In other words, the 'new men' of the 1950s introduced generational conflict and inequalities in wealth and education, while asserting a different equality – that between the young and old, 'In a world where every man is for himself there is nobody to tell the young immigrant to pipe down and listen to his elders and betters'.[34]

But for those without education or steady employment, town life was excruciating, a circumstance 'like watching the guests go into a great feast for which one needs a special card of entry, a card which they have not got'.[35] As part of the daily reality of poor youth in the capital, Leslie mentions boredom, hunger, low wages, overcrowding, and discrimination. In addition to these were irritating evidences of an alien authority, which used the rule of law to fix low wages, oppose strikes, arrest thieves and tax defaulters, and to repatriate vagrants. Leslie wrote that for 'the nationalist (these exercises of state power) prepare the way – to an extent that few rural areas can – for the theme that if only the alien authority is removed wealth will accrue to the African poor'.[36]

Repatriating vagrants was considered the appropriate means to break up the emerging urban crowd. Police 'spiv' raids were reportedly welcomed by the majority of African regular residents of Mwanza, and had 'a most salutary effect in inducing respect for law and order'. In 1957, these raids resulted in 202 youth being repatriated to their home villages, and the actual imprisonment of a 'number of persons who had returned to the town after being ordered to live elsewhere'.[37]

In fact, for the year of 1957, the PC reported 'spiv' raids in all the largest settlements of the Province, employing dozens of special constables in the effort. With some satisfaction, the PC wrote,

> Action by the Police to cope with spivs has met with the approval of the law-abiding public, and consider-able cleaning up has been done in Mwanza, Bukoba, Musoma, Tarime, Shinyanga, Maswa and Geita.[38]

Colonial police thus took a leading role in enforcing the new definitions of delinquency and non-conformity, so that behavior perhaps once tolerated by the family or community in the rural areas now was met with hostility and punishment in the towns. The police and colonial agents were becoming increasingly sensitive to patterns of youthful movement and leisure. Urbanization and capitalism required new forms of discipline and, therefore new methods of control and punishment: the 'spiv' raid.[39]

The residents of Dar es Salaam witnessed many street-cleaning sweeps. In 1954 for example the police conducted 94 'checks' of people thought to be 'spivs', tax defaulters or 'drifters' from the villages; of a total of 5,478 persons checked, they repatriated 1,094 to their home villages. In 1955, 1,184 were repatriated from Dar es Salaam.[40] According to the fictionalized memoirs of one Dar es Salaam resident, 'at regular intervals green government trucks suddenly appeared at night in the streets and a general chase ensued...'. Those without employment cards were sent to the police station overnight, and if not claimed by employers were sent to their home villages.[41]

However, not every township of the Territory was similarly afflicted with 'spivs'. Although the DC for Arusha reported the 'round up of undesirables' as early as 1954, he reported in 1957, however, very few 'problems' with 'spivs', claiming 'increasing control has been exercised on undesirable characters in the Township. 1619 persons were checked and 95 of them repatriated'.[42] In 1959, the police repatriated only 78 youth, mostly young Chagga, who, the DC wrote, 'come here to seek their fortune, and fall into bad company'.[43]

Spiv round ups and repatriations were a direct confrontation with the unrestricted freedom of movement enjoyed by youth of the 1950s. The colonial state simply countered with its own enforced travel operations, delivering undesirables back to the hoped-for restraining influence of their home villages. This was justified in 1960 by the Territorial Police,

> With the rapid change in the economic and social conditions of the public, there is an *ever increasing population drift from the discipline and security of tribal areas to the towns.* This leads to new problems for the Force. The number of petty thefts, particularly in urban centres, continues to increase, to the annoyance and inconvenience of the great majority of the public [emphasis added].[44]

Territorial Police acted physically against young men whose mere presence in the streets aroused enough suspicion that they were instantly placed in an imagined criminal class, which, according to colonial constructions of African society, was neatly opposed to the interests of more established African urban residents. These images of delinquent youth coming at the very end of the colonial period may be set against an earlier era when youth were more autonomous of the moral judgments of the state, when age-related social roles were still defined exclusively within rural society. In the villages, family and community needs organized time; pre-industrial distinctions between work and non-work prevailed. But by the 1950s, as more youth gained access to some western education and freedom to travel, their behavior now became defined not only by their village seniors, but by a scattering of capitalists, government agents and police. Colonial and capitalist definitions of proper conduct now extended to African youth seeking, in their freedom of movement, to negotiate their own autonomous standards of behavior during their uncertain transition to adulthood. They deliberately sought this transition in spaces independent of village patriarchies.

In the towns the colonials pronounced distinctions between 'appropriate' or inappropriate use of time by young Africans, in a system of wage labor which distinguished now between 'work' and 'leisure'. Young arrivals in the 1950s seeking in the towns a way of ensuring their generational mobility were never exposed to so many complaints of their non-conformity and delinquency. The official British post-war policy of encouraging the creation of a stable working class meant that some young men were made welcome in the towns. Others were not; some were loafers, and others were respectable.[45] The very presence of loitering young African men, no longer considered 'tribal', nor yet worthy of urban respectability, was seen as a contamination of the ordered environment the colonials sought to create. They served no purpose and it was better to return them to the restraining control of their elders back home.

NATIONALIST YOUTH: A NEW IDENTITY

TANU nationalism provided junior arrivals in the towns in the 1950s a means of opening up some new space for renegotiating their status. This as a result of the fact those heretofore occupying a rather marginal position and suspicious identity in urban society might through activity in an independence movement win the acceptance of more established residents. Leslie reported that nearly 100% of the African population in 1957 supported or were sympathetic of TANU.[46] Leslie personally regarded urban youth as unpredictable, explosive, and ripe for generational rebellion. He considered a trend in fashion among Dar es Salaam young men in 1957—'the cult of the cowboy clothes' – as 'a revolt of the adolescent, in age and in culture, against the authority of the elders, of the established, of the superior and supercilious'. The clothes were,

> The safety valve of the dangerous mob element which is likely always to be part of Dar es Salaam. They are unformed Hitlerjugend, as yet, their uniform waiting for a Feuhrer to give respectability to their longing to be admired, to have a place in the sun.[47]

Leslie's association of TANU with Dar es Salaam's idle and 'dangerous mob element' was repeated by another observer in the 1950s, Tanganyika's Governor Edward Twining. Twining's remarks suggest that at the very top of British administration, colonials considered the threat of nationalism to be one of growing social indiscipline. Addressing an assembly of chiefs in Mwanza District in February, 1954, Twining remarked that the new generation of politicians were 'people who feel that they no longer want to have the traditional work of Africans living in the country, developing their land, and tending their cattle, but who come to the towns to live lives of parasites'.[48] The evil influence of the towns attract

> The African, often at his most impressionable age, into a fierce economic struggle conducted in western terms and for western rewards, where the sanctions of tribal life no longer have a meaning.[49]

Such an urban environment could only produce an opportunistic, morally bankrupt leadership, with a following of hopelessly 'detribalized' young Africans. In his own words, Twining considered TANU to be a 'thoroughly spurious national organization' with corrupt leadership 'actuated by malice and self-interest'.[50] In November, 1957, he addressed a meeting of the Tanganyika Sisal Growers' Association, saying:

> At all times there is bound to be a hooligan fringe in growing towns which is far from easy to deal with, even with the constant vigilance of the police, but there has been unmistakable evidence that this hooliganism has been growing in extent during the current year and frequently occurs under the name of some political party. It has led to intimidation and to a general defiance of law and order. Moreover, some of the petty leaders have arrogated to themselves the position of usurpers of the authority of the Native Authorities and even government itself.[51]

Among Africans, however, the role assumed by urban youth in TANU is remembered as, instead, disciplined, the very 'front line' of, on all levels, a peaceful and orderly nationalism. Public memories of the generation of young men trying to get ahead in places like Dar es Salaam in the 1950s, and who in so doing joined the TANU Youth League (TYL), are full of images not of criminality but of restraint. Although African townsmen in the 1930s once regarded their junior newcomer neighbors in town as hooligans, these complaints have since been publicly forgotten. What is remembered is the employment of apparent members of the urban crowd to, ironically, maintain law and order at party rallies, or their work as messengers, singers, and security personnel.[52] Urban youth represented a constantly available pool of labor and talent for the party. Led, among others, by Julius Nyerere's younger brother, Joseph, urban youth performed in TYL choirs and comic plays, and were crucial in party fundraising and membership drives. In their various capacities TYL activists sought to undermine colonial assumptions that unemployment was tantamount to crime and iniquity. The prominent role of the TYL within Tanganyikan nationalism was such that when Julius Nyerere addressed the Mombasa African Democratic Union in January 1958, a colonial intelligence officer noted that he advised Kenyan nationalists to

> Divide their organizations into sections containing elderly members, young members, and women, and to ensure that the control and leadership were retained by the young men, who were more progressive, energetic, and prepared to take greater risks.[53]

Encouraging urban youth to assume many of the mundane responsibilities and organizing tasks of the party must be considered one of the most successful strategies employed by TANU leaders in the 1950s. The well-remembered zealousness of urban youth was a clear message to their party elders that young people dislocated from rural life might in the towns still perform subordinate duties, and that such service deserved, as in old times, the patronage of their seniors. TYL activists performed security work, maintained discipline at nationalist rallies, sang songs of derision and complaint in traveling TANU choirs, sold membership cards, and assumed whatever other routine physical tasks their leaders thought desirable to assign them.

All this was active distancing on the part of youth from the taint and stigma of criminality. Nothing better illustrates this point than the complaints which surfaced in colonial correspondence in late 1960 which claimed that young men of the TYL, with the struggle for independence virtually over, were now angering local authorities in Tanga, Northern and Southern Provinces by usurping police powers. That is, they began to enforce either real or imaginary territorial laws by organizing night patrols of towns and roads, stopping and sometimes arresting ordinary Tanganyikans for alleged offenses, drilling like soldiers with imitation rifles, searching motor cars for illegal commodities, and holding illegal courts. The deputy governor John Fletcher-Cooke wrote in November that,

> During the last weeks there have been a considerable number of cases in which members of the TANU Youth League have, sometimes deliberately and sometimes, I think, in good faith, or at least unintentionally, usurped the functions of constituted authority. In the greater number of these cases of the League, acting in the capacity of 'vigilantes', have arrested drunks, prostitutes and the like, and have either handed them over to the Police or meted out the customary punishment on the spot.[54]

Vigilantism was an unambiguous assertion and very public statement of young men's respect for law and order. Due to party censure such cases declined in frequency by the end of 1960. For many TYL activists, however, they had already proved their point, and had separated themselves from (intangible) hooligan society. Their role in nationalist performance can thus be seen as part of their ongoing struggle to lose their marginal status in the first place and secondly as a means by which to later call on the patronage of their 'elders' in the party after independence.[55]

EARLY DISCIPLINE IN ZANZIBAR

Early British attempts to instill colonial discipline among Zanzibaris preceded any specific concern with youth as a distinct and perhaps dangerous social identity. These attempts came with the abolition of slavery in the Protectorate in 1897, when the British anticipated that the work habits of slaves would dramatically deteriorate as they obtained their independence. They therefore dictated on what terms Africans could obtain their emancipation, and the kind of work obligations to which afterwards they would be legally subject. 'Vagrancy' became a criminal offense. According to the statutes of abolition, in order to avoid prosecution as 'vagrants', former slaves needed to prove they had both shelter and some means of support.[56] This was not considered enough to stop former slaves from roaming the countryside, however. Courts were empowered to prosecute ex-slaves who according to their employers were not working hard enough in fulfilling their labor contracts.[57] Zanzibaris faced sentences of hard labor and imprisonment if caught 'wandering about' without 'visible means of subsistence'. Cooper writes that the prisons in Pemba were crowded with those found guilty of vagrancy.[58]

The poor living in the towns were most vulnerable to police harassment for vagrancy. They were rounded up periodically in a way similar to the *spiv* raids on the mainland.[59] The police convicted one out of twenty 'natives' in Zanzibar Town in 1906, for either assault, drunkenness, adultery, vagrancy or burglary. Cooper argues this attack on crime was actually more 'an assault on the social complex of idleness', among islanders perceived as 'rootless', 'incapable of working or upholding any standards of conduct... slaves had to be made fit for an orderly society and taught self-discipline'.[60] The government cracked down on drinking and dancing. Those activities were considered part of the general atmosphere in the islands of dissipation and indolence. The state banned or required special permits for all *ngomas*, African dance performances, and prohibited Africans access to imported alcohol, as well as their possession or consumption of local brews.[61]

By the 1920s, however, the government was taking a more routine approach to the problem of social indiscipline, still prosecuting people for drunkenness and vagrancy, but with much less spirit and imagination. Law enforcement had lost its social agenda. Cooper concludes that 'in the end, the Government's attempts to create a society divided into owners and workers amounted to periodic and ineffective harassment'.[62]

Thus in comparison with Tanganyika officials in Zanzibar took a relatively early interest in enforcing discipline, rather than just talking about it. Although 'de-tribalization' was not considered the issue, officials sought to exert control over former slaves as if, like youth in Dar es Salaam, they were a rootless, mobile community, without fixed residences, potentially autonomous of society. On both islands and mainland loafing and riotousness were deplored and periodic sweeps of urban neighborhoods yielded rich catches of vagrants; the major difference was that in Zanzibar 'vagrants' were imprisoned or put to work, whereas in Tanganyika they were sent back to their villages, at least temporarily.

As the following suggests, when colonial officials in Zanzibar did take notice of youth as a separate social identity after World War II, they imagined approaches to youth indiscipline fundamentally different from those of Tanganyika. First of all, because the British in Zanzibar believed social stability depended on proper relations within and between races and families, rather than 'tribes',[63] 'de-tribalization' was not demonized in Zanzibar as it was in other colonies. 'Delinquency' was not perceived as caused by 'de-tribalization'. Rather, colonial agents in the islands considered 'delinquency' as a peculiar trait of adolescence, exacerbated by parental neglect. The image that emerges is that youthful misbehavior in Zanzibar was considered part of the inherent indiscipline of the age, caused by the decline of family rather than 'tribal' values brought about by unrestricted youth mobility.

Furthermore, because urban centers in Zanzibar grew at a much slower pace than on the mainland, officials worried less about uncontrolled urbanization and did not commission studies on the social influences of the growing towns. A consensus never emerged suggesting that the moral order of the villages was so superior to that of the towns that youth should be encouraged to stay in the rural areas. Towns in Zanzibar were not described as sinkholes of iniquity. Nor was the spiv raid a practice in the terminal years of British authority; the young male crowds of the capital could not so easily be returned to their villages of origin, since so many of slave ancestry had no 'ancestral village', except on the mainland.

Instead, officials took measures in the 1950s to encourage 'rational recreation'[64] in town by establishing youth associations such as the Boy Scouts and football teams. Youth associations, officials believed, would promote values of fraternity, discipline, and social goodwill in the rising generation of the islands. They would attack the 'social complex of idleness', which so often was expressed through criminal behavior. They would provide the government some way of exerting control over youth leisure hours. Such an interest in youth associations was prior to the very late interest in this area shown by the government in Tanganyika. As late as 1959, provoked by the prominent role urban youth were then playing in TANU, the Ministry of Local Government in Tanganyika appealed to Governor Turnbull to sponsor more research on 'youth clubs' in order to dispel government ignorance of 'youth' as a social factor in the towns.[65]

In the islands, however, the British by the mid-1950s had established a Youth Association to coordinate the many diverse youth organizations in Zanzibar. But just as these attempts were underway it gradually became apparent to colonial agents that the major concern of the state should not be with the organization of youth leisure but youth labor. That promoting 'rational recreation' was not reducing crime; 'juvenile' crime levels were increasing, the British believed, because of rising unemployment. Worse, in the late 1950s British administrators lived and operated in a highly political atmosphere, the control of which was seen to be undermined by the presence of numbers of young men without any steady work in the capital of the Protectorate. As nationalist politicians sought to recruit urban youth into their competing political movements, the British became more anxious over those without steady work, who in their 'idleness' they considered most vulnerable to subversive propaganda, and most capable of violence.

Thus in the post-war period 'youth' in colonial discourse embodied a discreet social category. Not only was the idea of 'youth' invented as a political identity in Zanzibar in the 1950s, but the 'problem' of youth unemployment as well. Despite a decades-long tradition of casual labor in the Protectorate, British officials became alarmed over youth unemployment in the islands.

SPORTS AND SCOUTS

The colonial state sought to use youth associations to control youth leisure hours and reduce racial hostilities in the islands. The

British first established a Sports Association in 1928 'to control and foster local sports'.[66] The president of the Sports Association gave a speech in 1927, in a period when the construction of sporting facilities was becoming an accepted ongoing investment of the colonial state, in which he said the following,

> Not only do I desire to see our Recreation Park the finest and best equipped in tropical Africa, an object of pride to ourselves and a thing of amazement to visitors, but to an even greater degree do I want to see sportsmen of all nationalities and sects practicing and perfecting themselves at the several types of sport in a real spirit of friendliness and goodwill.[67]

At least on one level, then, the colonialists conceived of sporting events as great social occasions, when individuals living in a racially-stratified society might play together and in so doing forget ethnic antagonisms. The idea was that with Africans, Arabs, Indians and Comorians merging into temporary play communities, racial distinctions might dissolve. This sentiment was echoed by Wheatley, a British civil servant called out of retirement in the 1950s to supervise the construction of a new sports stadium in the capital. In 1955 he wrote to the president of the Sports Association, that he had 'given practically a lifetime' to encouraging sport in Zanzibar, and that this commitment was justified because,

> ... I sincerely believe that sport is mellowing and maturing the different tribes and peoples of East Africa and their leaders which we have discovered by the Inter-Territorial matches, be it cricket, hockey or football. This may be received by cynicism in some quarters but it is a fact and not an opinion. Sport is providing a good bridge between an East African peoples (*sic*).[68]

Laura Fair's informants confirmed that football leagues in the capital encouraged the reduction of ethnic antagonisms. That happened particularly after the British introduced area divisions into the leagues in 1941.[69] The British sought through sport to instill in Zanzibari youth a respect for colonial authority, time discipline, and team spirit, which, however, were values often contested by Zanzibari players.[70]

The Boy Scout program was considered by its founder Lord Baden-Powell a 'character factory'. It was a means of providing youth with disciplined forms of recreation.[71] The Boy Scouts also had as one of its objectives the creation in the Empire of inter-ethnic social ties, as a means of reconciling or transcending parochial communal interests. The Overseas Scout leader in London expressed this in 1921 in a letter to Zanzibari scout leaders; among the Boy Scout movement's principal aims was 'that of knitting the different parts of the Empire more closely together in the bond of a great brotherhood'.[72] At the end of World War II the islands' scouting program was limited to boys from Zanzibar Town only. Then in 1947 some colonial leaders began to support an expansion of the program into the smaller towns of the Protectorate: Makunduchi, Wete, and Chwake. The Provincial Commissioner asked the Welfare Officer, 'Will you please give your coordinated efforts to the development of this project which has great potentiality for developing in the rising generation a sense of responsibility, civic pride, and character'.[73]

Two months later the British Resident himself wrote a statement on youth, which proved to be twenty years before its time, anticipating the thinking of Zanzibar's Revolutionary Council in the 1970s:

> Finally I cannot stress too strongly the importance I place on the encouragement of Youth Movements and especially the Boy Scouts. At the risk of repetition, I emphasize that in the winning of the confidence of the rising generation, both male and especially female, lies our chief hope of progress, if not salvation.[74]

By 1949 the Boy Scouts were the largest youth organization for boys on the islands, expanding to eight troops organized on Zanzibar, and a further eight organized in Pemba. The Boy Scouts in the early 1950s acted as the 'principal coordinating agency' for all youth organizations. Those youth organizations included a number of Asian and Arab sporting and social clubs for young men in town. There were also some other African sport and dancing groups in the capital.[75] Apparently, however, the Boy Scouts were not effective in their role of coordinating the many youth organizations in Zanzibar, or in exerting the desired level of state influence on young men. In April, 1955, a meeting of individuals interested in youth issues was convened by the government to discuss 'amenities' for youth in Zanzibar Town, 'and the need for any further measures to eliminate undesirable pursuits among Zanzibari youth'. Early measures to 'eliminate undesirable pursuits' remain unclear, but a committee was formed 'to assess the extent to which the existing clubs do and could further fulfill the needs of youth by providing suitable activities during their leisure hours'. This committee, in order to influence and control youth leisure, was given the task of forming a Youth Council from representatives of various youth organizations registered in the islands. A meeting was finally held in December 1955, but it was poorly attended.[76]

A Youth Association was finally formed in October 1956 to coordinate existing organizations for youth, 'make provision for the needs of the youth', and to encourage clubs to have youth sections. By the end of 1957, however, the Association had a constitution and a committee, but no members.[77] In 1958 the colonials concluded the idea of a Youth Association was 'premature'.[78]

IDLENESS AND ITS CONSEQUENCES

The idea for such an association was shelved just as crime levels and nationalist agitation in the Protectorate suggested that a Youth Association to regulate the leisure pursuits of youth was not only premature but also inappropriate. Crime levels increased significantly in Zanzibar in the 1950s, and in police reports about the growing wave of criminality 'youth' were given prominent treatment. Youth leisure associations appeared to be having no effect on youthful indiscipline. In 1951 5,708 cases of crime were reported. That number steadily rose so that by 1960 9,974 cases were reported.[79] The Protectorate established a court for juvenile offenders in 1956, which by 1962 was hearing fifty cases a year.[80] In 1958 the Annual Report of the Zanzibar Police suggested three leading reasons for the rise in crime. Unemployment and increased poverty were listed as the principal reasons, followed by a lack of parental control over juveniles.[81]

Also in 1958 the report began a special section on juvenile crime, which was 'a cause of some concern',

> Joy riding by parties of juveniles in cars borrowed without the owners consent was prevalent in the early months of the year, as was also theft from parked cars and from clothing of bathers on the town beaches. Both these undesirable activities were successfully controlled, but investigations revealed a lack of parental control. Young boys were frequently found wandering or sleeping on the streets at a very late hour.[82]

In the next year came the following police report,

> Zanzibar Stone Town is the main centre of juvenile delinquency and a gang of boys and young adults was responsible for a considerable number of breakings.... Lack of parental control remains a major cause of delinquency.[83]

Despite rising levels of crime in the Protectorate, no raids on 'spivs', so commonplace in towns on the mainland, were reported in Zanzibar. This is not to suggest that 'vagrants' were not a presence in the capital, only that they had come to be more tolerated than in Tanganyika; they were even allowed a modest space within which to roam, their parents never very far away,

> In lean periods the influx of boys from the country into towns becomes a problem but as soon as the clove harvest commences they practically all disappear into the plantations to pick cloves. One factor that minimizes this evil is that the homes of these children are usually within reach in a day, thus contact with parents is maintained.[84]

According to the British the security of the town from wild youth depended, therefore, on direct parental supervision, as well as full employment. Nothing was ever done to strengthen the family, however, nor was there any structure established to relieve youth unemployment in the islands, prior to the revolution. The only evidence of any effort by the British to fight the 'social complex of idleness' was made just one month prior to independence, in November 1963. The Assistant Director of Education forwarded two ideas for providing work to youth: encourage young men to join the Special Constabulary and establish a youth work corps. These work corps would be organized into groups of thirty each, clearing, leveling and planting for the imminent independence celebrations. 'For the future it is hoped these work gangs can be kept in being to undertake work of a national character', such as maintaining housing and drainage systems in the capital.[85]

Following the independence celebrations the work corps suddenly collapsed, with no youth turning up for work and their interest dead. Arab government servants perceived the youth corps, not surprisingly, as an opportunity for political patronage. Secondly, the recruited youth thought they would be made uniformed tour guides for the celebrations, rather than common laborers. The District Commissioner for Zanzibar Town, ruminating on the collapse of this project, commented that the youth corps was not an 'impossible dream' but that the time had not yet arrived for its success.[86]

Much more was *said* about unemployment, however. In late September 1962, an international symposium on youth unemployment was held in Dar es Salaam, with representatives from various African nations and territories, including the Protectorate of Zanzibar, in attendance. The delegates from the islands reported to the symposium a situation that was familiar. In other parts of the continent the drift of school leavers to the towns had created an ongoing unemployment problem among youth that sought wage labor in preference to subsistence agriculture in the rural areas, where there was no unemployment problem. The delegates stated there was no 'concerted plan' to combat unemployment in Zanzibar, no schemes to absorb youth in the town, and no training of youth leaders.[87]

Various African delegations expressed their views at the conference on the problem of youth unemployment in their respective countries and territories, and, according to the symposium report, a consensus was reached by the delegates, not only on the historical origins of unemployment in Africa, but the moral, social, economic and political dangers in this situation in its relation to the continuing growth of thousands of young men without work. We quote the Republic of Congo (Brazzaville) on this point:

> 'It is obvious that, morally, the unemployed youth who needs money to enjoy the advantages the town has to offer is tempted to stray from the straight and narrow path and to obtain by stealing what he cannot obtain by working....
>
> While the villages are emptying and the number of agricultural workers is constantly diminishing, the towns are filling with the unemployed and the idle who contribute nothing to the economic life of the country but whom the country must nevertheless feed....
>
> Politically, the thousands of unemployed and idle young men, dissatisfied with their lot, constitute an obvious prey for subversive propaganda. It is easy to persuade the workless that the Government does not care about them, is doing nothing to help them and has abandoned them to their fate. Political agitation can turn the young unemployed into potential shock troops for all manner of insurrectionary movements'.

Following the conference, the Zanzibari delegates with these alarming reports of subversion in mind lamented to the British Chief Minister in Zanzibar. They were 'aggrieved' to find that the Protectorate was one of the only territories that had made no efforts to deal with youth unemployment, and which still had 'to accept the fact that the problem of unemployed youth exists in Zanzibar'.

They continued to say,

> This problem seems to have two aspects. We can look at it as a problem that is connected with finding useful employment for young people in order to avoid repercussions of unemployment and the political and social implications that go with it. Secondly, we can look at the employment of youth as a means of contributing to the economic development of the

country and this we feel is a very important aspect indeed....

We would like to point out to the Government that unless a scheme or schemes are devised in Zanzibar in order to combat unemployment of young people, the problem will before long assume proportions which may be impossible to control with our limited resources....

The consensus of opinion of some delegates was that the migration of young school leavers to the towns was related to their general refusal to accept the restrictions of traditional rural family life and the rigors of subsistence or near subsistence farming.

A part answer to the problem, therefore, is the need to seek a means whereby some of these young school leavers can be encouraged to accept farming as a career....

The proposals of the returning delegates to devise 'schemes' and establish institutions to compel school leavers to return to farming were never acted upon by the colonial state, but they were similar to the disciplinary measures adopted by Zanzibar's Revolutionary Council only three years later. Their proposals included the introduction of youth camps to persuade school leavers to abandon the 'idleness' of the town and become farmers. The delegates believed that in the camps a system of 're-education for those young people who have left school and are unemployed will go a long way to inculcate in them the right attitude towards work and economic production'.

The specific form of training they recommended was based upon the reports of Nigerian delegates at the symposium: youth would be 'voluntarily' resettled in camps which would provide training in 'intensive' and 'scientific' farming principles. The camps, organized on democratic lines, would make school leavers into 'modern farmers'. In these 'farm institutes' the students would live in temporary shelters erected by themselves, and would be subjected to 'strict' discipline, and 'a certain amount of regimentation'. 'Good habits of hard work, perseverance and obedience should be fostered among the trainees', the Zanzibari delegates recommended.[88]

To complete this general atmosphere of spartan obedience and discipline, youth would also receive some kind of education 'aiming at inculcating in the trainees civic responsibility...'. Therefore, in the islands, just prior to independence, proposals were forwarded to establish camps or 'institutes' which would instill knowledge of 'scientific' farming techniques, and encourage a sense of civic responsibility, discipline and regimentation, and a disinclination to drift towards the towns. Such proposals were drawn up as antidotes to the colonial image of a class of idle and dissatisfied youth disturbing the towns.

These plans constituted a daring new approach to the 'problem' of youthful indiscipline, since the colonial state wasn't simply as in a spiv raid physically returning the urban crowd to the countryside, to hopefully fall once again under the venerable supervision of their village seniors. Rather, the camps offered, despite their emphasis on propaganda, discipline and austerity, an escape for young men from their dependent junior status in the countryside. The camps occupied a no-man's land between town and country where young men might entertain hopes of social promotion from their good work in the camps, independent of family restrictions. For this reason the youth camps inaugurated after the revolution were a far more successful experiment than spiv raids in Dar es Salaam in containing youthful indiscipline.

The provocation for such extreme measures of social engineering was the prominent role urban youth were playing, by 1962, in the nationalist politics of Zanzibar. That role was often labeled 'subversive' by colonial agents. To illustrate the connection in the colonial mind between youth unemployment and subversion, it suffices here to mention the short-lived and inconsequential Zanzibar Communist Party, founded in July 1962. Abdulrehman Muhammed held a press conference in the Princess Hotel in the capital to declare the beginning of the struggle to eradicate imperialism, capitalism and feudalism. Muhammed had recently returned from travels to Cairo, Beijing, London and Leipzig. It seems that while in London he suffered two nervous breakdowns. He was committed to a mental institution twice.[89]

According to British agents the new party fed on the temporary social discontent created by unemployment and low wages in the Protectorate. They were the result of a poor clove harvest.[90] British intelligence reported in 1962 that the new Communist Party shared common political views with many of the young activists of the other two leading parties of Zanzibar. They warned that,

> The possibility must be accepted that these individuals will one day find it to their advantage to band together and they will form a definite threat to any Government in Zanzibar especially if formed from among the present leaders.[91]

In October 1962, British intelligence reported that,

> The Zanzibar Communist Party is gaining ground slowly. Their fertile field is among the unemployed youths such as school leavers who roam about the streets and those who entertain imaginary grudges against the Government. Such a field provides a condition of mind that can absorb and accept communist ideologies. This is achieved by trying to convince the new recruits that their unfortunate plight is chiefly due to the present capitalist form of Government that rules Zanzibar.[92]

Seven months later, in May 1963, the following report was produced:

> There are signs that the government handles the unemployment situation, but still vagrancy is prevalent particularly with regard to Standard VIII students. Communist agents are making a capital out of it.[93]

Because of a lack of quality leadership and poor financial support, the fledgling Zanzibar Communist Party never took hold in the capital. It also ended never making its presence known in the islands except among some young men in the town, and to colonial agents assigned to observe the political agitation of 'frustrated' youth. The party had no perceivable political impact, and it died away by mid-1963.[94] The short history of the Communist Party in Zanzibar suggests the real fear among colonials that youth with some education who had drifted from village to town would be influenced by other youths. They were particularly weary of those youth who had traveled far more extensively, and who had gained prestige by accessing 'modern' learning in universities of various northern capitals.

In order to undermine such subversion by the more traveled and educated, colonial agents felt a need, then, to establish their own institutes of learning which would encourage work and civic responsibility, submerging young men in an environment alternative to that surrounding the students returning from overseas. These would attack youth interest in travel by creating alternative spaces of modernity and 'scientific principles' in the countryside, the backyard of the colonial state. Away from both town and village, outside of the limits of village patriarchy, these intermediate spaces were well-suited to the intermediate social positions of young men without jobs in town, neither children nor adults, no longer rural but not fully urban either. There, young men would learn how to work and be freed from their idle vulnerabilities to imported political dogma.

CONCLUSION

John Iliffe asserts that 'it was in the towns that Europeans first lost control of Africa'.[95] In the twilight of imperial rule, British agents worried over the perceived decline of social control once exerted by African 'tribes' or families, and the subsequent emergence of a mass of unemployed urban youth, who had little respect for law and order and were attracted by anti-colonial politics. It became common for the British in the 1950s to equate nationalism with youthful delinquency, and idleness with political agitation. Because of family decline and unrestricted travel, towns were becoming, not showcases for modernity, but pockets of crime, resistance, and immorality.

In relatively peaceful territories like Tanganyika, colonial officials feared 'unemployment' would cause the disintegration of law and order, which, at the very most, might require greater police-intervention and vigilance. In Zanzibar the stakes were somewhat higher, because in addition to crime the state feared that 'unemployment' might result in the political *subversion* of the young. For this reason colonial attempts in the islands to control youth leisure hours were shelved in the face of more serious concerns over the political and social impact of long-term 'unemployment' on youth in town.

The plans suggested in 1962 by colonial agents in order to establish youth camps in the countryside were a signal that the perceived deterioration of social discipline among youth was of concern to the colonial state. As a result, government circles were willing to consider officially taking on parenting roles in the Protectorate. After the revolution, the supposed idleness and lack of desire to 'build the nation' of young people compelled the revolutionary government in Zanzibar as early as 1965 to act on the 1962 proposals. What colonial agents only began to discuss became, in the period of Abeid Karume, an accepted fact, and foundation for state institutions designed to discipline, regiment, and punish the youth, in order to preserve the power of the new ruling clique. In socialism, even the colonial vocabulary of 'new men' and hooligans survived in an atmosphere where the new development ideology became so urgent. Even revolutionary leaders placed these categories of youth at the forefront of national discourse, and were willing to act as surrogate fathers to ensure the proper transition of youth to adulthood.

Notes

1. David Henry Anthony, 'Culture and Society in Transition: A People's History of Dar es Salaam, 1863-1939'. Ph.D. Dissertation, University of Wisconsin-Madison, 1983, 160-170.

2. *Ibid.*, xviii, 12.

3. E.C. Baker, *Report on Social and Economic Conditions in the Tanga Province*, Dar es Salaam, Government Printer, 1934, 15.

4. *Ibid.*, 7.

5. *Ibid.*, 16.

6. *Ibid.*

7. *Ibid.*, 17.

8. Anthony, 'Culture and Society', 187.

9. *Ibid.*

10. *Ibid.*, 159-60, 187, 190. For a biography of Fiah, see N.J. West-cott, 'An East African Radical: The Life of Erica Fiah', *Journal of African History*, 22 (1981), i, pp. 85-101. Fiah, despite his lack of agitation for actual independence from Britain, was an important transitional figure in Tanganyikan nationalism. Jomo Kenyatta compared him in this respect to Harry Thuku; see p. 101.

11. John Iliffe, *A Modern History of Tanganyika*, Cambridge: Cambridge University Press, 1979, 535; R.H. Sabot, *Economic Development and Urban Migration in Tanzania, 1900-1971*, Oxford: Clarendon Press, 1979, 19.

12. See Frederick Cooper, *Decolonization and African Society: The Labor Question in French and British Africa*, Cambridge: Cambridge University Press, 1996, 2, 12, 14; Steven Feierman, *Peasant Intellectuals: Anthropology and History in Tanzania,* Madison: University of Wisconsin Press, 1990, 23-4, 165, 167, 229.

13. John Iliffe, 'Wage Labour and Urbanisation', in *Tanzania Under Colonial Rule*, ed. by M.H.Y. Kaniki, London: Longman Group, Ltd., 1980, 301.

14. Frederick Cooper, *From Slaves to Squatters*, New Haven: Yale University Press, 1987, 114.

15. See, for a comparable process in 18th century England, John Gillis, *Youth and History*, New York: Academic Press, 1974, 182; Cooper, *Decolonization*, 19.

16. Tanzania National Archives (TNA) 504/1/53, #10 Bagamoyo District Annual Report, 1953.

17. TNA P.4/3 Southern Province Annual Report, 1954, 4A.

18. TNA P4/3 1957 #none, Masasi District Annual Report, 1957.

19. *Ibid.*

20. TNA P4/3 1958 #31, Southern Province Annual Report, 1958.

21. TNA P4/3 1958, #14 Masasi District Annual Report, 1958.

22. TNA A 6/6 Associations – Public Bodies, #310, 31/1/57, and #326, 15/5/57.

23. TNA P4/3 1959, #13 Masasi District Annual Report, 1959.

24. Interview, John Nzunda, Dar es Salaam, 8/2/96; see also *Sunday Observer* (Dar es Salaam), 6/16/96; *Maisha Wikiendi*, (Dar es Salaam) 3/23/97.

25. Andrew Maguire, *Towards 'Uhuru' in Tanzania: The Politics of Participation*, Cambridge: Cambridge University Press, 1969, 134.

26. TNA 20, Ukerewe District Annual Reports, 1955-59.

27. TNA 5449, #5, Mwanza Annual Reports, 1957.

28. *Ibid.*

29. J.A.K. Leslie, *A Social Survey of Dar es Salaam*, London: Oxford University Press, 1963, 22, 256; see also Cooper, *Decolonization*, 137-40, 336-47.

30. *Ibid.*, 1, 104.

31. *Ibid.*, 31.

32. *Ibid.*, 12.

33. *Ibid.*, 215.

34. *Ibid.*, 104, 217.

35. *Ibid.*, 105.

36. *Ibid.*, 106, 109; for a further colonial description of the hardships of unemployment in Dar es Salaam, see M.J.B. Molohan, *Detribalization*, Dar es Salaam: Government Printer, 1957, 49; Molohan blames the capital's social problems almost entirely on Africans. Loneliness and frustration were due to the decline of tribal ties and the increased desire to 'cut a figure' among young African men of the town. Also he cites hunger, which was caused by low wages and thriftlessness. Unemployment was due to a labor surplus; indebtedness was caused by extravagant social and family obligations. In addition he mentions amorality, irreligion, indiscipline in the home, and a lack of respect for law and order. Many of Molohan's conclusions in this area were based on Leslie's research.

37. TNA 5449, #5, Mwanza Annual Reports, 1957.

38. *Ibid.*, #28.

39. These insights come from Gillis, *Youth and History*, 177.

40. Tanganyika Police Annual Reports, 1954-63, Government Printer, DSM.

41. M.G. Vassanji, *Uhuru Street*, Oxford: Heinemann, 1991, 30; raids on 'loitering' youth in the capital, like unemployment, began in Dar es Salaam as early as the 1920s, well in advance of other towns in the Territory. See Anthony, 'Culture and Society' 92-93; Leslie claimed that in the capital in 1957 the DC each month repatriated 'several hundred boys and young men', mostly for tax evasion. See Leslie, *Social Survey*, 126.

42. See TNA R3/3 Vol 1, Annual Reports, Arusha District.

43. *Ibid.*

44. Tanganyika Police Annual Reports, 1954-63, DSM: Government Printer.

45. See Gillis, *Youth and History*, 134, 182-3; Jean and John Coma-roff, *Of Revelation and Revolution: Christianity, Colonialism, and Consciousness in South Africa*, Chicago: Chicago University Press, 1991, 64; Gary Cross, *A Social History of Leisure Since 1600*, State College Pennsylvania: Venture Publishing, 1990, 50ff; Richard Whipp, 'A Time to Every Purpose': An Essay on Time and Work,' in *The Historical Meaning of Work*, ed. by P. Joyce, Cambridge: Cambridge University Press, 1987, 210-223.

46. Leslie, *Social Survey*, 268.

47. *Ibid.*, 112.

48. Maguire, *Uhuru*, 157.

49. PRO CO 822, 1361, Twining to Colonial Secretary, 3/16/57.

50. *Ibid.*

51. PRO CO 822, 1627, Twining at TSGA mtg. Nov 15, 57.

52. Recent scholarly work is in the process of describing TANU's popular support among various social groups; see, for example, Susan Geiger, *TANU Women: Gender and Culture in the Making of Tanganyikan Nationalism, 1955-1965*, Oxford: James Currey, 1997.

53. Public Records Office, London, (PRO) CO 822, 1362, #194, report of the Director of Intelligence and Security, Nairobi, January 17, 1958.

54. PRO CO 822, 2063, secret and personal correspondence of deputy governor John Fletcher-Cooke, November 10, 1960; see also PRO CO 822, 2876, 'Incidents and Disturbances in Tanganyika, 1960-62'; TNA A6/4 , 'TANU, Pangani', #242, from Provincial Commissioner, Tanga, to various police officers, and DC of Pangani, 10/19/1960.

55. For this understanding of the role of young migrants in the TYL, I am indebted to the recollections of numerous TYL veterans. Interviews, Rashidi Kawawa, Dodoma, 4/21/95; Moses Nnauye, Dodoma, 5/3/95; Suleiman Fundogoro, Dar es Salaam, 8/2/95, 8/8/95; Suleiman Ngoma, Dar es Salaam, 8/2/95. 7/30/96; Fatuma Mohammed Ali, Dar es Salaam, 8/2/95; Ismaili Mwita, Dar es Salaam, 8/2/95, 8/8/95; Saidi Mwaba Ifunya, Dar es Salaam, 8/7/95; Ridwha Seffu, Tanga, 11/30/95; Abdallah Rashid Sembe, Tanga, 12/2/95; John Nzunda, Dar es Salaam, 8/2/96; Percival Patrick Mandawa, Dar es Salaam, 8/28/96; Mwishehe Mogana Simba, Dar es Salaam, 8/29/96.

56. Cooper, *Slaves To Squatters*, 72.

57. *Ibid.*, 86.

58. *Ibid.*, 116; during the all-important annual clove harvest, the government until World War I operated a system of forced labor; see 95.

59. *Ibid.*, 119.

60. *Ibid.*, 114.

61. *Ibid.*, 115.

62. *Ibid.*, 121.

63. A.H.J. Prins, *The Swahili Speaking Peoples of Zanzibar and the East African Coast*, London: International African Institute, 1967, 101; Norman R. Bennett, *A History of the Arab State of Zanzibar*, Cambridge: Methuen and Co., 1978, 235. Laura Fair is particularly blunt about this, when she claims that 'The stated goals of British colonial administration in Zanzibar was the preservation of Arab rule'; see Laura Fair, 'Pastimes and Politics: A Social History of Zanzibar's Ng'ambo Community, 1890-1950'. Ph.D. Dissertation, University of Minnesota, 1994, 253.

64. Cross, *Social History of Leisure*, 87ff.

65. PRO CO 822, 1641, #15, Ministry of Local Government and Administration to Governor Turnbull, 5/5/59.

66. Zanzibar National Archives (ZNA) AB 12/24A, Annual Report of Sports Association, 1937, #82a. Fair, 'Pastimes', 338.

67. ZNA AB 12/24 A Sports Associations, #50, speech given at annual general mtg. of fund, 13/2/27.

68. ZNAAB 12/24B, #128, Wheatley to President of Sports Association, 18/1/55, Wheatley arrived in Zanzibar in 1926 and was heavily involved in the Sports Association from its inception.

69. See Fair, 'Pastimes', 336, 349, 350.

70. Fair, 'Pastimes', 327ff.

71. Cross, *Social History of Leisure*, 116.

72. ZNA AB 12/88 vol. I, #19, Commissioner, Overseas Scouts to 'Sir' 28/6/21.

73. ZNA AB 12/89, #279, Provincial Commissioner to Welfare Officer, 13/1/47.

74. *Ibid.*, #280, 14/3/47, British Resident to unknown.

75. ZNA BA 27/1, Annual Report of Social Welfare Department, 1949.

76. ZNA AB 12/11, Youth Movements, #1, 2, 5, 7.

77. ZNA BA 27/9, Annual Report of Social Welfare Department, 1957.

78. ZNA BA 27/10, Annual Report of Social Welfare Department, 1958.

79. ZNA BA 47/17 and 47/25, Police Annual Reports, 1952 and 1960.

80. ZNA BA 27/8-14, Annual Reports, Social Welfare Department, 1956-62.

81. ZNA BA 47/23, Police Annual Report, 1958.

82. *Ibid.*

83. ZNA BA 47/24, Police Annual Reports, 1959.

84. ZNA BA 19/12 Labor Department Report, 1957.

85. ZNA AK 23/2, 'Youth League', # 1, 2, 5, 18, 20.

86. *Ibid.*

87. This ideas and the following material comes from ZNA BA 108/10, 'Symposium on Unemployed Youth'.

88. *Ibid.*

89. Airgram, American Consulate to Department of State, #13, 24/7/62, Central Decimal File, Box 1709, LBJ Library.

90. PRO CO 822, 2132, #290, British Resident to Secretary of State, 26/7/62.

91. PRO CO 822, 2046, E61B, central intelligence committee appreciation, September 1962.

92. ZNA, AK 31/15, #30, Intelligence Report for Zanzibar Urban District, 19/10/62.

93. ZNA AK 31/15, #101, Intelligence Report for Zanzibar Urban District, 22/5/63.

94. Airgram, Picard to Department of State, #13, 24/7/62, Central Decimal File 1960-3, Box 1709, LBJ Library.

95. John Iliffe, *A Modern History of Tanganyika,* Cambridge: Cambridge University Press, 1979, 381.

Chapter 3

'HAVE YOU NOT HEARD THE WORDS OF OUR ELDERS?': SENIOR BAMANA WOMEN'S ADAPTATION TO CULTURE CHANGE IN RURAL MALI

Julianne E. Freeman

INTRODUCTION

In the Beledugu region of Mali[1] senior Bamana women are vital to the well being of their families and wider communities. They work as midwives ushering women through childbirth, they are caretakers watching over young children and their compounds, as well as educators giving daily lessons. They are advice-givers on such issues as marriage and family disputes, they act as healers drawing on their knowledge of medicinal plants to remedy the illnesses of family members and neighbors. They farm rice and plant gardens providing additional crops for family consumption, they spin cotton and produce clothing for their families. They give meaningful benedictions to younger people who support them, they direct female initiation to ensure the safe passage of girls into womanhood, and they play a range of important roles in the marriages of their sons and daughters. Thus, their knowledge is deep. It is a kind of wisdom grounded in the practice of everyday life. In fact, it is often said that 'every compound needs an older woman'.

Working primarily with three senior Bamana women, whose own work involved them in the fields of child care, midwifery, traditional healing, craft production, grand-parenting, and celebrations of marriage and initiation, I came to learn something very important. I came to learn that the practical knowledge that older women have of health and illness, childbirth and child rearing, and the nature of social relationships, is grounded in their roles as wives and mothers (Short 1996). While the work of marriage and motherhood demands much of younger women (in the pressure to adapt to a startlingly heavy work-load and the need to suppress their individual desires in favor of the common good), it builds an important foundation for their roles in later life.

It is therefore important to consider the daily activities and experiences of senior women, especially in the light of the fact that their roles are dependent on the structures of the family as well as on the currency of what elders regard as Bamana knowledge. Such knowledge is perceived as opposed to *tubabu* or Western knowledge. In this chapter I investigate the embeddedness of senior women within the family and how senior women's practical and embodied knowledge ensures their place in the social group. I also consider ways in which the particular areas of expertise that senior women gain over a lifetime are challenged by forms of Western knowledge, taking a brief look at the practice of midwifery at a rural maternity hospital as my primary example.

My work in a Beledugu town and surrounding villages, exploring the experience of senior womanhood, involved me in the lives of three senior women, in particular. I observed their social interactions and their work, learned about and participated in their daily work activities, accompanied them to women's celebrations, and socialized with them as an adopted member of their families.[2] As people learned about my project I encountered many reactions to my chosen subject of study. There were some men who laughed. Perhaps they did so because the topic of senior womanhood seemed unimportant to them. Perhaps they did because of the preposterousness of a project carried out by someone so far removed in age and cultural experience from the lives of senior Bamana women. However, there were some, both men and women, who were fascinated by this project--the later sentiment often accompanied by statements about the power and centrality of senior women within village life.

Previous gerontological research in West Africa has focused primarily on social organizational factors that affect the elderly, such as the seniority principle (Bascom 1942, Paulme 1969) or demography (Adeokun 1982, Apt 1975), rather than on the lived experience of elders. Thus, leaving much to be learned about the activities elders engage in, the shared perceptions of the role elders play within the community, the experience of being an older member of the community, etc. The collection of older women's life histories (Andreski 1970, Romero 1988, Smith 1981) or descriptions of attitudes toward elders (Barbier-Wiesser 1972, Camara 1979) are exceptions to the emphasis within the gerontological literature on the social and titular roles of elders, who are primarily older men. In Mali, some gerontological researchers have addressed men's roles almost exclusively (Rosenmayr 1988, Traore 1985). While the focus on women's lives in anthropology is clearly established (e.g. Abu-Lughod 1993, Boddy 1989, Friedl 1989, Weiner, 1976), attention to the lives and experiences of older African women is a more recent focus of anthropological inquiry in general (see e.g. Coles 1990, Short 1996, Udvardy and Cattell 1992).

OLDER WOMEN AND THE FAMILY

One of the older women with whom I worked is Sira, a mother, grandmother, midwife, healer, and respected elder of her village. Though her husband died many years ago, she continues to live in her husband's compound, as is customary, alongside her sons, grandsons, and many daughters-in-law.[3] On any given day you will find Sira under the *gwa* (or lean-to) in her compound. The way to her *gwa* is found from a main village path, up a narrowed and gradually inclined passage between two adjacent compounds, that opens into the central courtyard of Sira's compound on the left. On the slight down slope are the rooms of Sira's children and daughters-in-law, and in the center of the compound sit a pair of mortars, and an adjacent granary. Continuing to the right, piles of firewood belonging to individual wives of Sira's sons and grandsons, line the compound wall, and just beyond, under the shade of the *gwa*, Sira often sits on a mat or a low stool. There she receives visitors, addresses their many concerns, and is found in times of need. Sira is well established in her family. The distance you walk to find her within her compound suggests the degree to which she is embedded in family life both through her own care-taking and the care and respect she receives as an elder member of the family into which she married. Whenever I visited Sira I would inevitably find children at her feet, asleep on her mat, leaning against her, or playing somewhere in her general vicinity.

Conversations with elders reveal beliefs about appropriate spaces for members of the family based on age and gender. Older women occupy their *blo*, or antechamber of their small house or room within the compound. Older men often sit in the passageway to the compound, also called a *blo*, an intermediary space between the family compound and the shared space of the village path. These unique activity spaces for elder men and women suggest distinct roles for men and women. Men come to represent the family in village politics, while older women work for the family and are less involved in the politics of the village, especially of older, land-owning men. Older women are in fact expected to stay home.[4] People explained to me that it is not proper or dignified for an older woman to walk about. Those in need of her should come to her compound. Older women's knowledge of medicines and illness and the smooth operation of compound activities make them both very much needed and feared. The fear of senior women stems from a fear of their potential to use their accumulated knowledge of health and illness in malevolent ways. Knowledge associated with the expertise of older women, in addition to the natural power that women possess through their reproductive and sexual capacities, contributes to many people's fear of older women (though no longer reproductive) as witches.[5] Not only are older women expected to spend most of their time within the compound due to their family's need for their expertise, but older women are also expected to stay home; thus the possibility of witchcraft accusations is lessened. By controlling the movement of an elder female relative and thus the contexts in which she uses her life-sustaining knowledge, the good reputation of an older woman and her family may be preserved.

Spending my days beside older women it was not hard to notice that many of them were not only home but also sitting down much of the time. Their position of sitting was in contrast to the action of younger women who often hurried around the compound, busily cooking, cleaning, nursing, and provisioning the household with fresh water and clean clothing. The significance of this act of sitting was brought to my attention in conversations with older women about their lives. All were emphatic about the hard work of cooking and raising children and about how old age brings a woman the opportunity to sit, if there is a daughter-in-law present to take over the bulk of the work. Both older men and women take more opportunities to rest. The act of sitting suggests a respected status for both older men and women in the compound. Children, however, rarely stay put. In the words of one older man, they 'flit about like birds'. Growing older and becoming an elder involves a process of settling down into the responsibilities of adulthood, working, and then, finally, resting. On the other side of the important phase of hard work, and far distant from childhood, elders are calm, their 'minds are seated' (*'u hakiliw sigilen don'*).

Sitting is just one physical and bodily expression of the social position and power that elders occupy. I often noticed the slow pace that still active senior women adopted to walk across the compound, structured not, primarily, by debility but by a lived wisdom, the subtlety of movement expressing their relative position and power. The way a person walks across the compound and the space that a person occupies in the compound are related to physical and cultural dimensions of age and gender. A Bamana proverb suggests that elders may adopt a unique way of moving: '*don bè kè ni kamankun ye, mogokoroba don bè kè ni kamankun ye*' ('the dance of elders is done with the shoulders').[6] As this proverb suggests, elders adopt ways of moving that are commensurate with their physical age, lived experience, and social position. In conserving movement, elders express an understanding of the essence of a given activity, in the case of dancing this can be done with the shoulders.

Through specific activities, such as midwifery, an older woman may establish an important role for herself within the village community. Sira is in great demand in her village of 600 inhabitants where she is the head midwife. I would often arrive to find her talking with a neighbor or a daughter-in-law. Or washing a newborn child that she had delivered, wetting first its front then expertly turning the infant by grasping one of its arms and placing the child on its belly across her legs so that she could wash and massage the child's back. The massage helps to give

the child the needed flexibility to withstand the abrupt movements that it will endure in the hands of young caretakers (called
denwminadenw - children holding children). The incantations,
which Sira pronounces effortlessly, are the most important part
of the daily bath, as they are believed to protect the infant from
sorcery attacks.[7] This final step in the ritual bathing is an example
of embodied practice that establishes younger women's need for
a senior woman's important skills.

Elders also have ultimate recourse to much power through
the pronouncement or denial of benedictions, those powerful
words that position elders closer to the after world and to the
power of the divine, which they summon. Much like incantations, benedictions bind younger people to their elders and obli-
gate the younger generation to look after their parents and older
relatives.[8] One senior woman succinctly expressed this important position that elders hold, in her advice to a man who had
recently married. 'Have you not heard the words of your elders?'
she asked. 'You must not put couscous in water, add sugar, and
eat that, leaving out the old people. Apart from the mother and
father, benedictions are not found elsewhere'.

As in all societies, Bamana parents are faced with the looming
reality of being replaced by their children. While parents have
socially sanctioned authority over their children, the parent-
child relationship is not entirely an authoritarian one. Reciprocal
joking and mild teasing exists between parents and their children, as I often witnessed. One day, for example, Sira's oldest son,
Abdullahe, brought her a kola nut, a sign of respect toward elders.
Sira looked at the kola nut and complained as Abdullahe walked
away, that it was not a good one. He countered from across the
compound that she did not need a nice, new kola nut, since she,
herself, was old. It was not rare to hear such an appraisal of older
women by their sons. I also often heard the same response to the
objection of another older woman, expressed every time her son
brought her a ragged mat on which to sit: 'an old person is meant
to sit on an old mat', the son would always reply.

Meyer Fortes wrote of the paradoxical familiarity between
parent and child. He explained that, '...the authority parents have
over their children must be reconciled with their love for them...'

(1949:197). The teasing and familiarity may not only reflect love but also the tension between adjacent generations who are more often in more frequent contact with one another and in direct competition over resources, fame, etc., than are people of alternate generations (see e.g. Nahemov 1987:108-115). Perhaps because the actions of adjacent generations reflect upon one another, this relationship is expressed in terms of rivalry in Mali. I was told that parents are the rivals of their children. *'i ba ka kan ka kè i sinamuso ye'* – 'Your mother must become your rival'. [*'i fa ka kan ka kè i faden ye'* – 'Your father must become your enemy or rival'.] This proverb, which is meant to express that children must strive to become better than their parents, expresses the tensions between parents and children, whose relative powers and achievements reflect upon one another.

While elder women may be surrounded by children, daughters-in-law, and supported and respected within their families, they are faced with the challenge of having lost much of their productive capacity. Some of the elder women with whom I worked joked that they felt useless. One senior woman consistently reprimanded her daughters-in-law whenever they hit their children in front of her, as it undermined her authority and sense of power. In other more serious conversations many explained that growing older is hard because, as elders, they often spend the day *thinking*. Reflection upon one's life experience and the building of wisdom is hard work as well. Accepting dependency on others is clearly a difficult challenge that most elders face.

CULTURE CHANGE

Certainly for many senior women the source of much of their 'thinking' or worries lies in their insecurity about the future. Having given up the productive roles of cooking and millet farming they face total dependence on their children to take care of them. Ntife, a mother of two adult sons, often expressed concern about the future and how she and her family would be supported. Her youngest son worked as a mechanic in town, but his earnings were unpredictable. The oldest son, who had completed school, was still in search of an occupation. Ntife had a means of income as a producer of the traditional mud-painted cloth, but that was also sporadic, and dependent on her physical ability. She complained often of shoulder stiffness and pains in her legs, as the amount of time she could continue to work on cloth was becoming increasingly limited. The fear of her sons' inability to find well-paying jobs seemed to be embodied by the stiffness of her limbs.

While Ntife's children struggled, other women I met were completely abandoned by their children. One woman, Kaja, had given birth to seven sons and they had left, one by one, seeking employment in various urban centers throughout West Africa. With the exception of one son, she did not know exactly where they had gone. This all too-common practice brings much shame to the children, thus ensuring that her sons will probably never return. Fortunately, Kaja was still active; she washed cloths and gathered wood for a meager living, often relying on the generosity of neighbors and friends for additional support.

In addition to the economic hardship that pervaded the Beledugu, I was aware of the contrast in the experience of older and younger people. An older bard, with whom I spent many afternoons, explained that even when he went to important village events he noticed that people had lost some understanding of the Bamana language. There was an essential problem in the translation of his knowledge, and it struck him deeply. People's minds were perhaps elsewhere, and his words no longer had the impact that they used to have. Bamana knowledge, he explained to me, was only one type of knowledge. There was also 'tubabu' (Western) knowledge (also equivalent to school knowledge) as well as the older Islamic knowledge. Other elders also spoke of the striking presence of 'tubabu' knowledge. While they were careful not to critique too harshly this kind of knowledge that I shared with their French colonizers, they all pointed out that it was entirely distinct from 'Bamana' knowledge.

I became aware of many ways in which senior women's knowledge came up against the influence of Western modes of thought. One day when we were sitting under her mango tree, Ntife told me about the origin of children,

> When a woman is about to conceive, the soul of the
> little child comes to sing next to her house. If you hear
> the noise, '*kenw, kenw, kenw*,' you bring food to it; it
> is the *ja*[9] (soul) of the not yet born...When the child's
> *ja* arrives, it comes at night, in the hope of drinking
> water from your jug. If it does not see the cup [on the
> water jug], the child's *ja* leaves and goes to another
> person's compound where it drinks until satisfied,
> and stays...Whenever you see a pregnant woman, she
> became pregnant because, at the time, the *ja* of her
> child came to sing in her house. The water jug must
> not stay empty during the night.

Ntife's son had been married for several years. His wife, who had
not yet conceived, had painful menstrual cramps each month, a
sign that she was not well enough to become pregnant. Ntife's
concern with this was evident in the way she spoke solemnly to
me, there under the mango tree, about her daughter-in-law's difficulty conceiving. The problem for Ntife was that her young,
educated son, refused to believe that the sound she described to
me was that of a child's *ja* in search of a home. Ntife told me that
the next time she heard the sound she was going to bring her son
over so that he could hear it for himself and perhaps begin to
have faith in and reinforce the efficacy of the prophetic sound.

MIDWIFERY AND THE MATERNITY HOSPITAL

Paralleling the contrast between Bamana and *tubabu*
knowledge, my investigation of childbirth revealed a divergence
between older women's knowledge and practice of midwifery, and
the Westernized approach to midwifery practiced at the nearby
maternity hospital. Traditionally, the practice of midwifery is the
occupation of older women. All senior women are supposed to
know how to deliver a child, though some, in reality, are more
timid in the face of this important task than are others.

I made many inquiries into midwifery. The first began in
a small animist village. There I interviewed a group of senior
women about their work in general, and their knowledge of
midwifery in particular. About five women who had come to the
public square to meet me for the first time, sat on the stools that

they had brought, and looked at me with one hand over their mouths. Such posture is a distinctly older woman's posture which communicated the modesty and reserve somehow appropriate to older (*hòròn*--noble) women. The women told me of their work of making potash, spinning cotton, giving advice, and looking after children. Yet before they would tell me anything about midwifery they summoned Kama, the head midwife.

Kama approached the circle of women with what I perceived as an air of confidence, her white *boubou* (long cotton garment) flowing behind her as she took measured steps in the direction of the four other older women and myself, seated rather tentatively on our stools. Kama interviewed me about why I had come and about what I had hoped to learn from the senior women of their village. Again I explained my interest in their work, as best I could, especially my interest in their activity of midwifery. Upon hearing this, Kama moved our discussion into a small hut, out of the earshot of the uninitiated children. We sat as best we could, on the earthen floor of the hut where the village stored supplies for communal work projects. In front of me one of the women sat on the handle of a hoe, while the others sat on the stools they had brought from their compounds. Kama led the way in explaining the basic methods used to deliver children in the village, while the other women pitched in to clarify and actually illustrate their methods. They explained that given a lack of materials, and even the absence of plastic, the laboring woman sits directly on the dirt floor, and the child is born into the hands of the midwife. The woman who sat on the hoe facing me even acted out how an older women sits to support the laboring woman's back, and how the midwife positions herself to catch the baby. All the senior women emphasized that women of the village give birth while squatting or sitting down, their backs supported by a woman from behind, unlike at the maternity hospital which requires that women give birth lying on a table, flat on their backs. To them, the way of lying down was entirely foreign. Perhaps this was due in part to the fact that lying down is a position of inactivity, while sitting is a position of work, from which many tasks are carried out. Throughout my inquiry into the practice of midwifery, the local maternity hospital was characterized as an entirely different kind of place to give birth than was the village. The difference was found in the position of lying down, and by women's access to medication at the maternity hospital.

On several occasions I went with Ntife to the maternity hospital as she accompanied neighbors and friends there. While older women did not actually deliver children at the hospital, they were always enlisted to help out with the more mundane tasks, such as ensuring the laboring woman's general comfort and scrubbing down the delivery room after the birth. Ntife was particularly sought after for the concern and compassion she showed toward the women. The presence of older women within the maternity hospital, however, did not take place without controversy.

Ntife explained to me that when the maternity hospital was first built it was staffed, at night, by a traditional midwife, who Ntife described as *'farafin'* (meaning both African or dark-skinned and illiterate), as opposed to *'ecoliden'* (lit. 'child of the school' or Western-educated person). She worked there for many years before people became suspicious of her and she was fired in the wake of an increasing number of women dying in childbirth. The trained health workers (or aides) who now work at the maternity hospital under the head midwife have remained distrustful of older women in general, fearing that an older woman may try to use her power to cause harm to a mother or an as yet unborn child. So fearful were the aides that their professional reputations would be ruined by the interference of elder women and their midwifery practices. Thus, older women were not allowed inside the delivery rooms. This even pertained to Sira, the head midwife of a nearby village, who had walked the entire 10 kilometers to the maternity hospital after sending her granddaughter, who was having a difficult labor, to the maternity hospital. Sira's journey was an amazing feat for a frail older woman, who, herself, joked about it, saying that she cannot even make it to the adjacent mango grove (in the vicinity of her rice field, about 100 yards from her compound) if not on the back of a bicycle. Sira, however, told me that she was not upset about being barred from the delivery room. Rather, she was happy that her granddaughter had successfully made it through her first childbirth. While the aides mistrusted older midwives, the local perception of the maternity hospital was equally ambiguous. While it was lauded for the access to medications that it provided, many complained about having to deliver lying flat on their backs and about the meanness of some of the health care aides who worked there. Many also feared having to go to the maternity hospital due to a wide spread belief that women who give birth there have a greater chance of dying.[10]

Ntife had to work around the restrictions at the maternity hospital because when she accompanied women there, her tasks were not simply profane. Ntife managed to forge relationships with many of the aides who gained her trust and would allow her to enter the labor room. There, Ntife did her secret work. One night I observed that she sat quietly watching Kadi, a woman who had come to give birth. Kadi sat almost motionless kneeling on the cement floor. Across from her, I sat next to Ntife. I too watched Kadi, then Ntife, then Kadi. Twelve hours we had been there and the noise of the day had turned into the silence of the night. Ntife waited. I waited. Occasionally Ntife looked at me. Once she chuckled, out of nervousness for the event, for my presence, or perhaps in contrast to the seriousness of the moment. Another time her eyes met mine only momentarily. Ntife rose from where she was sitting to massage Kadi's belly. The aide who was on duty that night was clear across the courtyard as Ntife ran her fingers over Kadi's belly and uttered her incantation three times, beckoning the little one to come out and play.

Since Ntife was able to befriend the health care aides she was able to practice midwifery and to make a difference. The efforts she made for each of the women were duly noted. While much younger, these women were all strong believers in the power of this kind of activity.

CONCLUSION

As the example of midwifery illustrates, the difference in practice and knowledge exhibited at the maternity hospital by women of different ages and training is striking. The training of the aides contrasts the local knowledge of older women in a way that is perhaps increasingly common in the Beledugu.[11] The older women's methods at the maternity hospital represented a different yet admittedly powerful approach. Their power was acknowledged in the prohibition against most senior women entering the delivery rooms at the maternity hospital. The example of the maternity hospital brings to light one arena of senior women's practical knowledge that is challenged by forms of Western technology and ideology. It has yet to be seen whether the maternity hospital threatens the viability of careers in midwifery, however grueling and low paying, for senior women.

Older Bamana women are widely acknowledged for their experience and expertise in the day-to-day activities that take place in their husband's compounds, where they came of age, and gained much of the knowledge that makes them so needed in their older age. One older woman commented to me that a woman could not become the head of women of any village unless she leaves her natal village and makes the transition to her husband's village. This undoubtedly requires hard work. Yet this hard work often pays off in the end. Senior women build knowledge of the basic necessities of life and survival. In older age, they are thus poised to pass on this knowledge to younger women who are just starting out their lives of hard work and motherhood. The foundation of senior women's knowledge is deep in its pattern of formation and in its acknowledged power. Senior womanhood, though not without ambiguity, is undoubtedly hard work, through which senior women secure a place for themselves in the family and community. Those who can adapt most readily to the challenges that culture change brings them may be the most successful as elder members of their communities.

Notes

1. Translated as 'the place of pebbles', the Beledugu is a savannah region of Mali which lies to the north of the capital city of Bamako. The predominant ethnic group is Bamana, a people who in this region pride themselves as farmers, and as a fiercely independent group, renowned as one of the last to stage a resistance against French colonialists. The Beledugu region is also know for its 'leaves' or medicine, and the inhabitants' knowledge of sorcery and magic. While Islam is the predominant religion, many con-

tinue to follow older, indigenous religious practices, characterized by ancestor worship, animism, and animatism, either as their sole religious practice or, more commonly, in conjunction with the practice of Islam.

2. This research was funded by a Fulbright-Hays Doctoral Fellowship and Indiana University Graduate School Grants-in-Aid-of-Research carried out from November of 1991 to May of 1993. Funding for preliminary research in the summer of 1990 was funded by summer research fellowships from Indiana University's Department of Anthropology and Women's Studies Program.

3. Marriage patterns in this Bamana region are patrilocal and exogamous.

4. Catherine Coles (1990) found the opposite pattern among older Hausa women who actually gain the freedom to travel more freely in older age.

5. Many people I spoke with were fearful of the gathering of older women, fearing that their encounters were about witchcraft and the sharing of secret knowledge.

6. Kassim Kone brought this proverb to my attention in a discussion about this paper.

7. As the infant mortality rate is very high, many parents fear that their children will not live to their first birthday. Sorcery is believed to be the cause of most children's illnesses, thus protective incantations, such as that uttered by an older midwife, are deemed a most important ingredient for the child's overall welfare.

8. The reciprocity between parent and child is expressed in countless ways. An elder has his or her responsibilities to the family, such as watching over the compound, and settling disputes wisely, while the younger families members are supposed to provide food and other necessities for their elders. Children also have the right to forbid an elder from traveling. Several older women simultaneously complained and boasted to me when their children forbade them to travel, recognizing that their children placed such restrictions on them out of both a need for their presence in the compound and a concern for their safety and welfare.

9. *Ja* is the human part of the person, center of confidence and fear (Bailleul 1981). Here I translate this as soul. The word *ja* is also used to refer to a person's shadow or image.

10. Traditional midwives were also vulnerable to gaining a negative reputation. In one village the head midwife was suspected of being

a witch since many women under her supervision had died in childbirth. As a result, pregnant women of that village planned to deliver their children in town at the maternity hospital.

11. Sira, the village midwife with whom I worked, actually received some training in the town where the maternity hospital operated. She proudly displayed her midwifery kit, though it was clear from the unused gauze and pristine razor blade nicely preserved in her box of supplies that the kit was a symbol of her skill and accomplishment as a midwife rather than a tool that she actually used to deliver babies.

References

Abu-Lughod, Lila. 1992. *Writing Women's Worlds: Bedouin Stories.* Berkeley: University of California Press.

Adeokun, Lawrence. 1982. 'Demographic Determinants of Intra-Family Support for the Aged in Nigeria', in *Aging Well Through Living Better*, pp. 311-315. 10th International Conference of Social Gerontology. Vol. 2. Deauville, France.

Andreski, Iris. 1970. *Old Wives Tales: Life-stories from Ibibioland.* London: Routeledge & Kegan Paul.

Apt, Nana. 1975. 'Urbanization and the Aged', in *Changing Family Studies*. C. Oppong, ed. pp. 176-182. Legon: Institute of African Studies.

Bailleul, Père Charles. 1981. *Petit Dictionnaire Bambara-Français, Français-Bambara.* England: Avery Publishing Company.

Barbier-Wiesser, François-George. 1972. 'Les Vieux-Sonts-ils Toujours (en Afrique) les "Greniers du Village", Testes Rassembles au College d'Enseignment General d'Oussouye', *Afrique Litteraire et Artistique* 22:69-74.

Bascom, William. 1942. 'The Principle of Seniority in the Social Structure of the Yoruba', *American Anthropologist* 44:37-46.

Boddy, Janice. 1989. *Wombs, Aliens, and Spirits: Women, Men and the Zar Cult in Northern Sudan.* Madison: University of Wisconsin Press.

Camara, S. 1979. 'Vieillir Chez les Mandenka ou les Metamorphoses de la Vie', *Ethno-Psychologie* 34 (3-4): 327-338.

Fortes, Meyer. 1949. *The Web of Kinship among the Tallensi.* London: Oxford University Press.

Friedl, Erika. 1989. *Women of Deh Koh: Lives In an Iranian Village.* New York: Penguin Books.

Nahemow, Nina. 1987. 'Grandparenthood among the Baganda: Role Option in Old Age?' in *Growing Old in Different Societies: Cross-Cultural Perspectives.* J. Sokolovsky, ed. pp.104-115. Acton, Massachusetts: Copley Publishing Group.

Paulme, Denise, ed. 1969. *Classes et Associations d'Age en Afrique de l'Ouest.* Paris: Librairie Plon.

Romero, Patricia, ed. 1988. *Life Histories of African Women.* London: Ashfield Press.

Rosenmayr, Leopold. 1988. 'More Than Wisdom: A Field Study of the Old in an African Village', *Journal of Cross-Cultural Gerontology* 3 :21-40.

Short, Julianne E. (Freeman). 1996. Musokorobaya: Practice, Embodiment, Transition, and Agency in the Lives of Senior Bamana Women of Mali. Ph.D. Dissertation, Indiana University. Ann Arbor: University Microfilms.

Smith, Mary. 1954. *Baba of Karo: A Woman of the Muslim Hausa.* London: Faber & Faber.

Traore, Gaoussou. 1983. 'A Profile of the Elderly in Mali', *Gerontologie Africaine* 3: 11-23.

Udvardy, Monica and Maria Cattell. 1992. 'Gender, Aging and Power in Sub-Saharan Africa: Challenges and Puzzles', *Journal of Cross-Cultural Gerontology* 7 (4): 275-288.

Weiner, Annette. 1976. *Women of Value, Men of Renown: A New Perspective in Trobriand Exchange.* Austin: University of Texas Press.

Chapter 4

GENDER, AGE AND POWER: HIERARCHY AND LIMINALITY AMONG ABALUYIA WOMEN OF KENYA AND THEIR IMPLICATIONS FOR DEVELOPMENT

Maria G. Cattell

WOMEN AND SOME COMPLEXITIES OF POWER

Power is multifaceted, taking many forms and varying in intensity – as is true of its obverse, powerlessness. 'Power ... is made up of a multiplicity of intersecting elements which offer themselves as instruments and effects of power, and also as points of resistance to that power' (Moore 1986:194). Rarely monolithic and absolute, power is commonly experienced as partial and incomplete. Power waxes and wanes through individuals' lives as they grow up and grow old, experience varying socioeconomic circumstances, and participate in different relationships (Udvardy and Cattell 1992). Age, accumulated resources (tangible and intangible), and social class can be significant factors in women's opportunities for power. Power is also linked to cultural ideologies about gender, age and personhood, and about marriage and the family. It is linked to access to economic and socially valued resources in the local political economy. Beyond that, it is linked to complex and widespread social, economic and political processes occurring in regional, national and international arenas (Hakansson 1994).

For many women the exercise of power and experiences of powerlessness occur most commonly in daily life, particularly in family relationships and everyday household and work settings. Concerns often focus on personal autonomy, or the capacity to make decisions about one's own actions; the ability to gain and control material resources, such as food, clothing and money for self and children; and human resources, or getting others to do what you want them to do.

One interesting puzzle is the way dominant classes or groups maintain their dominance without constant coercion, or why subordinate groups or classes accept and even actively participate in their own oppression. Margot Lovett (1992), for example, in discussing gender relations and marriage among the Ha (Hutu) in colonial western Tanzania, makes the case that Ha women acquiesced in their own domination because they understood their lack of options. Realizing their powerlessness, they were reluctant to challenge overtly those who were more powerful, i.e. their fathers, brothers and husbands. The resistance of Ha women took the form of individual efforts to better their own situation, for example, trying to get the house or clothes owed them by their husbands or obtain a divorce. They did not attempt to challenge or change the system of marriage and gender relations that kept them subordinate. Ha women made these efforts in socially sanctioned ways (returning to their natal home, petitioning the colonial court) which gave them little room to maneuver and often failed. Nevertheless, the Ha case demonstrates that the weak do not experience unmitigated powerlessness and that they operate within a system which gives them some rights, however limited.

Further, while resistance by subordinates may sometimes take the form of open challenges and outright rebellion (Scott 1985), most often resistance is something less than a rebellion and is carried out in the course of everyday life. In the 'everyday resistance' of Bedouin women in Egypt, for example, male domination is countered through secrets and defiance within the boundaries of women's spaces, in the presumptively male sphere of marriage decision making, and through subversive discourse (Abu-Lughod 1990). Bedouin women's resistance on various fronts enables them to make decisions about their activities and to control their limited resources. In addition, they are often successful in their attempts to control marriage decision making, which figures large in Bedouin social and economic life.

While there is good reason to focus on the subordination of women *vis-a-vis* men, such an approach does not tell the whole story of the complexities of power in women's lives. This is perhaps especially true in Africa, where space, knowledge and opportunities are highly gendered and women may have their own systems of knowledge and power within their families (Cattell 1989a). The power of African women is recognized in myths and in their roles as ancestors and as warriors and rulers ('queen-mothers', 'rain-queens') in various political arenas (LeBeuf 1963), including the West African 'dual-sex' political systems (Amadiume 1987, Leith-Ross 1939, Okonjo 1976, Shanklin 1989). African women's power in ordinary daily life may be less apparent, especially given the large literature on their oppression and powerlessness, but it does exist. As an example, among the Samia of Kenya, older widows are currently refusing the customary form of remarriage known as widow inheritance, in which a widow marries a clansman of her deceased husband. Often women announce their refusals in strategic public discourses at funerals. Here their ability to resist remarriage relies in part on their positions as senior women but also on the consent of the very males they resist (Cattell 1992a, 1996a, 1997a). Some ethnic groups have gender ideologies that allow biological females to assume the gender roles and social power of son or husband (e.g. Amadiume 1987).

In their struggles for power, women, like others who are poor, oppressed and marginalized, tend to employ the 'weapons of the weak', to use James Scott's (1985) phrase, though African women have sometimes resorted to large-scale aggressive and militant tactics.[1] But women's small-scale struggles, their everyday resistance, may in fact give them considerable power within their own sphere and sometimes in the male sphere as well, as in the example of Bedouin women mentioned earlier. Such power is not simply a concession by powerful men, but something women achieve among themselves, in their own power system, as well as through acts of resistance to male domination (Dickerson-Putman and Brown 1998).

I do not want to downplay the very real problems of women struggling to have some control over their own lives *vis-a-vis* domineering males. But I would like to suggest that power is more complex than viewing females only as subordinate in patriarchal systems. First, they are not always subordinate in the patriarchy, since gender is not the only determinant of relative power. And, as mentioned earlier, women may participate in their own systems of power. I will examine such a system here: the age hierarchies of Abaluyia women of western Kenya.

RESEARCH METHODS

My anthropological fieldwork in Kenya has consisted primarily of participant observation including informal and in-depth interviews and field-designed survey questionnaires. I have focused on aging and old age, the lives of the elderly, and family life in circumstances of rapid socioeconomic and cultural change. The research extended over two years from November 1983 through November 1985, with return visits of four to six weeks in 1982, 1987, 1990, 1992, 1993 and 1995. It was carried out in rural western Kenya among two Abaluyia subgroups, primarily the Samia and to a lesser extent their neighbors the Banyala, and among families of my rural informants in the cities of Kisumu and Nairobi.

I have lived among Abaluyia and have been incorporated as a member into two families in Samia and one family in Bunyala.[2] I have observed and interacted with numerous people in many homes, on roads and footpaths, and in other public places such as markets, churches and schools. I have shared daily activities, serious illness, theft, house fires, the struggle to educate children, marriages, births and deaths. My contacts have included females and males of all ages with a range of social and economic characteristics.

The result is a wide-ranging knowledge of Abaluyia society and culture in Samia and Bunyala, knowledge recorded in extensive and varied written fieldnotes and also in what Simon Ottenberg (1990) calls 'headnotes', or unwritten data, data recorded only in one's memory. The fieldnotes include narrative field journals and many topical notes describing events and conversations, biographical interviews, a household census in one village, focused interviews (mini-surveys on a particular topic), and a lengthy questionnaire used for a survey of 416 women and men age 50 and over.

ABALUYIA OF WESTERN KENYA: A CENTURY OF CHANGE

The Samia of Samia Location (now Funyula Division) and the Banyala of the Bunyala area live in ridge and valley terrain around the northern and eastern shores of Lake Victoria in Kenya. Many more Samia live in Uganda. They are two of the 16 or 17 culturally and linguistically related communities grouped into the Abaluyia people, the second largest ethnic group in Kenya. In 1989 Abaluyia numbered about 3,000,000, of whom about 60,000 were Samia and about 38,000 were Banyala (Kenya 1994: 6-2, 1-160).

A century ago the Samia, Banyala and other Abaluyia lived in small kin-based groups in fortified villages. In the late 19th century they were subsistence farmers and cattle and goat herders who were largely untouched by the world economy or outside cultural influences, except for local migrations. Then in 1883 the British explorer-geographer Joseph Thomson (1885) trekked through the area. Thereafter western Kenya changed radically with colonialism and then nationhood (in 1963), the rapid development of cash cropping and labor migration, urbanization, and the hegemony of European ideologies and institutions such as Christianity and formal education (Cattell 1989b, Seitz 1978, Soper 1986).

Today in Samia and Bunyala there are churches, schools, a hospital, telephone and electric lines, police, government administrators, market centers, roads, public transportation. However, work and lifestyle remain fundamentally rural. For example, agricultural work is done by hand labor with hoes, machetes and other hand tools. All roads are dirt, 'footing it' is the most common mode of transportation, private telephone and electric hookups are rare, though there has been a marked increase in homes with television sets (run off car batteries) in recent years.

Nowadays almost all Banyala and Samia, females and males, are peasant farmers who grow both subsistence and cash crops. As elsewhere in sub-Saharan Africa, women are the major food producers. People also engage in commercial fishing, trading (especially trading farm produce at local markets) and other income-generating activities including operating small shops and, for a few, wage employment. As a number of older people told me, 'When I was young, things were free; but today it is a world of money'. As people age they continue farming as long as they are physically able, from necessity and also from the desire to be considered useful, i.e. responsible adults who provide for their dependents.

Another major change is that poverty is widespread in the area. In the 1880s food was abundant in western Kenya (Thomson 1885). Today, hunger and malnutrition are not uncommon (Cattell 1996b, K'Okul 1991). Many young people are responding as their fathers and grandfathers did, struggling to take advantage of opportunities in the different economies of urban wage employment and peasant farming. Thus people (especially men but increasingly also women) move back and forth between city and farm, between urban and agrarian lifestyles. They maintain contacts with kin and develop their rural homes for eventual retirement to their homeland, the only place where most Kenyans have any hope of owning land (cf. Moller and Welch 1990, Stucki 1992).

These changes have occurred during the lifetimes of those who are now elderly, who themselves were innovators participating in the changes – especially males. As boys and young men they went to school, served in the military in World Wars I and II, went outside their home area seeking wage employment, spent time in newly urbanizing areas, and learned to speak Swahili. In general, they had much greater exposure to the new influences than did women. Women, for the most part, stayed in the rural area, headed households and worked harder than ever to make ends meet in conditions of increasing poverty and scarcity (cf. Hay 1976).

ELEMENTS OF HIERARCHY: GENDER, AGE AND KINSHIP

Hierarchy is pervasive among Abaluyia. Daily interactions occur in social contexts shaped by the sexual division of labor and the complex interplay of gender, age and other factors such as kinship, the elements from which hierarchy is constructed. Power over others is exercised in various ways, such as making decisions about work and family life (what crops to plant, which food to cook, whether to take a sick child to the hospital), giving advice, ordering others' daily activities, and sending people to do errands. Individuals may compete with each other for power, or they may cooperate in influencing the activities and behavior of others to increase the likelihood that 'wealth' will flow their way, where wealth refers to goods, money, services and other benefits (Caldwell 1982).

Higher status individuals expect respect and obedience from those of lower status. Respect is shown through obedience, verbal and behavioral deference, and avoidance of physical contact and discussion of certain topics. The quiet obedient child who quickly fulfills assignments is the exemplar of a respectful junior, though expectations of obedience are not confined to children. Wives should be respectful and obedient to husbands; junior wives should follow the lead of the first wife, and so on.

While age and generational (kinship) statuses are significant in shaping hierarchy they are not always congruent, for example when a niece is older than her aunt. In such cases it is not always clear who is the senior person in a given relationship. Such status ambiguities can lead to ambiguities concerning the proper flow of respect and obedience, command and advice, goods and services. Power may even 'flip flop' over an individual's life course, with shy young girls, who are among the least powerful, becoming strong-minded, relatively powerful adult women and finally, powerless again when they become frail old women.

Furthermore, with age and experience females become more adept at resisting the domination of others and asserting themselves. Thus individual adults' expectations of obedience and respect may be accepted at times but sometimes are evaded, contested or even ignored (Cattell 1992a, 1994a).

An inescapable aspect of the structuring of social events and individuals' daily associations is the gendered nature of work. Nearly everyone plants, cultivates and harvests both food and cash crops, but most other work is distinctly women's work or men's work. Women carry out a variety of activities related to food preparation, domestic tasks and child-care. Men's work involves clearing fields for planting, herding livestock, and house building and repair. From adolescence on, much of a woman's waking hours are spent with children and other women in their gendered work settings where women are autonomous, making all relevant decisions among themselves.[3]

While most relationships are ordered by norms of respect behavior, gender is not the only determinant of power relations between any two individuals. Age and kinship position can override gender considerations. A middle-aged man who 'rules' his wife (almost certainly younger than himself) will defer with great respect to his elderly mother. Men will say that 'women are *abakeni* (strangers, i.e. not of their husbands' lineage) and not very important'. However, older women may in fact have a great deal to say in family decision making processes and in other social arenas in this overtly patriarchal society (cf. Herbert 1993, Udvardy and Cattell 1992).

Unlike some Abaluyia groups well known in the literature (Sangree 1966, Wagner 1949, 1956), the Samia and Banyala did not and do not have circumcision age grades or a formal age group system which plays in a major role in ordering relations among individuals and groups. Also, social maturity is not achieved in a group process marked by communal rituals but individually and gradually, through marriage and parenthood. Maturity evolves into old age, marked by the end of a person's reproductive career (including, for women, the end of menstruation) and loss of physical strength, the latter associated with the ability to grow food and provide for one's family, that is, to meet adult responsibilities.

An old person (*omukofu*) is to be respected and obeyed by anyone junior in age and generation. A very old person (*omukofu muno*), by definition frail or disabled, is to be respected, cared for and even feared, as being close to the spirits of ancestors (*emisambwa*). Even after death, individuals have power in their families, for *emisambwa* can influence the health and well being of their descendants.

Family positions and roles are important for contemporary Abaluyia, as they were earlier in the century (Wagner 1949, 1965). Every child is born into the clan (*oluyia*) and patrilineal descent group (*enyumba*) of the father and remains a member for life. Clans and patrilineage tend to be localized because sons

usually bring their wives to live on their father's land.[4] This patrilocal residence pattern is reinforced by the reality of contemporary
land shortages that tie males to land inherited from their fathers
(females rarely inherit, or even own, land). Thus brothers and
half-brothers[5] often live on adjacent farms, their sons and grandsons remain on the same land (further subdivided), and male
'cousins' live nearby. *Enyumba* (patrilineages) are usually three
generations deep, breaking up into new *enyumba* with the death
of the last brother or half-brother in the senior generation. Thus
many family homesteads (*amadaala*) are occupied by groups of
brothers and their families, and older people live with sons, sons'
wives and grandchildren.

Even in this strongly male-oriented situation, maternal ties
are significant. They are institutionalized in a variety of ways,
including the special relationships of mother's brother and sister's
son and the ongoing visits and exchanges between mothers and
daughters (and daughters' children) even after daughters marry
and move away (Cattell 1994a).

Because females are peripheral in patri-lines, wives are deper-
sonalized in husbands' genealogies through use of clan rather than
personal names and, after one or two generations, are dropped
from genealogical recitations. Living females, however, have
important duties in their natal lineages throughout their lives.
Married daughters/sisters (*abakoko*) are called home by fathers,
uncles or brothers to participate in discussions and rituals during
family crises such as marriage decision making and funerals. This
gives women identities and rights not derived from their husbands nor under a husband's control (cf. Hakansson 1994).

Females are valued for their hard work, for bringing bridewealth to their families, and as potential sources of support for
elderly parents (a duty formerly considered to be primarily that
of sons). Girl children are valued, but a girl is subordinate to
almost everyone during her early years. Gradually, however, a
woman acquires prestige and power as she moves up the kinship
ladder. By the time she is 'old' (any time from about age 50 on)
a woman is likely to have spent years directing the activities of
daughters-in-law and often also managing the family farm during
her husband's absences for employment or when she is widowed.[6]

She is likely to be a woman respected by kin and community for her hard work and achievements as well as for her senior position in her family. Age and generational seniority, more than gender, are the foundation for respect and the right to claim the obedience and services of juniors and family support in old age.[7]

INSIDE THE KINSHIP HIERARCHY: ABALUYIA WOMEN AND POWER

One important way in which Abaluyia girls and women experience power and powerlessness is through their roles in women's age hierarchies within the kinship system of power. In this system women's opportunities for autonomy and control of resources improve with age and advanced kinship or generational status, theoretically and in practice. Juniors frequently challenge seniors (as they do in all societies, see Foner 1984), so women learn to negotiate and manage their relationships with each other. Sometimes, however, hierarchy is muted or not particularly relevant. An exception to the rules is the relationship of grandmothers and granddaughters with its strong element of egalitarianism in spite of age and generational differences. Another is what happens as an older woman becomes increasingly frail, when the situation of upward mobility through the life course reverses and the frail elder is socially and economically marginalized – a situation she shares in some ways with adolescent girls.

The most salient female relationships are among sisters and between mother and daughter, mother- and daughter-in-law, and co-wives, where age hierarchy is ever present, and grandmothers and granddaughters, where hierarchy is muted. The following brief descriptions of these key relationships include both the norms of behavior and some ways subordinates resist the power of the dominant. It is worth bearing in mind John Caldwell's (1982) ideas about 'wealth flows', which in sub-Saharan Africa usually flow up, from children to parents. In a broader sense, there is a multitude of wealth flows in Abaluyia society, within many different relationships, where one of a dyad may command the goods, labor, respect, in short, the wealth, of the other. And of course wealth is power.

Sisters. Age and seniority are important determinants of status. For example, siblings always know the order of their birth, and often the order of birth of other sibling groups. If a person asks, 'Who are your brothers and sisters?' you usually get, without prompting, the names in order of birth. Among siblings, hierarchy is perhaps strongest in childhood, when older siblings order younger to do errands and chores just as adults command children. Later in life, diplomacy becomes more important in getting siblings to do as you wish.

Since brothers usually remain on their father's land, the ties among brothers remain strong (or conflict is strong!). Women, on the other hand, marry 'out' to their husbands' homes.[8] In spite of this separation, sisters may continue to cooperate in support of each other and other females in their families. One dramatic example of this occurred in one sibling group when the oldest brother's daughter was about to graduate from college. The young woman's father did not plan to celebrate her achievement. But the father's older sister, with the cooperation of other sisters, organized her younger siblings (including the reluctant father and two other brothers) for a family celebration. As firstborn, and as a successful career woman, the oldest sister had the clout and the respect to bring this about in spite of some reluctance from 'below'. For example, from the graduate's father who had to close his business for a day or two and spend a lot of money for food and drink.[9] While the celebration pleased the graduate immensely, it also emphasized female solidarity in the family and forced family recognition of the young woman's accomplishment.

More commonly, sisters (and other females) support each other in daily chores such as child-care, cooking, carrying water; through small exchanges of food or other goods; helping out when visitors are in a home, and in other ways.

Mothers and Daughters. The mother-daughter relationship is one of mingled respect and affection. It begins with the dominant mother but in time evolves into a relationship of rough equality. Girls, much more than boys, are expected to help their mother with child-care, domestic and farming chores. Since all these are under the mother's supervision, a girl is primarily disciplined by her mother. Mother is the senior, the teacher, the one responsible for her daughter's behavior. At the same time, mother-daughter (and mother-son) relationships are likely to be strongly affectionate compared to relationships with fathers, who are more authoritarian and distant.

In the daughter's adolescence tensions and problems focus on her education and sexuality. Such indigenous society seems to have channeled these tensions in several ways. When the old women of today were girls, grandmothers and older sisters shared responsibility with the mother for a girl's education. Sexuality was more closely controlled by senior generations, parents arranged marriages (forced in some or perhaps many cases), brides were tested for virginity. The 10, 12 or 14 year old bride went to live in her new husband's home, where she was under her mother-in-law's tutelage and domination. Such arrangement probably helped defuse tensions between mother and daughter by transferring them to the in-law relationship as the mother-in-law guided her daughter-in-law's behavior and continued her education in women's skills.

As a woman becomes secure in her marriage and higher social status as a mother and mature woman, her relationship with her mother can become relatively equal. Married daughters are likely to return home for visits, alone or with their children, especially if there are visitors or a funeral or other occasion when extra help is needed. A daughter may stay for several weeks during which she enjoys working and socializing with her mother. While a woman must always respect her mother, as a mature woman she can associate with her mother as a friend and co-worker, as someone with whom she shares many life experiences, and as someone she loves.

In contemporary society some new tensions have entered mother-daughter relationships, as girls marry at later ages and often have a child before marrying.[10] Premarital pregnancies lead to increased social and emotional pressures and heavier work burdens for the middle generation. The girl's family must manage the stigma of premarital pregnancies and often it is the girl's mother who takes responsibility for the child (Cattell

1989b, Kilbride 1990, Kilbride and Kilbride 1990, 1997). If the girl later marries a man other than the father of her premarital child, she leaves the child with her mother when she goes to live in her husband's home (few Abaluyia men will accept another man's child in their home).

Mothers-in-law and Daughters-in-law. Relationships between mother-in-law and daughter in-law are quite different from those of mothers and daughters. A new young wife is engaged in a power struggle with her husband's mother over the work the mother-in-law supervises and over the affections and material support of the man who is son to one, husband to the other. A young wife is under the thumb of her husband's mother and is junior to every adult in the home; she may even have more than one mother-in-law to answer to if her husband's father has more than one wife (about a third of Samia men are polygynists).

Furthermore, as a stranger newly come to the home, she is unlikely to have supporters other than her husband. To avoid criticism and problems she has to work hard and be modest in behavior and obedient to the will of others. She cooks with her mother-in-law in the senior woman's kitchen and gets her own kitchen only after she has given birth to three children. Having her own kitchen signifies that she is a mature woman who can make her own decisions concerning food choices, preparation and serving, which gives her additional power within the home (Cattell 1992a).

Later in life, her role may reverse; the young bride who was very subordinate may assume the dominant position in her home. If her husband spends most of the year working in an urban area, she may become the de facto manager of the home and farm and the one providing care to her elderly, frail, widowed mother-in-law. If she and her mother-in-law have had a good relationship over the years, the older woman is likely to receive good care from her daughter-in-law, usually with help from grandchildren. But if theirs has been a difficult relationship, the old woman may suffer: her daughter-in-law may be slow in bringing water or may dole out very small portions of food. She may even forbid her children to do errands for their grandmother. Thus the older woman misses out on help with chores, companionship, and the valued social role of grandmother. She is demeaned, marginalized and made to feel useless. She is a woman without power.

In the 1980s and 1990s many things about marriage and family life are changing in ways which appear to be reducing the powerlessness of brides. For one thing, young people often choose their own spouses nowadays. Young couples may live in an urban area, away from the close control of their parents. Even those women who remain in the rural home are resisting the pattern of mother-in-law domination with some success. They do so, for example, by building their own kitchens earlier in their marital careers and eating in their own houses with their husbands rather than in their mother-in-law's kitchen with other women of the family. Young wives do this with the support of their husbands in what seems to be another aspect of the general loosening of the senior generation's control over juniors.

Co-wives. In polygynous marriages, the first or 'big' wife ideally manages women's labor for the benefit of an entire homestead. However, tensions and conflicts among co-wives are notorious. There is even a special word for jealousy among co-wives *esikharikhari*. The senior wife may resent her new co-wife, especially if the husband brought the new wife without consulting his first wife. A junior wife may resent the senior wife's control. There may be anger if the husband gives a dress to one wife and not another, or if he pays the school fees of one wife's child and tells another wife that her child can just stay home and help her with work. Co-wife conflicts often are expressed through children, for example, a woman may forbid her children to eat food prepared by a co-wife, or one woman may be unduly harsh toward another woman's child. Stories of wicked stepmothers occur in folk tales and in autobiographical accounts of childhood.

But cooperation among co-wives is the ideal and also often the reality, especially among women who have been co-wives for a long time. They may act in concert against their husband, quarreling among themselves so there is no peace in the home, refusing to cook their husband's food, and generally making life miserable for him until he gives in to their wishes. Longtime co-wives may even unite against a young third wife and try to drive her from the home (case study in Cattell 1992c). They may also support each other as widows. That is the case of Samia widows who are saved (born again) Christians and refuse to follow indigenous funeral customs, including widow remarriage, which, as saved people, they perceive as 'things of Satan' and, as women, as a renewal of male domination (Cattell 1992a).

Older Women. Even this brief consideration of female age hierarchies among Abaluyia reveals complex relations of dominance and power among females. Relationships in female hierarchies entail many ambiguities and involve cooperation and solidarity, competition and conflict. Further, as we have seen, the nature of the power relationship between any two women may shift over the life-course and dominance/subordination may be reversed.

Michael Schatzberg (1992) made the point that for Africans, power involves not only the control of resources (including people's labor), but also their consumption. Thus a person's fat body results from and is evidence of the social and political power that enables the person to consume food in plenty. By Samia standards, a mature woman (*omukhasi omudwasi*) is one whose breasts and abdomen have grown fat. While this bodily transformation undoubtedly results from repeated pregnancies, the woman who has become fat physically has also become fat socially. She is a mother, with children that she can put to work and send on errands; she has her own kitchen, makes decisions about which crops to grow and which foods to prepare for meals. She is a consumer of wealth, as anyone can see by looking at her.[11]

Older people, however, lose muscle mass at an accelerated rate (part of normal physiological aging) and so become thin and weak physically at the same time they are becoming socially 'thin'. Some years ago, when a very thin, very frail Samia woman in her mid-80s said to me, 'All we old people think about is eating'. I took her statement literally, especially as I knew her small energies were expended in daily quests for food. But it may bear thinking about in terms of losses of status and power experienced by the elderly, particularly with the rapid and radical socio-economic changes of the past century. In this context, her remark can be understood as a commentary on the losses of old age, including the loss of personal autonomy and social 'fatness' or power.

BEYOND HIERARCHY: GRANDMOTHERS AND GRANDDAUGHTERS

The relationships of Abaluyia grandmothers and granddaughters are, in a sense, outside the system of female hierarchy. Grandmother-granddaughter relationships are characterized, ideally and often in practice, by informal behavior, emotional warmth and love, friendly teasing, and the grandmother's indulgences such as gift giving and tolerance of 'misbehavior' including discussion of sexual matters. Grandmother and granddaughter may call each other *mwalikhwa* (co-wife) as a sign of their social equality, a fictitious equality because in fact the grandmother is very senior to the granddaughter.

A. R. Radcliffe-Brown (1940, 1949) called such relationships 'joking' and contrasted them to 'respect' relationships that are more formal and bound by rules. Most relationships (with the parental generation and one's in-laws in particular) are of the respect type.[12] Joking relationships provide an alternative to the constraints of respectful behavior. Not surprisingly, nearly everyone speaks of grandmothers with marked warmth and affection.

Abaluyia grandmothers have the important duty of 'advising' or teaching granddaughters (and younger grandsons), advising being the preeminent role of elders. Grandmother-granddaughter relationships simultaneously embrace friendly equality and the grandmother's authority as an old woman, a person of high kinship rank, a person of knowledge. The muting of this authority in a joking relationship undoubtedly facilitates girls' learning and has important affective benefits for both parties.

However, ambiguities and uncertainties in the relationships of grandmothers and granddaughters have resulted from the changing roles of girls and women in modern Kenya. Older women's cultural expertise and social authority have been badly eroded in today's world (Cattell 1989a). For example, in the past, grandmothers advised girls about sexual and marital behavior, subjects not usually discussed with parents, who must be respected. In effect, grandmothers controlled significant aspects of adolescent sexuality (see note 10) and the intergenerational transmission of knowledge (cf. Cohen 1985, who describes a similar situation among neighboring Luo people).

Today young children commonly sleep with grandmothers, but adolescent girls often sleep in their mother's kitchen (a separate small building because of fire hazards). Here girls can talk among themselves about things that matter to them. Today's granddaughters want the knowledge of schools and books in order to compete for employment. Most grandmothers are illiterate and never experienced formal employment. Today's unmarried young women want to know about 'family planning' (contraception), not how to remain a virgin until marriage, as grandmothers would advise them. As one grandmother told me, 'Nowadays it isn't easy to advise the young'.

Nevertheless, while they remain vigorous, many Abaluyia grandmothers continue to make contributions to their families, including the new role of taking responsibility for children of their unmarried daughters (cf. Sangree 1986).

IN THE INTERSTICES: LIMINALITY AND MARGINALITY IN ADOLESCENCE AND OLD AGE

The social equivalence of grandmothers and granddaughters may sometimes dissolve into a shared liminality, especially as granddaughters become adolescents and grandmothers become frail. Their liminal periods have different boundaries, however, and very different outcomes, psychologically and practically.

The concept of liminality, or being outside the bounds of normal social structure, is that of van Gennep (1960) as reinterpreted by Victor and Edith Turner (Turner 1967, 1969, 1974; Turner and Turner 1978). The Turners applied van Gennep's notion of ritual liminality or marginality, of being between two social statuses, to ordinary (non-ritual) social situations. In the Turners' view, social structure is an arrangement of positions or statuses that order social relations. This contrasts with anti-structure or liminality, marked by social ambiguity, structural invisibility and secular powerlessness. Persons in similar social positions, whether they are ritual liminars or socially marginally elders, are likely to develop a sense of *communitas* or psychological bonding achieved through feelings of comradeship and unity.

In indigenous Abaluyia society, adolescent liminality was institutionalized: young males were warriors, young females were wives apprenticed to mothers-in-law. They had clearly defined roles though little if any power. In contrast to youths, elders (women and men) were the decision-makers and voices of authority. In a society organized on the principle of seniority, growing older meant growing wiser, wealthier and more powerful, except, presumably, when elders became frail, that is, physically and/or mentally weak. Grandparent-grandchild joking relationships may be a cultural indicator of some less desirable aspects of old age in indigenous society. They hint at the structural and social equivalence, powerlessness and mutual liminality of the old and the young.[13]

The new political and socioeconomic conditions under colonialism in the early 20th century began the erosion of the prestige and power of elders, a process that appears to be continuing today. The situations of young people have gone through a double shift. In colonial times many young men had access to the new resources of education and wage employment, which gave them social and economic power not controlled by local elders. More recently access to education has broadened to include girls and young women. However, because of Kenya's weak economy, education no longer guarantees employment. Today's young people often find themselves at loose ends, unable to succeed in the modern world and lacking the socially useful, though marginal, roles they had in indigenous society. Combined with the present economy of poverty and scarcity, it seems likely that both youth and old age have become more ambiguous and uncertain times of life than they were in the past.

Thus among Abaluyia in the 1980s and 1990s, both old age and youth are periods of marginality, ambiguity and powerlessness, in contrast to adulthood, which is characterized by social maturity and responsibility (Cattell 1993). Adolescents and elders are in transitional life stages in which adulthood is pivotal, but from sharply different perspectives. Adolescents are not ready for the responsibility toward which they are moving, whereas elders, as they lose strength and become frail, are less socially and economically useful and are moving beyond adult responsibilities.

If adolescents are not yet adults, they can at least look forward to achieving that status, they have opportunities, hopes, and plans. Elders are in the potentially devastating situation of losing their adult status as they move toward frailty, death and ancestor-hood. As some elders said, when asked about their plans for the future, 'Plans? I have no plans. I am just waiting to die'. Old people who are becoming weak, physically and/or mentally, sometimes are described as 'like a child again'. Their adulthood has been compromised by their inability to participate fully in adult life. As they lose their strength and come to be cared for by others, they may be like children again, in some ways, but of course they are not really children. Some in their families may think they are living too long, depriving children of their life force. They may be feared because of their greater spiritual powers because they are so close to the ancestors, and at the same time looked down upon because they are ignorant of modern ways, unable to help others and carry out the proper roles of elders.

In 1985 I asked many Samia people from adolescents to the very old how they viewed their lives at three points: a few years ago, now, and a few years in the future. Interviewees were asked to place themselves on a scale represented by a 7-rung ladder. Most adolescents were optimistic about their future, expecting it to be much better than their present. Of 69 secondary school students, 38% expected to be at 6 or 7 (the top of the ladder) within five years. Only 11 of the 416 elders (less than 3%) thought they would be at the top.[14] Roughly a third of the old people said their future would be worse, that they would be at the bottom of the ladder or that they did not know what it would be.

Gender differences among the adolescents were not significant. Young women were as optimistic as the young men, not surprising since all were in secondary school and looked toward a hopeful future in which educational achievement would be rewarded with economic opportunity. However, older women, reflecting their lifetimes of lesser opportunity and present greater poverty (relative to men), felt less in control of their lives and less optimistic about their futures than older men.

All this suggests that young people and elders are well aware of being outside the centers of their societies, and well aware of the different futures they face.

IMPLICATIONS FOR DEVELOPMENT, PERSONAL AND SOCIETAL

What does all this suggest for the present and future of Abaluyia girls and women, especially older women, and their roles in development? I do not have a program to present, only a few suggestions for approaches which might help both women (including older women) and their society to develop.

Seek Indigenous Solutions. Look for indigenous responses to local needs; listen to local people, including older women, those who do much of the work and struggle daily to care for themselves and their families.

However, even with participatory and locally based research and action, the input of the *relevant* local people must be sought (Adagala and Bifani 1985). Too often, 'local people' means men, and does not mean women. Consulting only men constitutes a serious oversight, given that African women have primary responsibility for child-raising and food provision and are also the major agricultural producers on the continent. For example, even in so 'simple' a matter as obtaining fuel-wood for cooking, there is a tendency to ignore the experience and opinions of the girls and women who gather the wood and do the cooking. Thus a Samia man, who sees many trees on a hill but does not try to collect the wood or cook with it, sees plenty, and reports that obtaining fuel-wood is not a problem. The girl or woman who goes to the same hill and finds only poor quality wood for her cooking perceives scarcity, but her experience that obtaining fuel-wood is a problem is ignored in reforestation programs (Aloo 1993).

Similarly, seeking indigenous solutions should aid in restoring older people to a more central place in their society, provided the western ideological view does not dominate. This view, common among development workers, writes off the elderly as 'having no use value in the process of capital accumulation.... [so that] many are relegated to the social margins of their society' (Neysmith and Edwardh 1984:40, see also Treas and Logue 1986). Older Africans, especially in the rural areas where the majority of them live, continue to engage in productive work as long as they are physically able. Older Africans also continue to participate in family life, as in the earlier example of grandmothers raising grandchildren born outside marriage. Their experience and contributions should be valued in development efforts.

RECOGNIZE OLDER WOMEN'S CONTRIBUTIONS

There is a call to re-value and to recognize the contributions to development of women and of older women in particular. As they continue struggling for survival and advancement for themselves and their families in a rapidly changing world, Abaluyia women of all ages need support, recognition and opportunities (e.g. for credit). Like women all over the world, they are 'overworked and underpaid' (Tiano 1987:216) and also, too often, invisible in development processes. Recognizing older women's contributions will help the older women maximize self-help, family contributions (from them and to them), and their participation in rural development.

Older women are accustomed to continuing their active roles in the rural economy and within the family as long as they can. Indeed, they insist upon it, knowing its practical value to themselves and its value to their self-esteem, and knowing that their long-term security depends on it within the family support system based on interdependence and reciprocity. Indeed, this is not peculiar to Abaluyia, for kinship is a primary coping strategy throughout Africa (see Iliffe 1987).

In Samia, however, older people are often regarded as impediments to development, as it happens throughout the world (see Treas and Logue 1986). Many younger Samia expressed the idea that older people do not understand today's world, like an 18-year-old secondary student: 'There is some education such as boiling drinking water that when you tell old people about it, they just say, 'We have been surviving without boiled water'. In fact, education, schools and new knowledge, the knowledge of books, of outsiders, are seen by both young and old as increasing intergenerational differences and misunderstandings. While older people, especially grandmothers are usually loved and respected, they are not necessarily viewed as up-to-date. To be thought out of touch with today's world puts one's usefulness in the past, so older women's contributions to development may be taken for granted and go unrecognized.

Recognition of their work as contributions to development might help reduce the liminality or marginalization of older women, a knottier problem than the marginalization of adolescent girls. The potential usefulness of adolescent girls is readily recognized and much discussed; increasingly, families regard their daughters as worth educating so their future contributions to their families will be improved. The usefulness of older women is less apparent. Being regarded as no longer adult is vastly different from being not yet adult. To be considered out of touch with today's world puts one's usefulness in the past.

Older Samia women want to participate in development. Like younger people, they talk about *maendeleo*, the Swahili word for 'development' or 'advancement' that is a kind of national slogan and call to action. To these women, however, development means not only advance and improvement on a large scale, but also bettering one's own situation and that of one's family in areas such as nutrition, health and education. Some older women attend adult literacy classes (17% of the 200 women age 50 and up, in my 1985 survey of old people in Samia), and many struggle to feed and educate grandchildren. Many older women continue food-producing and income-generating activities: in my survey, 38% of older women said they grew cotton (the major cash crop in Samia) and the same proportion said they engaged in petty trading. A number of older women have been leaders in the community-based primary healthcare program developed at Nangina Hospital.

While these activities may not directly advance development in the sense of capital accumulation (a conceptualization of development defined by already developed nations), they do make contributions to the real, practical development which comes through improving the health and nutrition of people whose poverty and needs are great. The work of older women frees the labor of younger family members (cf. Cronk 1990, Rix 1991, Roberts and Thomas 1994) and helps to meet the needs of children. In these efforts older women are helped by cash remittances from family members, especially sons and, to a lesser extent, daughters.[15] Such remittances are almost always spent on consumption goods rather than on rural development (Rempel and Lobdell 1978), but insofar as they help improve a family's standard of living, they constitute another contribution to development.

USE WOMEN'S LEADERSHIP SKILLS

Use women's leadership skills and strengthen women's organizations, including local mutual aid societies and larger scale organizations that can give women a significant political voice in the national arena (Amadiume 1987).

While they know a lot about powerlessness, Abaluyia women also know how to lead. As women move up the kinship ladder they learn to exercise power through negotiation and decision making as they manage girls and other women in doing 'women's work' in the household and on the farm. This is not merely 'kitchen politics', as one man dismissed it, but the skills necessary for women to carry out their essential work. Many women also gain experience managing the entire farming operation while husbands are absent for extended periods or when a woman is widowed. Ironically, women's knowledge of child-care, crop production, food storage and preparation, and farm and family management has not lost its importance to daily life, though such knowledge is not valued when it comes to achievements in the world of urban employment.

Rural Abaluyia women have other opportunities for leadership in business (some are very successful entrepreneurs), in religious groups and in their communities. In Samia it is often women who become Community Health Workers and thus leaders in health promotion in their home areas. Women often are the leaders in the numerous self-help groups found in rural areas. Among women's groups in particular, only women may be officers (by government decree) though men may be members.

In 1995 I interviewed Teresa Mudimbia, who, as county coordinator, oversees more than 2,000 women's groups in Busia District. I remarked that people often say old people won't learn, that they just want to do things in the old ways. 'Yes', responded Ms. Mudimbia, 'they just say forget about old people. But in fact many women group leaders are old women'. Why should older women so often be group leaders? The knowledge and experience of older women favors them for leadership roles, especially in groups requiring or benefiting from cooperation among women. In addition, older women are senior. Cultural expectations are that senior people (women as well as men) deserve respect and that their advice should be sought. Also, older women are far more likely to have the time for activities outside the home than younger women with heavy child-care responsibilities.

INTEGRATE CULTURAL PATTERNS AND VALUES

There is a need to integrate indigenous knowledge, roles and cultural values into the modern situation and development efforts. There is also a need to build on cultural patterns such as the grandmother-granddaughter relationship and the advisory roles of elders.

In surveying old people in Samia, my research assistants a number of times heard some variation of the following: 'I thought I would just die with my information. I am always here. Come back whenever you can and ask me more questions'. Young people, in their turn, were surprised at how interesting it was to sit and really listen to the old people talk about the past, Samia customs, and their own lives and opinions. 'I never knew so much about my own culture', they told me, sensing the importance of issues of cultural identity with which many Africans today are grappling.

Could such encounters be formalized in the Kenyan educational system, as once they were institutionalized in the lessons taught by grandmothers in their houses? Many textbooks incorporate cultural materials from Kenya's various ethnic groups. Surely schools could find ways to encourage students to listen to individual old people, as my research assistants did. Home assignments and bringing elders into classrooms would offer support to the culturally recognized but often frustrated roles of grandmothers (and grandfathers too) as advisers and teachers to the young. Such a program, based on an existing relationship pattern, should help to diminish views of older women as marginal or as impediments to development. At the same time it would enrich the cultural knowledge of younger generations and emphasize indigenous values in social life.

All too often youths who are no longer in school 'just stay at home' with little useful work to do, little chance of getting employment anywhere, and, for girls, the likelihood of becoming unmarried mothers. But adolescent liminality can be socially useful, as it was in indigenous Abaluyia society, where youthful energy was turned to socially desirable purposes. Perhaps some of the energy of young people could be directed to the service of elders who need assistance, following cultural ideals that children care for elderly parents, but with a community as well as family orientation. There are obstacles to such an idea; an important one is that altruism and helping others tend to be a family matter. One helps one's kin, expecting to be helped in turn. For example, a frail old Samia woman twice had a small house built for her by community health workers from Nangina Hospital's primary healthcare program.[16] When the old woman needed a third house, the health workers resisted. They had done enough, it was her family's duty to provide. Unfortunately the old woman had no living son (the proper person to build her a house), and she waited a long time until finally a stepson (the son of a co-wife) built one for her.

AFTERWORD

Some difficulties by both adolescents and elders may be resolved at the local level, with good will and hard work. However, it is also the case that most people in Bunyala and Samia are poor because they are caught in a situation not of their own making and not amenable to local correction. Parker Shipton (1990:381), discussing African famines, notes the irony that what causes famines, i.e. 'the market', 'the state', also resolves them. Similarly, one cannot dismiss notions of economic development involving capital accumulation simply because they are 'western'. Markets and states are not going to disappear, nor is their influence on everyday life in no-longer-remote African villages going to disappear. Furthermore, indigenous people, too, have economies of capital accumulation. Ask any pastoralist who wants more cattle, ask any farmer who longs for more land and more bursting granaries!

In the long term, issues of food security, access to other resources, health, social equity and a good life will be resolved only through 'real' economic development and the elimination of poverty. One way to move in this direction is to take better cognizance of the value of indigenous interests and ideas, and of the value of everyone's contributions, including those of older women, who have much to offer their families and societies. Perhaps economists' conceptualizations of capital accumulation could benefit from African ideas of social capital, or wealth in people, and recognition that 'indirect' contributions to economic development, such as grandmothers' caring for grandchildren, are significant and necessary contributions to economic development.

ACKNOWLEDGEMENTS

I am grateful for the invaluable help over the past 12 years of my Abaluyia field assistants, especially John Barasa 'JB' Owiti from Samia, who has been with me from my first visit in 1982 and, since 1985, Frankline Teresa Mahaga from Bunyala. Thanks also to the Medical Mission Sisters, Nangina Hospital, Nangina Girls Primary School, and Samia officials, among others, and to my late husband Bob Moss. Above all, *mutio muno* to the many people of Samia and Bunyala who allowed me to share their lives in various ways. The research was partially funded by the National Science Foundation (grant BNS8306802), the Wenner-Gren Foundation (grant 4506), and Bryn Mawr College (Frederica de Laguna Fund grant). I was a Research Associate at the Institute of African Studies, University of Nairobi, in 1984 and 1985. Portions of this article derive from an invited lecture on 'Women of Power: Age Hierarchies in Modern Kenya', given at Cleveland State University in June 1993, and from papers given at the annual meetings of the African Studies Association (Cattell 1992c, 1993) and the Society for Applied Anthropology (Cattell 1994b).

Notes

1. For example, in 1929 tens of thousands of Igbo women (Nigeria) marched on colonial administrative centers, broke into prisons and released prisoners, attacked Native Courts and engaged in other activities which the British labeled 'riots' but the Igbo called the 'women's war' (Van Allen 1976). More recently, in the former kingdom of Kom (in what is now Cameroon), Kom women carried out a large-scale uprising and took over governance of Kom; they ruled from 1958 to 1961 (Shanklin 1989).

2. Banyala are the people, Bunyala is the place. In the Samia language, Basamia are the people, Busamia is the place. In English the prefixes Ba- and Bu- are dropped for Ba/Busamia and retained for Ba/Bunyala. I know of no reason for the difference; it's just the way it is done.

3. Younger women work all day long; men of all ages and older women often have leisure time for relaxing and socializing. Roberts and Thomas (1994) found similar situations in two other Kenyan but non-Abaluyia communities in Elgeyo-Marakwet and Meru districts.

4. This localization of descent groups was confirmed in 1985 by a household census in Siwongo village.

5. Polygyny is widespread, with about a third of older men being polygynously married (Cattell 1989b); thus many men have half-brothers, that is, sons of their father's co-wife (or wives).

6. About two-fifths of Kenyan farm households are headed by women (World Bank 1989).

7. Of course family support in old age is complex and, these days, increasingly problematic. It depends on many factors which I will not go into here (see Cattell 1989b, 1990, 1992b).

8. That is, postmarital residence is patrilocal. This is both the ideal and a common reality.

9. One sister did not participate, but her resistance to this celebration was expected since her relations with various family members had been strained for several years.

10. Premarital pregnancies have become common in Kenya in recent decades (Kenya 1980; Khasiani 1985), perhaps 10% of Kenyan schoolgirls are affected (World Bank 1989). Today girls are less under the control and protection of their families because of the

many socioeconomic changes of recent decades. For example, today most Kenyan girls attend school for at least a few years (World Bank 1989). School takes children away from their families, especially adolescents in secondary school, since most secondary schools are boarding schools. Adolescent girls, in school or not, are virtually powerless in a society whose patriarchal ideology condones rape and gender violence (Steeves 1997). They are easy prey for males, from their age peers to teachers and other older men. In this setting old rules of sexual behavior, imparted by grandmothers and enforced within tight-knit communities, no longer are significant constraints on sexual behavior.

11. When I visited Kenya in 1993 I had gained a little weight since my visit the previous year. Almost everyone commented: 'Oh, Maria, you are fat. That is good'. In America that would be an insult, but in rural Kenya to be called fat is a compliment! It means you have food and good health. Few people are fat in the sense of being obese (with its negative connotations, at least in the US) probably because of everyday dietary insufficiencies associated with poverty, seasonal food shortages and occasional famines. Interestingly, while mature Abaluyia women generally are heavy of breast and abdomen, fat men are less common, except for the occasional 'potbelly', which also suggests social fatness.

12. Exceptions include a girl's *senge* (father's sister), who could be a co-wife and an equal and, along with grandmothers, is expected to teach girls about sexual and marital behavior, and a woman's brothers-in-law, who are potential husbands if she is widowed and 'inherited' (remarried within her husband's family).

13. Claims that elders were 'always respected and cared for' in indigenous African societies are based on current ideals and values rather than on knowledge of past social realities. We do not really know how frail elders were treated in the past (Cattell 1997b, Peil 1995).

14. All 11 elders were 'saved' (born again Christians) for whom a good future is to be 'with Jesus'. For them, hardships in this life and death were unimportant; what mattered most was that they would spend eternity with Jesus.

15. Most remittances in Kenya go to older people (Knowles and Anker 1981); roughly half the older women in my survey received such remittances.

16. Samia houses built of mud-and-thatch need to be replaced about every 10 years.

References

Abu-Lughod, Lila. 1990. 'The Romance of Resistance: Tracing Transformations of Power through Bedouin Women', *American Ethnologist* 17: 41-55.

Adagala, Kavetsa and Patricia Bifani.1985. *Self-employed Women in the Peri-urban Setting: Petty Traders in Nairobi*. Nairobi: Derika Associates.

Aloo, Theresa C. 1993. 'Fuelwood and Tree Planting: A Case Study from Funyula Division in Western Kenya'. Ph.D. Dissertation, University of British Columbia. Ottawa: National Library of Canada.

Amadiume, Ifi.1987. *Male Daughters, Female Husbands*. London and New Jersey: Zed Books.

Caldwell, John C. 1982. *Theory of Fertility Decline*. New York: Academic.

Cattell, Maria G. 1989a. 'Knowledge and Social Change in Samia, Western Kenya', *Journal of Cross-Cultural Gerontology* 4: 225-244.

———. 1989b. 'Old Age in Rural Kenya: Gender, the Life Course and Social Change'. Ph.D. Dissertation, Bryn Mawr College. Ann Arbor MI: University Microfilms.

———. 1990. 'Models of Old Age among the Samia of Kenya: Family Support of the Elderly', *Journal of Cross-Cultural Gerontology* 5: 375-394.

———. 1992a. 'Praise the Lord and Say No to Men: Older Samia Women Empowering Themselves', *Journal of Cross-Cultural Gerontology* 7: 307-330.

———. 1992b. 'Informal Systems of Old Age Support in Developing Countries: Anthropological Perspectives'. Background paper for World Bank policy research report, *Averting the Old Age Crisis* (1994).

———. 1992c.. 'Burying Mary Omundu: The Politics of Death and Gender in Samia, Kenya'. Paper presented at the annual meeting of the African Studies Association, Seattle.

———. 1993. 'Moral Personhood and Gendered Adulthood among the Samia of Western Kenya'. Paper presented at the annual meeting of the African Studies Association, Boston.

————. 1994a. "Nowadays It Isn't Easy to Advise the Young": Grandmothers and Granddaughters among Abaluyia of Kenya', *Journal of Cross-Cultural Gerontology* 9: 157-178.

————. 1994b. 'Liminal Beings: Old People and Adolescents in Samia, Kenya'. Paper presented at the annual meeting of the Society for Applied Anthropology, Cancun, Mexico.

————. 1996a. 'Does Marital Status Matter? Support, Personal Autonomy and Economic Power among Abaluyia Widows in Kenya', *Southern African Journal of Gerontology* 5 (2): 20-26.

————. 1996b. 'Gender, Aging and Health: A Comparative Approach', in *Gender and Health: An International Perspective*, edited by Carolyn Sargent and Caroline B. Brettell, pp. 87-122. Upper Saddle River NJ: Prentice Hall.

————. 1997a. 'African Widows, Culture and Social Change: Case Studies from Kenya', in *The Cultural Context of Aging: Worldwide Perspectives*, second edition. Jay Sokolovsky, ed., pp. 71-98. Westport CT: Bergin & Garvey.

————. 1997b. 'Ubuntu, African Elderly and the African Family Crisis', *Southern African Journal of Gerontology* 6(2): 37-39.

Cohen, David William. 1985. 'Doing Social History from Pim's Doorway', in *Reliving the Past: The Worlds of Social History*, edited by Olivier Zunz, pp. 191-235. Chapel Hill: University of North Carolina Press.

Cronk, Lee. 1990. 'Family Trust', *The Sciences* 30(6): 10-12.

Dickerson-Putman, Jeanette & Judith K. Brown, eds.1998. *Women Among Women: Anthropological Perspectives on Female Age Hierarchies*. Urbana and Chicago: University of Illinois Press.

Foner, Nancy. 1984. *Ages in Conflict: A Cross-Cultural Perspective on Inequality Between Old and Young*. New York: Columbia University Press.

Hakansson, N. Thomas. 1994. 'The Detachability of Women: Gender and Kinship in Processes of Socioeconomic Change among the Gusii of Kenya', *American Ethnologist* 21 :516-538.

Hay, Margaret Jean. 1976. 'Luo Women and Economic Change during the Colonial Period', in *Women in Africa: Studies in Social and Economic Change*, edited by Nancy J. Hafkin and Edna G. Bay, pp. 87-109. Stanford CA: Stanford University Press.

Herbert, Eugenia. 1993.. *Iron, Gender and Power: Rituals of Transformation in African Societies*. Bloomington and Indianapolis: Indiana University Press.

Iliffe, John. 1987. *The African Poor: A History*. Cambridge: Cambridge University Press.

Kenya, Republic of. 1980. *Kenya Fertility Survey 1977-78 First Report*, vol. 1. Nairobi: Central Bureau of Statistics.

———. 1994. *Kenya Population Census, 1989*, Volume I. Nairobi: Central Bureau of Statistics.

Khasiani, Shanyisa Anota.1985.. *Adolescent Fertility in Kenya with Special Reference to High School Teenage Pregnancy*. Nairobi: The Pathfinder Fund.

Kilbride, Philip L.1990.. 'Adolescent Premarital Pregnancies among Abaluyia of Kenya: The Grandparent Role'. Paper presented at annual meeting of African Studies Association, Baltimore.

——— and Janet Kilbride.1990. *Changing Family Life in East Africa: Women and Children at Risk*. University Park: Pennsylvania State University Press.

——— and Janet Kilbride. 1997. 'Stigma, Role Overload, and Delocalization among Contemporary Kenyan Women', in *African Families and the Crisis of Social Change*. Thomas S. Weisner, Candice Bradley and Philip L. Kilbride, eds., pp. 208-23. Westport CT: Bergin & Garvey.

Knowles, J. A. and Richard Anker.1981. 'An Analysis of Income Transfers in a Developing Country', *Journal of Development Economics* 8: 205-226.

K'Okul, Richard N. O. 1991. *Maternal and Child Health in Kenya: A Study of Poverty, Disease and Malnutrition in Samia*. Monograph of the Finnish Society for Development Studies No. 4. Uppsala: The Scandinavian Institute of African Studies.

LeBeuf, Annie M. D. 1963. 'The Role of Women in the Political Organization of African Societies', in *Women of Tropical Africa*, edited by Denise Paulme, pp. 93-119. Berkeley and Los Angeles: University of California Press.

Leith-Ross, Sylvia. 1939. *African Women: A Study of the Ibo of Nigeria*. London: Faber.

Lovett, Margot.1992. 'On Power and Powerlessness: Marriage and Political Metaphor in Colonial Western Tanzania'. Paper presented at the annual meeting of the African Studies Association, Seattle.

Moller, Valerie and Gary Welch. 1990. 'Polygamy, Economic Security and Well-being of Retired Zulu Migrant Workers', *Journal of Cross-Cultural Gerontology* 5: 205-216.

Moore, Henrietta L. 1986. *Space, Text and Gender: An Anthropological Study of the Marakwet of Kenya*. Cambridge: Cambridge University Press.

Neysmith, Sheila M. and Joey Edwardh. 1984. 'Economic Dependency in the 1980s: Its Impact on Third World Elderly', *Ageing and Society* 4: 21-44.

Okonjo, Kamene. 1976.. 'The Dual-Sex Political System in Operation: Igbo Women and Community Politics in Midwestern Nigeria', in *Women in Africa: Studies in Social and Economic Change*, edited by Nancy J. Hafkin and Edna G. Bay, pp. 45-58. Stanford CA: Stanford University Press.

Ottenberg, Simon. 1990.'Thirty Years of Fieldnotes: Changing Relationships to the Text', in *Fieldnotes: The Makings of Anthropology*, edited by Roger Sanjek, pp. 139-160. Ithaca & London: Cornell University Press.

Peil, Margaret. 1995. 'Family help for the elderly in Africa: a comparative assessment', *Southern African Journal of Gerontology* 4 (2): 26-31.

Radcliffe-Brown, A. R.1940. 'On Joking Relationships', *Africa* 13: 195-210.

———. 1949. 'A Further Note on Joking Relationships', *Africa* 19: 133-140.

Rempel, Henry and Richard A. Lobdell.1978. 'The Role of Urban-to-Rural Remittances in Rural Development', *Journal of Development Studies* 14: 324-341.

Rix, Sara E. 1991. 'Older Women and Development: Making a Difference'. Paper presented at Expert Group Meeting, Integration of Aging and Elderly Women into Development, Vienna.

Roberts, Bruce D. and Samuel P. Thomas. 1994.. 'Ageism and Development in Africa: An Analysis of Two Kenyan Societies'. Paper presented at the annual meeting of the American Anthropological Association, Atlanta.

Sangree, Walter H. 1966. *Age, Prayer and Politics in Tiriki, Kenya*. London: Oxford University Press.

———. 1986. 'Role Flexibility and Status Continuity: Tiriki (Kenya) Age Groups Today', *Journal of Cross-Cultural Gerontology* 1: 117-138.

Schatzberg, Michael G. 1992. 'Power in Africa: A Cultural and Literary Perspective'. Paper presented at the annual meeting of the African Studies Association, Seattle.

Scott, James. 1985. *Weapons of the Weak: Everyday Forms of Peasant Resistance*. New Haven: Yale University Press.

Seitz, Jacob. 1978. 'A History of the Samia Location, 1890-1930'. Ph.D. Dissertation, University of West Virginia. Ann Arbor MI: University Microfilms.

Shanklin, Eugenia. 1989. 'Anlu, the Kom Women's Rebellion of 1958-1961: A Matriarchal Moment in Human History?'. Paper presented at Conference on Matriarchal Moments in Women's History, Trenton State College, New Jersey.

Shipton, Parker. 1990. 'African Famines and Food Security: Anthropological Perspectives', *Annual Reviews in Anthropology* 19: 353-394.

Soper, Robert (ed.). 1986. *Kenya Socio-Cultural Profiles: Busia District*. Nairobi: Ministry of Planning and National Development.

Steeves, H. Leslie. 1997. *Gender Violence and the Press: The St. Kizito Story*. Athens OH: Ohio University Center for International Studies.

Stucki, Barbara R. 1992. 'The Long Voyage Home: Return Migration Among Aging Cocoa Farmers of Ghana', *Journal of Cross-Cultural Gerontology* 7: 363-378.

Thomson, Joseph. 1885. *Through Masai Land*. London: Edward Arnold.

Tiano, Susan. 1987. 'Gender, Work, and World Capitalism: Third World Women's Role in Development', in *Analyzing Gender: A Handbook of Social Science Research*, edited by Beth B. Hess and Myra Marx Ferree, pp. 216-243. Newbury Park: Sage.

Treas, Judith and Barbara Logue. 1986. 'Economic Development and the Older Population', *Population and Development Review* 12: 645-673.

Turner, Victor. 1967 [1964]. 'Betwixt and Between: The Liminal Period in Rites de Passage', in *The Forest of Symbols: Aspects of Ndembu Ritual*, pp. 93-111. Ithaca: Cornell University Press.

———. 1969. *The Ritual Process: Structure and Anti-Structure*. Ithaca: Cornell University Press.

———. 1974. *Dramas, Fields, and Metaphors: Symbolic Action in Human Society*. Ithaca: Cornell University Press.

——— and Edith Turner. 1978. *Image and Pilgrimage in Christian Culture: Anthropological Perspectives*. New York: Columbia University Press.

Udvardy, Monica and Maria G. Cattell. 1992. 'Gender, Aging and Power in Sub-Saharan Africa: Challenges and Puzzles', *Journal of Cross-Cultural Gerontology* 7: 275-288.

Van Allen, Judith. 1976. 'Aba Riots' or Igbo 'Women's War'? Ideology, Stratification and the Invisibility of Women', in *Women in Africa: Studies in Social and Economic Change*, edited by Nancy J. Hafkin and Edna G. Bay, pp. 59-85. Stanford CA: Stanford University Press.

Van Gennep, Arnold. 1960 [1909]. *The Rites of Passage*. Translated by Monika B. Vizedom and Gabrielle L. Caffee. Chicago: University of Chicago Press.

Wagner, Gunther. 1949, 1956. *The Bantu of North Kavirondo*, Vols. I & II. London: Oxford University Press.

World Bank. 1989. *Kenya: The Role of Women in Economic Development*. Washington, DC: The World Bank.

Chapter 5

'TREAT YOUR ELDERS WITH KINDNESS AND RESPECT': CULTURAL CONSTRUCTIONS OF AGE AMONG MIDDLE CLASS CAIRENE EGYPTIANS

Bahira Sherif

The last two decades have seen an increasing scholarly interest in specific issues such as gender. However, the anthropological study of aging cross-culturally is still in its infancy. In the past, classical monographs of non-Western societies may have included a short section on the family life cycle, including old age. Contemporary studies focus almost exclusively on issues such as trans-nationalism, post-colonialism etc., with little anthropological research is being conducted with a specific focus on the actual changes in people's lives and attitudes over the life course. Yet, particularly in many complex non-Western societies, changes over the life course have profound effects on the lives of men and women in terms of status, access to resources and opportunities, and potential problems and disadvantages.

This chapter examines some of the perceived and real changes accompanying the aging process among middle and upper-middle class elderly Muslim Egyptians. This study draws on fieldwork conducted in Cairo, Egypt among two generations of families with the older generation ranging from about 55 to 80 years of age, and the younger generation ranging between 25 and 45 years of age.[1] Furthermore, this study draws on historical and religio-legal sources dealing with the relationship between 'adult children' and their parents in order to provide a cultural backdrop for understanding how contemporary decisions among 'adult children' and aging parents are being negotiated. This chapter illustrates the fact that perceived changes in status vary on an individual level and do not necessarily lead to generalizations for whole groups of people. This study also suggests that old age does not automatically afford an individual with respect and a social position, as is so often implied in the literature on the Islamic world (see for example Aswad and Bilge 1996, Barakat 1985, Bill and Leiden 1984). Instead, it is argued that the consequences of aging differ for men and for women, and are influenced by other variables such as health, financial status, and the marital state of adult children.

AGING AS A GENDER SPECIFIC PHENOMENON

Among middle class Egyptians the attainment of adult status for both men and women comes through marriage. It is only at the point of marriage that it becomes socially acceptable for an individual to leave the natal home and to start his or her household. Marriage marks the end of what is commonly perceived as a 'carefree' youth and leads to the acquisition of whole new sets of responsibilities. Primarily, a couple is expected to start a family in the first year of marriage and to carry the full economic and moral responsibility of raising that child and subsequent children. Further changes in status within adulthood are not clearly marked until the last child has left home and the elderly parents are faced with a redefinition of their roles. In contemporary Cairo, this redefinition is becoming exceedingly complicated, due to rapid changes within society.

Among contemporary middle class Egyptians, the elderly, in particular, are caught in a precarious position. On the one hand they have been socialized and told that older people, especially men, attain their highest status with age and become the dominant decision-makers within the extended family. On the other hand, elderly men are increasingly aware that their adult children, influenced by media, economics, and other forces, do not turn to them with the same respect once accorded to older people. For example Lutfi, an 80 year old retired government official, states,

> When I was young my father and my uncles always had the ultimate say - whether it be over my job, my marriage, or even, at times, about raising my children. I would not have dreamt of discussing major decisions without them. Today I see a different atti-

tude, both with my sons and my nephews. They are good men and visit me regularly, but I do not know how they spend their money, what they are teaching their children, and what they discuss with their wives. When I ask them, they laugh and tell me that I am old and that the world has changed. My opinion is not considered valuable by them. I hear the same from my friends. This is bad - they are forgetting their religion.

Older retired men spend a great deal of time bemoaning the 'good old times' with other male siblings or peers. They will often state that the youth of today are *wahish* (bad), and do not know how well off they are. There tends to be little empathy for how young people are dealing with contemporary problems such as pressing economics, traffic or child-care. Elderly middle class men often complain collectively about their perception of diminished authority in their families. Few of these men complain publicly about their wives, and, instead, focus on their adult children as the source of conflict.

Elderly women face an almost completely separate set of issues. They derive their status primarily by having children - in particular one or more sons - and by having raised them in a 'moral' manner. Even among very highly educated women, motherhood is seen as the final step in the attainment of complete adulthood. Children are perceived as providing emotional and financial security for their elderly mothers, and old age, on an individual and societal level, becomes particularly harsh for women who have not been able to bear children. Widows are particularly subject to a strict societal code that forces them to move back home to their adult children in order to uphold the reputation of their families. Childless widows, therefore, are often perceived as a burden on the whole extended family.

Among many middle class families, women's social status increases with the number and age of their children.[2] Furthermore, for contemporary older women, a son's achievement reflects back on the mother in terms of status and prestige in her community. In addition, even today, elderly women derive much of their power, importance, and status by arranging marriages for their children and other related young men and women. While, traditionally, arranging a marriage carried with it the subsequent reward of a daughter-in-law's labor and the increased status of the mother-in-law within the family, those relationships are changing in today's Cairo. Potential brides, fearing the power of the mother-in-law have become very savvy in terms of exploiting the tight contemporary housing market to their advantage. Future daughters-in-laws tend to encourage their grooms to find apartments as far away as possible from the natal family, often with the pretense that, as a young couple, they needed to start off in a 'modern, clean apartment'. Since, among this class, older couples usually live in rent controlled apartments in the older sections of town, and since these apartments are not easily accessible, young couples are able to establish new residences in the outskirts of the city, where new apartment developments are constantly being built.[3] This often leads to tensions within extended families, as parents feel that their sons are being 'taken away' and are not accessible anymore. As the case of Mona illustrates, this is becoming an increasingly common tactic for new wives to gain control over their husbands,

> When we first got married, Said wanted to live near his parents. He said his mother could cook for us since I work full-time. I knew this was not a good idea - much better to live far away, and then his mother will not meddle in our business. In the old days, my mother had to live with her mother-in-law, and this was terrible. She had to work all the time. Today everything is different. So now we live in the new part of the city, and the commute makes it very difficult for us to see Said's parents more than once a week. We have a very good relationship with them in this way.

Nevertheless, not all the younger people are as burdened by their elderly in-laws or parents as suggested by Mona's comments. For some young people, the close relationship between adult children and elderly parents actually eases the burden that is felt through contemporary pressures of dual-earner couples. Several of the subjects of my study cited the usefulness of having either parents or in-laws living near by, in particular for aiding with child rearing. Elderly women are frequently seen as extremely useful, due to their ability to provide child care for contemporary working daughters or daughters-in-law, while also passing on cultural traditions and helping with the cooking.

In certain instances, younger couples also cited the presence of parents as potentially helping to settle marital disputes and providing financial backing in meager times or for emergencies. Nevertheless, most of the young people interviewed for this study were not eager to discuss intimate details of their marriages with their aging parents, again and again citing 'changed circumstances' and a 'lack of understanding' on the parent's part as the motive. Instead, they often felt that either siblings or a removed aunt or uncle were more useful as advice givers in stressful times. Both men and women tended to rely on same sex relatives as their primary basis for emotional support, while the issues of honor and reputation arose again and again as deterrents to involving friends or co-workers in familial disputes. As it was seen in the case of Lutfi, elderly parents tend to be aware of their marginal place in terms of giving advice, and often feel resentment about the consequences of 'modernization'. They usually hold the view that, both socially and religiously their children have strong obligations to them. They sense that Western concepts such as 'individualism' instead of 'collective decision making' could potentially be destructive to their social order. Elderly parents, therefore, turn increasingly to legitimizing their roles by advocating religio-legal tenets that deal specifically with the relationship between adult children and their parents.

THE RELIGIO-LEGAL RELATIONSHIP BETWEEN ELDERLY PARENTS AND ADULT CHILDREN

In order to begin to understand the cultural context of aging in contemporary Muslim Egyptian society, it is instructive to examine some of the laws and Islamic discourses that concern themselves with aspects of the relationship between adult children and elderly parents. According to the law, the relationship between parents and children parallels the rights and obligations that are established through marriage. The *shari'a* has developed specialized topics that reflect the highly protective attitude of the Qur'an towards minor children and aged parents. Specifically, the primary legal relationship between parents and children centers on the question of adequate maintenance of dependent children and needy parents. The economic and social welfare of children is a major responsibility of parents, and it is enforceable under Islamic law (Fluehr-Lobban 1987: 184, Nasir 1990: 108). Conversely, it is the legal responsibility of children to take care of their aged parents, both financially and socially. As we have already seen ethnographic evidence indicates that, for many Egyptian middle class families, the welfare of both children and old people centers round the economic and social capabilities of the extended family.

According to both the Qur'an and religious law, children attain not only certain rights through birth but also specific duties. According to both the Qur'an and the Islamic jurists, just as parents have obligations towards their children, children have obligations towards their parents. For example, al-Ghazali (1959: 171) wrote:

> In general, the rights of the parents are greater than the rights of the children, because to honor its parents is a duty for the child, and in the words of God, this duty is called together with service to God since it is said: Thy Lord hath decreed, that ye worship none save Him, and (that ye show) kindness to parents (Qur'an 17: 23).

According to the classical discourses, poor behavior of children toward their parents was seen as a reflection of the parents' behavior towards their parents. A popular belief still expressed publicly, states that the respect a child shows to its father will be equal to the respect that the father had shown to his parents (al-Tabarsi 1956: 252-253). Furthermore, al-Ghazali wrote that, 'When a youth honors an old man, then God reserves for the young man a youth who will honor him in old age' (1959: 148).

The classical jurists based many of these arguments on the Qur'anic belief that children are obligated to take care of their poor and needy parents and to love and honor them always:

> ...And that ye show kindness to parents. If one of
> them or both of them attain old age with thee, say
> not 'fie' unto them nor repulse them, but speak unto
> them a gracious word (Qur'an 17: 23).

This Qur'anic injunction with verses 29: 8 and 31: 14 have been
further interpreted by the classical jurists to mean that children
have a particular responsibility for taking care of their surviving parent if one has passed away. In another scenario, they are
responsible for their mother if she has been divorced by their
father and is in financial need (Degand 1988: 117). According
to all schools of thought, the financial situation is the primary
determinant of the extent to which the child or children are
responsible for a parent.

Based on the Qur'anic ruling, 'And give the kinsman his
due...' (17: 26), the classical jurists determined that sons and
daughters are equally responsible for taking care of impoverished parents. They stated that the gender of the child who was
providing economic support during a period of great financial
strain was inconsequential to the parents during this time. For
example, al-Misri emphasized that 'it is obligatory for one to
support one's parents, whether one is male or female, when one
has money in excess of one's own living' (1994: 547). Based on
the Qur'anic rulings that referred to children without specify-
ing gender, the jurists stressed that both sons and daughters were
to be responsible for maintaining a good financial relationship
between themselves and their parents. However, they were also
responsible for showing their parents respect and love at all times
(Degand 1988: 117). The gender and the age of the child only
began to take on any relevance to a child's obligation to parents,
if he or she had to work outside the sphere of parental protection
and observation. Otherwise, there was no difference between
sexes in terms of obligations to the parents.

From both Qur'anic and classical sources, one can see that
parents are, as a matter of course, entitled to either the labor or
assets of their children when suffering economic adversity. In
order to ensure this right, the jurists stressed various strategies to
persuade children to fulfill their obligations. These include the
stressing of Qur'anic injunctions (17: 26) regarding the financial

obligations of children to parents and the need to strengthen emotional ties between children and parents, as well as the threat of divine punishment. Again and again, the jurists emphasized that family ties needed to be maintained and strengthened, and that this could occur only through a shared sense of respect and obligation for each other. This idea is perhaps best expressed by Ibn Qayyim,

> It is no sign that one is honoring one's parents when a man allows his father to sweep the threshold or to carry the goods of others on his head, in order to use the money that is earned in this manner for his survival, while the son is filthy rich and has access to enormous wealth. It is no sign that he honors and respects his mother if he lets her serve others, wash their clothes and carry water to them... , whereby he (the son) says: both parents are employed and healthy, they are neither chronically ill nor blind (1950, 4: 67).

Ibn Qayyim went on to ask if either God or the Prophet indicated that the duty to respect one's parents should be fulfilled only if one or both were either chronically ill or blind. He pointed out that such conduct could not be ordained by either law (*shar'an*), the commonly used language (*lugatan*), or the custom (*'adatan*), and does not convey honor and respect for the parents or an appreciation of close family ties (*silat al-rahim*).[4]

By discouraging parents from drawing from public funds for poor people (*zakat*), and by encouraging children to take care of their parents, both the Qur'an and the jurists emphasized the value of familial ties to society. If at all possible, individual problems are to be solved within the family circle. In order for the larger society, the *umma*, to be harmonious and run smoothly, individual problems must be solved on an individual level and must not become a burden to the greater community. This community is governed by the concept of a moral, sacred order in which the obligations of individuals to society take precedence over individual concerns, and in which men and women contribute to the harmonious whole. Debate and conflict are expected to be part of normal social life, but conflict should be resolved by a return to the whole, by the achievement of consensus.

The writings by the jurists and the Qur'anic injunctions regarding the relationship between elderly parents and adult children need to be understood as providing a backdrop against which individual decisions are negotiated among contemporary Muslim Egyptians. They, along with social norms and traditions, provide a framework and a set of beliefs which individuals draw upon when faced with complicated situations and changes over the life course.

RELIGIO-LEGAL TENETS IN PRACTICE

Apart from a fear of divine retribution, the values of many middle class Egyptian families strongly support the legal norms of filial duty. As we have seen, both the Qur'an and the Islamic law stipulate that financially capable children must care for their needy parents. Furthermore, according to Egyptian social norms, maintenance means more than just providing the bare necessities. If a child, in particular a son, becomes wealthier than his parents, social norms require that he help his parents in maintaining a life style which is higher than that to which they were accustomed. Among several of the families in my study, sons who had made considerable amounts of money by working in either Saudi Arabia, the United Emirates, or Libya were now helping their parents with gifts of modern appliances such as washing machines and video machines. They were also financing the *hagg*, the pilgrimage to Mecca. It is considered incumbent upon men, in order to maintain their prestige, to contribute to the well being of their parents. Nonetheless, there are exceptions.

A somewhat deviant situation was presented to me by one couple who were in their late thirties and, by Egyptian standards, quite well to do. The husband, an engineer, told me that his wife really disliked his family and refused to interact with them. He, on the other hand, was extremely attached to both of his parents and his two sisters, and secretly, left his office every day to pay a visit to one or another member of his natal family. Before going to see his parents, he always made sure to buy a gift of sweets, *shish kabab*, or even a piece of jewelry for his mother. This couple was a favorite topic of conversation within the larger family: Some people pitied the husband for his unfortunate choice of a wife, while others criticized him for not being 'a man' and 'not taking a stand' against his wife.

While, according to classical discourse, it is just as obligatory for daughters as for sons to help maintain their parents, at least among my sample of middle class families, this was an uncommon occurrence. Women tend to express ambivalent attitudes towards the financial maintenance of parents. Among two of the younger couples I spent time with, the women expressed regret at not helping their own parents financially, but they stated that their husbands felt their own economic situation to be too tight. I did observe that other women in similar situations tried to take care of their parents in other ways, such as rendering help in the case of illness or mental or physical weakness.

My ethnographic evidence illustrates that the pull of the natal family tends to remain very strong for many middle class, adult, Egyptian men and women. The conflicting loyalties of spouses to the conjugal unit and to their natal families arise as a source of tension at various points in their lives. Nevertheless, social norms that advocate family reputation and family honor work to modify the influence of the conjugal family and men and women tend to maintain a consistently close relationship to their elderly relatives. As will be seen, the relationship by older people with their adult children remains of crucial importance for economic, social, and emotional reasons.

NEGOTIATING AGING, ECONOMICS, AND ILLNESS

During the course of my fieldwork, I repeatedly heard about several cases in different families where various generations contributed some of their resources for the care of an impoverished older relative. In one case, the elderly uncle of one of my informants lost his money through a bad business deal and suffered ill health, as well as financial pressures. (He was also responsible for a wife and six daughters.) His older brother, who, himself, had ten grown children, held a family meeting and asked his children, as well as his other siblings, to contribute a small amount of their various incomes to a fund for his brother. Through this pooling of resources, they managed to raise enough money to get the financially stricken man into a new business and to pay for his family's upkeep. Within the period of one year, he recovered financially and worked out a payment plan whereby he was able to pay back his entire family over a number of years. While some of the individuals present at the first meeting were initially not very thrilled at the prospect of contributing their money on behalf of this man, they eventually changed their minds when the uncle guaranteed that they would eventually be repaid. With many persuasive speeches in which he called on various Qur'anic sayings and the promise of the pleasures of the afterlife, the uncle presented this case as '*the* opportunity to do good in life'. Notwithstanding the resistant minority, many other family members displayed a sincere concern for the stricken elderly man and his family. Of course, as in all societies, not all the families I observed in Egypt have such harmonious ways of interacting. It does seem, however, that religious injunctions, coupled with Egyptian social norms, ensure that, at least for a great majority of individuals, physical and economic security lies primarily in extended family membership.

The most complicated scenario for every family in my study, with regard to aging, dealt either with an elderly female relative who was financially devastated by the death of a spouse, or an elderly relative debilitated by illness. Many of these middle class families had devised personal strategies for coping with these issues. Nevertheless, they admitted unanimously that aid always came from several members within the extended family. In particular, when dealing with an impoverished widow, family relatives tried to soften the blow by pooling resources and setting up small funds from which these women could draw for their expenses. Quite often a widow's male relatives would approach the family of the deccased husband to ask also for their contributions, as well. Since the social reputation of each family was always at stake, it tended to be very difficult for the members of the deceased person's family to decline such a request.

The issue of taking care of an ill elderly relative is currently becoming one of the most complicated issues for contemporary middle class Egyptians to deal with. With so many women working outside of the home amidst this sector of society, the care-taking responsibilities that traditionally were the domain of the woman are increasingly being relegated to other elderly relatives. Combined with the day-to-day hassles of living in contemporary Cairo, this additional burden is being felt most keenly by older women. Namaat, a recent widow with no children, exemplifies this issue,

> First my husband became sick and I took care of him
> - day and night I took care of him. Then he died, and
> six months later my older brother was widowed and
> he became sick. Now I travel by bus every day to his
> apartment, bring him food, make tea for him, pick
> up his medicine, and listen to him complain. I am
> 75 years old, and nobody cares that I must move in
> all this traffic and heat. The rest of the family points
> out that I have no children and no responsibilities.
> They always tell me that it is Allah's will that I help
> my brother. Who will take care of me should something happen?

Namaat's situation is typical of many middle class families. Within those families, adult children, even if they live in the same apartment house, feel that they are too busy and overworked to take care of a sick relative, and that it is the responsibility of the elderly female relatives to be the caregivers. Furthermore, many adult children tend to feel that they do not also need to take on care-taking responsibilities if they are already contributing financially to an elderly parent. It must be pointed out that there are many variations to this pattern, and I also observed several scenarios in which adult daughters where caught in the middle between raising their own children and taking care of an elderly relative. Strikingly, this burden fell almost exclusively on the female members of the family.

GRANDPARENTS AS PRIMARY PROVIDERS

A little recognized phenomenon in contemporary Cairo is the increasing number of grandparents bringing up their grandchildren. While divorce figures by Western standards remain minuscule, they are rising compared to even twenty years ago.

Recently divorced women who, according to social custom, are expected to move back to their paternal homes, are increasingly working outside of the home. As a result, they are letting their young children being raised by their parents. Day care is virtually non-existent in Egypt, and traditional norms still advocate that the best caregivers for children are members of the extended family. Elderly parents, therefore, find themselves becoming increasingly responsible for their adult daughters and their children once again. Cultural norms that advocate group decision making about familial issues help support scenarios in which a mother and parents share in the raising of young children. Amidst this class, it is becoming increasingly common for a father to have bought several apartments in one building, with the goal of potentially having his children living under one roof. Particularly in the case of divorce, this type of arrangement is favored by parents and the adult daughter. It often means that other siblings will also be living in the same house. Thus, what we find is that, while rapid social change is bringing about more frequent incidence of divorce and, with it, a disruption of traditional norms, many middle class extended families are adapting themselves to contemporary circumstances.

CONCLUSION AND IMPLICATIONS

An examination of the Islamic religious and legal ideals of the relationship between children and parents reveals a strong emphasis on the guardianship of the individual throughout the various stages of his or her life. The definitions presented by the medieval jurists stress the responsibility of the parents for the child, which begins at conception. In return, children are obligated to care for their aged parents.

In these times of economic stress, it is especially evident among middle class couples that it is the financial responsibility of family members that has brought to the surface a widening in the gap between religious and legal ideals and popular practice. When examining the strategies employed by these couples, we see once again an elective usage of laws, beliefs, and traditions that is, in and of itself, not surprising, but which does reflect the constant negotiation of acceptable forms of behavior.

In the group of Egyptian families that are the subject of this study, one finds that legal rules, combined with social parameters, ensure the material protection of children and aged parents. Nonetheless, the social emphasis on retaining strong ties with one's natal family can also be a source of extreme stress for individuals. In particular, many middle class Egyptian males bear a heavy financial responsibility by having to provide for their wives, children, aged parents, and single, widowed, or divorced female relatives. It is within this realm that we see most clearly a departure from classical discourses in contemporary practice. While Qur'anic injunctions and classical writings encourage every individual, regardless of gender, to be equally responsible for caring for their aged parents, many contemporary middle class Egyptians feel that this economic burden is appropriately carried only by males. The women in my study emphasized both through words and actions that their economic contributions were to be allocated entirely to the upkeep of their immediate families, i.e. their husbands, their children, and themselves.

In contrast to men, women are primarily the emotional and physical caregivers in their families. Elderly women, feel themselves to be especially burdened with the stress of caring for ill spouses and siblings, while also being asked to watch over their daughters' children. These women are profoundly impacted by changes in contemporary Egyptian society. On the one hand, the traditional dominance and power which they held in their households has faded, and on the other hand, they are increasingly responsible for the long term care of their contemporaries, their children, and their grandchildren.

Relationships within the extended family, both in a social and economic sense, play a very important role among the Muslim Egyptians of my study. Nevertheless, while, as we have seen, the rights and obligations between children and parents are generally clearly defined, the economic relationship between the individual and his or her extended family is not as obvious, and is usually negotiated individually from case to case. Nevertheless, social norms, intertwined with religious beliefs and personal sentiments, ensure that individual members of families ultimately work together in order to cope with the issues facing elderly relatives. It is this network of family relations that, until today, gives elderly middle class Egyptians their greatest personal and economic security.

Notes

1. Initial fieldwork was conducted between 1988 and 1990. Additional research was continued in 1992, 1994, and 1996.

2. Among this class and generation of couples, 5 - 6 children are common. However, among the younger generation, and due to the contemporary economic situation, 2 children have become the norm.

3. Initially, renting an apartment is a very complicated procedure for young couples, due to the lack of availability and the large deposit (or 'key' money) that needs to be put down. Many couples marry and wait 2-3 years until they actually move in together because of the tight market.

4. *Silat al-rahim* is used by the jurists to refer to the caring and helpful stance that relatives show to one another. However, *sila* can also mean a present that may be offered, at any time, not just when a familial tie exists. One can assume from these semantics that the word is used because of its double meaning. It is applied by the jurists to emphasize the duty of the children to provide for the maintenance of their parents.

References

Aswad, Barbara and Barbara Bilge. 1996. *Family and Gender among American Muslims*. Philadelphia: Temple University Press.

Barakat, Halim. 1985. 'The Arab Family and the Challenge of Social Transformation', in Elizabeth Fernea, ed., *Women and the Family in the Middle East*, pp. 27-48. Austin: University of Texas Press.

Bill, James and Carl Leiden. 1984. *Politics in the Middle East*. Boston: Little Brown.

Degand, Angela. 1988. *Geschlechterrollen und Familiale Strukturen im Islam: Untersuchungen Anhand der Islamisch-Juristischen Literatur*. Europaeische Hochschulschriften. Frankfurt: Peter Lang.

Fluehr-Lobban, C. 1987. *Islamic Law and Society in the Sudan*. London: Frank Cass.

Geertz, Clifford. 1983. 'Local Knowledge: Facts and Law in Comparative Perspective', in Clifford Geertz, ed., *Local Knowledge*. New York: Basic Books.

Geertz, H. 1979. 'The Meaning of Family Ties', in Clifford Geertz, H. Geertz and L. Rosen, eds., *Meaning and Order in Moroccan Society*. Cambridge: Cambridge University Press.

Al-Ghazali, Abu Hamid ibn Muhammad. 1959. *Das Elixier der Gluckseligkeit*. Translated by H. Ritter. Koln-Dusseldorf.

Ibn, Qayyim. 1369/1950. *Zad al-ma'ad fi huda hair al-'ibad* (*The proviant for the hereafter and the right path to the wellbeing of the servants [of God]*). 4 vols. Cairo.

Levy, Reuben. 1969. *The Social Structure of Islam*. Cambridge: Cambridge University Press.

Al-Misri, Ahmed ibn al-Naqib. 1994. *'Umdat al-salik wa- 'uddat al-nasik. Reliance of the Traveller: The Classic Manual of Islamic Sacred Law*. In Arabic with facing English text. Translated by Nuh Ha Mim Keller. Revised Edition. Evanston: Sunna Books.

Nadim, Nawal. 1977. 'Family Relationships in a Harah in Cairo', in Saad Eddin Ibrahim and Nicholas Hopkins, eds., *Arab Society in Transition*, pp. 107-20. Cairo, Egypt: American University Press.

Nasir, Jamal. 1990. *The Islamic Law of Personal Status*. London: Graham and Trotman.

Pickthall, Mohammad Marmaduke, trans. 1976. *The Glorious Koran: Text and Explanatory Translation*. Albany: State University of New York Press.

Sokolovsky, Jay. 1997. *The Cultural Context of Aging*. Westport: Bergin and Garvey.

Al-Tabarsi, al-Hasan ibn al-Fadl. 1376/1956. *Makarim al-akhlaq* (The Noble Characteristics). Cairo.

Chapter 6

PERCEPTIONS OF AGE: CONVICTION, CONTEST AND CONTROVERSY IN SIDAMA

Seyoum Y. Hameso

[T]he elders ... reach their position in Sidamaland, settling disputes of everyday life, making policy rules about production, assisting the government in collecting taxes, and performing the rituals that negotiate the changing meaning of the cultural code. Indeed, they are the ones closest to the influential dead elders who, through dreams, remind the living of their obligations to that code.... [T]here is a group of specialist mediators who are leaders of the major clans (*mote*), the generational classes (*gadana*), and a few esteemed old men who have survived two cycles of the generational class system (*woma*). [T]his is a social system which I have characterised as a geron-tocracy (John Hamer 1994: 128)

INTRODUCTION

The discourse of age and time-related notions is bound to be fluid in an African setting where time is a less measured concept made visible only in terms of relative temporal move-ments often marked by events and celebrated in rituals. Thus, the Sidama cultural perceptions of age have a lot to do with social patterns within the African world.

A question arises. Why should the notions related to age systems be studied? John Hamer (1998b: 5) noted the impor-tance of age systems in the political leadership and social organi-zation of Sidama society. While violence against enemies, in the past, required an element of passing of age, he recently argued that gerontocracy as a tradition and mirror for the future serves useful structures and values. Thus, gerontocracy is useful not just for Sidama but also for the Western commitment to democracy and as a way of solving a 'coming problem of social existence' or partly a 'means of accommodating to the aging population'. Comparing it to the modern style roles and in the defense of gerontocracy, Hamer added,

> [I]t seems impossible that Westerners, especially Americans, with their stress on public involvement mediated by electronic media and emphasis on the priority of individual rights, could ever be concerned with a seemingly hierarchical rule by old men and women. Paradoxically, however, gerontocracies, like the Sidama in the Eastern Horn of Africa, with their emphasis on decentralized decision-making and consensual rule, practice far more community participation and rational discourse than the people of nation-states (*Ibid.*)

From the field research carried out in the late sixties and early seventies, and judging from his observations, Hamer came out with the view that the Sidama have a highly elaborated form of gerontocracy. The relevance of the study of notions related to age and aging, elsewhere, is noted by Mario Aguilar (1998) for whom the 'perceptions of age are a daily and habitual concern of every person in any given society or nation'. Kertzer and Madison (1981: 109) have also argued that 'age is rivaled only by sex as a universal principle of social differentiation'.

For the Sidama, 'the time perspective ... is based on the age-grade system' (Brogger 1986: 114). Here, as in other African societies, the common perception had been that old age is often associated with positive imagery. Since tradition endowed age with wisdom, status, prestige, and authority, being *gercho* (elder) readily elicits respect and recognition. In many parts of colonial Africa this fact had quickly been grasped. Indirect rule, in particular, is known to have relied not only on the mediation of 'respected' elders but also on local chiefs (Hameso 1997d). Such perception survived the times of turmoil: colonization, controlled decolonization and the post-colony.

Within our discussion of the conception of time and the process of aging, this chapter aims at three objectives. The first objective is to explain and interpret the Sidama world, past and present. The second is to examine the perception of time and age in the same world. The third is to explore change dimensions of these perceptions within the interactions of 'other worlds'. In so doing, the goal is not to comprehensively deal with all aspects of the Sidama world.

THE SIDAMA WORLD: PAST AND PRESENT

> To appreciate a people's explanation of life and misfortune, one needs to have a general picture of the wider framework of their existence (Jan Brogger 1986: 21).

The Sidama live in the North-East of Africa or the present day Southern Ethiopia where there is tremendous social tension over identity. Sidama is estimated to have a population of 4 million people.[1] Sidama as a country is bordered by the Oromia, Wolayta, and Gedeo nations. For the last several hundred years, the Sidama people have subsisted by mixed horticulture and cattle herding whereas for much of the twentieth century they became involved in coffee cash cropping. Land is the most important asset and the people have intense attachment to it for economic, social and political reasons. Before the colonial ventures and partly even afterwards, each member of the society owned certain acreage of land enough to support its family. There was also communally owned land called *danawa* reserved for grazing and other common uses including holding to newcomers and young couples. The local *songo* decided on the use and distribution of the *danawaland*. The land holding system hardly accommodated greedy feudal landlords until the introduction of the *naftanya* system from the north. The egalitarian ethos helped maintain fraternity, peace and the moral order in society.

Having diverse natural terrain, Sidamaland is suitable for a variety of flora and fauna. The *wesse* plant, resembling a banana tree, is typical to Sidama and its neighbors. Grown in most parts of the Sidama, the tree takes three to six years for consumption in the form of *wassa*, the staple food item. *Wassa* serves not only a consumptive purpose but it is also central to communal and social roles. It is eaten within the family and in community gatherings (such as marriage, mourning, and different ceremonies and events) where a group or a dozen of community members share food from one or more *xiltes* (dishes made of clay). Once it is properly set in place, the *wesse* plant does not require intensive and regular weeding. The latter is often done by men while the final task of readying the plant for consumption is the responsibility of women.

Here the role of gender is such that an apparent sexual division exists in relation to age. Both old men and women command respect in Sidama society. From old men comes a *cimesa* chosen according to his age and his Luwa, while from old women comes a *qaricho* chosen by her age. Even though society is largely patrilineal, there are also protective and caring attitudes towards women (Hoteso, 1990: 101). Though women are not formally members of the Luwa system, they are central to its survival through their responsibility for the reproduction of the household and the management of much of its subsistence labor. Women do not participate directly in councils but, whenever having a grievance, they are represented by a spokesman of their choice. Thus just as aging accords a position of honor for men, so it does for women. Jan Brogger (1986: 54) observed that elderly women behave with self-assurance, even smoking the water pipe, which is regarded as the prerogative of the male elders, consistent with the increase in their authority. These patterns and attitudinal frameworks still exist despite perceived and real changes in the perception of age.

Another important crop that affects Sidama life is coffee whose production, distribution and consumption has direct bearing on the economic welfare, social dimension and political arrangements within and outside Sidama.

POLITICAL ECONOMY: CONCEALED PAST AND CONTESTED IDENTITIES

Written records on Sidama life relate to a contemporary phenomenon of keeping archives. For a considerably long period of time, however, historical research has been severely circumvented by centrist and despotic Ethiopian-cum-Amharic rule that has undervalued and undermined knowledge creation and dissemination about subordinated peoples and cultures. Nevertheless, the Sidama political economy is bound to rely on oral tradition, rituals, and symbols most of which still remain a matter for further research.[2]

The conquest of Sidamaland by the army of Menelik of Shoa in 1893 impacted the Sidama world in more than one way. Firstly, that conquest brought about the colonial system known in local parlance as a *gabbar-neftanya* or tenant-settler, or even a slave-master relationship resulting in economic dispossession (Bulcha 1997: 27-68, Keller 1987: 45). Secondly, it promoted authoritarian and hierarchical Amharic values undermining the sense of consultative egalitarian underpinning of governance by the Sidama. The patterns and effects of this conquest coincided with European colonial rule in Africa. Thus like elsewhere in colonial Africa, Abyssinian settler colonialism confiscated Sidamaland and distributing it to armed settlers, known in local parlance as *naftanyas*. This dispossession was followed by Sidama resistance and subsequent coercion against dissent by the authorities. The empire (state) and the Coptic Orthodox Church were united in their imposition and reinforcement of a physical, cultural and spiritual domination in the colonized lands.[3] Again, like other forms of colonialism, the Abyssinian-cum-Ethiopian colonialism undermined people's culture so as to control their tools of self-definition in relation to others. It led to 'the destruction or the deliberate undervaluing of a people's culture and literature, and the conscious elevation of the language of the colonizer' (wa Thiongo 1986: 16). Unlike European settler colonialism that formally relinquished power and physically departed from many parts of Africa in the mid-fifties and sixties, the Abyssinian colonial rule remained in Sidama and elsewhere in the south.

The legacy of domination was maintained and promoted by Haile Selassie's 'modernizing' autocracy. The collective memory of the Sidamas of that era is the modernization of their oppression. Improved and improvised were the methods of exaction; namely, the system of tax collection, recruitment into the army and into a bureaucratic system (Hameso 1998: 112). The advent of the 1974 revolution also undermined the Sidama social organization and cultural underpinnings. The status of the elders and the role of the customary sanctions were relegated and replaced by communist-structured, strictly hierarchical administrative units. The customary *ollaas* and village councils were replaced by *qebele* administrative units, while *murichas* (social event organisers and informants) and *cinanchos* (co-operative work organisers) were replaced by *qebele* administrators.[4] The *qebele* (spelt as *kebele*) administration had little to do with the Sidama customary law and procedures, *seera*. Quite often the *qebele* appointees were accountable to the communist *derg* military regime and they were aspirants to write and speak Amharic, a language which was also imposed as a medium of education in schools (see Hameso 1997b). At the same time the regime denigrated the belief system and it worked to undermine the Luwa system. A hitherto preserved forests and public assembly-point trees, *gudumaales* were cut to make way for state-run coffee plantation and to implement draconian communist villagization programs. The burden on Sidama society was only worsened by economic oppression imposed as heavy taxation and low fixed coffee prices were compounded by forced military conscription.

The new regime that toppled the *derg* in 1991 drew its social base from the Tigrean people (led by the Tigrean People's Liberation Front) and obtained its inspiration from Albanian communism. In its rhetoric, and in order to get support with the intention of mapping its social and political control mechanisms, it bandied about the notions of 'peoples, nations, nationalities', decentralization and federations, and the use of national/local languages. Further, the regime took over the main thrust of the Ethiopian past, and the national rhetoric that in the past had already failed short of deeds. Thus, in Sidama, as elsewhere, the TPLF regime sought support from disgruntled elements in society. These included prisoners of war from the *derg* army, elementary school teachers (who were suffering from low pay and low morale), unemployed young persons who were unaccustomed to Abyssinian machination and treachery. The 'elders', the educated, the well informed, the politically conscious and those who questioned the legitimacy of the TLF rule were excluded from any public decision-making processes. The regime's propaganda machinery presented 'higher intellectuals and business persons' from the South as enemies of the people. As in the days of the *derg*, attempts at co-opting the local leaders and elders were made possible at the expense of corruption and loss of respect for their moral authority. As a result, support for the promotion of the Sidama language in its written form and some very basic economic change measures came from local initiatives supported by some aid agencies.

CULTURE, BELIEF SYSTEMS, THE MORAL CODE, AUTHORITY AND PERCEPTIONS OF TIME

> The Cushitic speaking Sidama have an unusually pervasive gerontocratic social structure, based on a generational class system directed toward the implementation and perpetuation of elderhood authority (Hamer 1996: 526).

The Sidama trace their cultural and linguistic origins to common ancestors. In terms of culture, they evolved as a uniform entity through the use of the Sidama language. In terms of *religion*, the Sidama believe in a creator sky deity, Magano, who 'once lived on earth but returned to the sky after people continued to complain about having to make a choice between reproduction and eternal life' (Hamer 1994: 188). Since then the chosen paths to Magano have been lower level deities serving as brokers. Stanley (1966: 219) suggests that,

> The Sidama religion is basically monotheistic combined with ancestor worship.... Even the worship of the tribal forefathers is largely based on the belief that they are powerful protectors of the clans, as effective intermediaries between God and their people.

Thus through ancestor worship, the living and the dead occupy interconnected worlds as the spirits of the dead visit the living in the realm of thought, mainly through dreams. The notion of reincarnation and life after death that is actively sought after in other belief systems exist in Sidama as well. For this and other reasons, various sacrifices are offered to 'feed' the dead. The sacrifice of animals and the letting of their blood on sacred sites (such as burial places and deep forests), the prohibition of eating pork, and the responsibilities of a first born to offer sacrifice on the death of his parents are similar to rituals present in other African religions. Within this system, the old themselves are perceived as being close to death and thereby to God. As a result, they command over the temporal space between an ordinary being and the supernatural.

The monotheistic belief tendency in one Magano (God) or *kalaqo* (divine creation) coincided with the teachings of the monotheist belief systems and this may explain the ease with which Christian missions were received. Such acceptance also facilitated by missionary education and their tendency to expand their numbers by proselytism and by converting members of other religions (See also Braukamper 1992: 195-197).

THE *HALAALE* MORAL CODE, THE LUWA SYSTEM AND GERONTOCRACY

The moral code in *halaale* plays an essential role in the Sidama belief and politico-cultural systems. The term *halaale* means 'truth' or 'a true way of life'. Hamer (1994: 126-144, 1996: 526-551) defines *halaale* ideology as principles of the moral code governing the relationship between people. This moral code involves specific values such as the importance of generosity, a commitment to truth in issues of conflict, fairness in delivering blame and punishment, avoiding disruptive gossip, responsible use of money, respect for property boundaries, and avoidance of adultery and sexual promiscuity. The significance of wealth acquisition relates to the esteem one acquires through a reputation for generosity and by redistributing these gains in hospitality and support of one's kin.

According to the *halaale* moral code, greed and arrogance are looked upon as inviting feelings of jealousy and fear. Therefore they are not viewed favorably. The purpose of guarding and interpreting the moral order and the moral code resides in the hands of the elders. Since life is a continual process, the *halaale* code does not end with the death of particular elders. They are believed to continue to influence the living by reappearing in dreams. Thus, Sidama elders who are dead do remind the living elders if failing to uphold *halaale* or if they are and negligent in 'feeding' them through animal sacrifice at appropriate shrines (Hamer 1994).

The *halaale* code as a moral system works effectively well through social sanctions. The elders have the monopoly of ultimate sanctions in the form of curses that are believed to be effective. Through an elder's curse a person receives social rejection 'by both the social and supernatural worlds', i.e. a physical and absolute removal from society. The Sidama world knows no capital punishment; and even murder is punishable only by *guma* or 'blood compensation'. Neither do the elders and the council possess direct means of coercion and physical force at their disposal. Brogger (1986: 109, 111) points out that 'the style of behavior and demeanor of everyday life .... is clearly not based on threats of physical force. It is not the cowed subservience based on fear of whips, gallows and dungeons which is displayed, but it clearly demonstrates a concern for public opinion and sensitivity to criticism'. Thus, without the use of physical force and violence, the moral order functions perfectly well.

The older generations have served the people for centuries by preserving the institutions and the code whereas the expression of *halaale* ideology is structured in practice by linking household to community, different generations, and the two genders on a complementary basis. Notably, the moral code augured well with another side of the Sidama ethos: that of 'decentralized decision-making and consensual rule', thus practicing community participation and rational discourse. Hamer (1998b) compares this with the authority of the Western style nation state that is 'devoid of justice' whose 'alternative could be a personalized, decentralized form of gerontocracy modeled on the system of the Sidama'.

Halaale is also supported by notions of *buude* or *jirtee* and *seeraa* that are interrelated administrative and cultural aspects that refer to social norms, values and the associated sanctions. In this respect, the politico-cultural aspect of the Sidama past goes back to the idea of kingdom (*woma*), principality (*mote*), and the Luwa systems.

THE *WOMA* AND THE *MOTE INSTITUTIONS*

The *woma* institution is the earliest form of political institution in Sidama governance. The term *woma* is associated with wisdom and it a has direct analogy with a queen of the bees whose production of honey and organization is considered as wise and sophisticated. A *woma* has his council called *woma songo* and as the head, or even as a father of the *songo*, his council reigns supreme. Brogger (1986: 108) referred to *songo* as a senate and suggested that 'the pressure on the individual is not exerted by the invisible hand of the market, but is based on the strong authority of the senate'.

The situation of *woma* varied from place to place and from clan to clan. While the existence of a *woma* is essential in society in all places, as the queen for bees, the age and the method of election of a *woma* developed distinct variations. In most parts of Sidama, including in Alata where there are several clans who are administered as federations, gerontocrats are elected from different sections of society to the role of *woma*. In other places such as Holoo and Sawolaa, the *woma* institution is dynastic and familial, hence inherited. In this case, at the death of a *woma* his son replaces him regardless of the son's age. If he is too young to assume authority, he is helped by regents and other gerontocratic advisers (Hoteso 1990: 146-147).

Another form of authority is the *mote* institution. The role of this institution is explicitly political. The leader, *moticha*, is elected to an administrative and a leadership position on the basis of his age and his knowledge. His election takes place after thorough consultations with members of several local councils or *songos*. A *Moticha* leads the national arena that also subsumes otherwise independent units of local councils such as *ollaa songos*. Members of the *songo* emerge from a body of wise persons (*hayoo*) elected from different Sidama clans. These councilors are, mainly but not necessarily, gerontocrats. They advise the *songo*, they represent a person in disputes or take cases/appeals to the *songo* of the higher order, the *mote songo*, or they lobby for a certain cause. Councils are run by customary law and members of the local *songo* need to understand the law by heart including the crime typology and the relevant punishment. While most routine and relatively dispensable works are accomplished at the local level, higher and controversial issues or disputes require the meeting of the *mote songo*. In such cases, the *moticha* resorts to *halaale* and those persons who tell a lie in front of him are believed to die after. Thus, fear of death forces them to tell truth.

Whereas the power of the *woma* had waned through time with the coming of feudal Ethiopian rule, that of the *mote* had waxed (Hoteso 1990). The role of the *woma* has become one of non-interference in political and administrative matters and consultative on cultural and religious issues. Today and in many places the position of the *mote* itself is largely undermined by the Ethiopian state system.

THE LUWA SYSTEM AND THE ROLE OF GERONTOCRACY

The Luwa system is another age-related institution performing ritual, cultural, defense and political roles and it has several similarities to the Gada system of the Oromo.[5] Hamer (1998b: 6) refers to Luwa as the generational 'class' system that structures society offering 'elderhood authority to the production activities of youth and the sexual division of labour'. As a method of governance, the system has elements of egalitarianism and consultative decision-making.

The Luwa system has five rotating age grades or 'classes'. They are *Darrara*, *Moggisa*, *Hirbbora*, *Fullaasa*, and *Wawwasa*. Members of different grades pass through time (every seven years) when their status changes. Brogger (1986) views age-grades as a compromise between a chronological age and a generation. A Luwa congregation takes place at a sacred site, usually a camp, where initiates stay for two months being fed by their fathers, away from labor and women. Their initiation follows the choice of their leader, *gadana*, by a committee of eight people who conduct the selection under strict secrecy. As a matter of principle, the members of the committee should assume no prior knowledge of each other nor should they have contact with the young man they select. In order to decide, they consult witches (*qalichas*) and philosophers (*masalto*) who set the criteria of the would-be leader's character, his features, including a hair-style and even teeth. Here, the significance of being a first born male, preferably from a first marriage is an added advantage. The person should be physically and morally perfect in order to sym-bolize the ritual power of the group. Desirable qualities of the *gadana* include wisdom, circumspection, and ability to mediate disputes. The final selection is based on the elder's majority vote. He reigns for seven years and these years become associated with his name and 'points in history will be identified with reference to the *gadana*' (Brogger 1986: 114).

In this manner, each 'class' consists of three sets of elders, ini-tiates, and pre-initiates where all men are linked to one another in a junior-senior relationship throughout the life cycle. The cyclical feature of the system means that all males will shift from a youthful status of providing deference and service for elders to the position of the latter in re/distributing wealth and knowledge. Even as youth, they are allowed to participate in elder's councils attending and learning while the old make decisions. Therefore, with an unavoidable sense of paternalism and guardianship of the moral code, the elders have a direct bearing on the youth that form the productive forces and the basis of creating wealth.

All these traditions reinforce the place of elders whose actions are as diverse as consultation, decision- making, conflict resolu-tion, monitoring social cohesion and the assurance of continuity amidst change. These actions are related to the notions of knowl-edge and wisdom. For example, from the granary of people's col-lective memory, the deposing of the tyranny brought about by queen Furra is ascribed to a remaining old man (after the rest were massacred on her orders) who advised the young and the fellow people on how to deal with tyranny.

As for conflict resolution and elders' role it is customarily land and property which occupy most of their time. As already suggested, their authority to solve conflicts and policy-making is stamped by a resort to curse and to the supernatural involving heavy sanctions. Comparably, policy making and conflict resolution in the West is 'highly specialized, hierarchical, and impersonal' (Hamer 1998b: 6). Times always change. And the perceptions of age have been altered due to several factors. Changes have influenced the Sidama's belief system, day-to-day activities, attitudes, and reactions as well as interactions within Sidama and with the Sidama Diaspora.

PERCEPTIONS OF AGE: CHANGE AND CONTINUITY

The usefulness of age-related systems in general, and of gerontocracy in particular depends on its ability to positively contribute towards the economic, political, social/ educational and belief systems.

It is a fact that in a society where story telling is the norm, where spoken rather than the written word carries heavy weight and where illiteracy is widespread, education and knowledge remains in the hands of those who have information. From early stages in life, women teach their children in several ways. Through rituals and meetings, old men pass on hard won experience from an equally hard and harsh struggle for survival against all odds. This will-power brings confidence to younger generations by the appreciation of the wisdom of their past that contributes to their current efficacy to solve contemporary problems. With the spread of formal education and the influence of the churches people have questioned the moral authority of gerontocrats.

The poor economic situation also affected the initiation of age-sets, as the two-month period stay of the Luwa initiates involves abstention from work and recourse to consumption. The Luwa fathers and step-fathers are bound to provide for their sons the necessary resources including mass feeding. The growing scarcity of resources worsens the economic situation and therefore discourages the celebration of cultural rites associated with age-grades and gerontocracy. Furthermore, concentration on wealth distribution, particularly, at low levels of economic welfare, reduces the current and potential wealth creation. It takes away the incentive to produce goods necessary for the future reproduction of society.

It would be unrealistic to idealize the past as smooth and conflict-free. There had been conflicts surrounding land ownership and grazing rights. Contradictions were also exhibited between emphasis on accumulation of wealth and its subordination to the moral code of generosity. In the 1960s, for example, when the cash economy was in its early stages, land conflicts consumed the wisdom of the elders in their routine struggle to maintain community harmony. Most disputes studied in those periods centered on theft, property boundaries and sorcery (Hamer 1972: 236). It would be incorrect to assume that the transfer of authority among generations took place smoothly. Stanley and Karsten (1968) admitted that the transfer of power between age-sets in Luwa was marked by a degree of violence. That violence was symbolized by mock-fights as part of the culmination of Luwa ceremonies in which fathers needed to give in. Hesitation on their part may have precipitated a crisis or even blow away suppressed feelings and conflicts.

Serious conflicts arose during the transitional cultural periods when age-sets went on ritual war expedition to neighboring areas to procure livestock. These took place in areas where a pastoral life style had been a norm. As the majority of Sidamas are now settled agriculturalists, these practices are extinct and in most areas the action of cattle raiding is made symbolic rather than real.

Tensions are also known to arise from incompatible individual and community commitments and interests. The fact that the elders judge truth and broker fairness in social relations and preside over the allocation of property is bound to be subjective and sometimes rough. While the process of arriving at truth and fairness requires protracted discussion that is itself problematic given time constraints and the need to gather circumstantial evidence, the final decision relies on the trustworthiness of those involved.

Apart from these concerns, several forces threaten gerontocracy in Sidama, both externally and internally. They include the expansion of the cash economy for export, the spread of religious missions, and the ever-present political pressure from the Ethiopian empire-state. Thus, Kurimto and Simonse (1998: 25) identified factors that contribute to the decline of age systems; namely, *modern education*, capitalist *cash economy*, and *state intervention*. *External influences* are an important part of these concerns.

EXTERNAL INFLUENCES

An example was given by Spencer (1965) in the case of the Ma- speaking Samburu of Kenya where gerontocracy was imperiled by outside forces. The British colonial administration controlled the Maasai peoples' dispute settlement processes, imposed taxes, and required the sale of cattle through official channels. However, the influence of an imposed colonial administration was limited and the Samburu continued their traditional gerontocratic authority over herding and community life since there was no other environmentally appropriate means of survival. Despite such resilience, the susceptibility to pressure is all prevailing. Abbink (1998: 161) pointed out in the case of the Oromo that the *Gada* system of government, once grafted on an agro-pastoral way of life, is susceptible to changes in social scale, economic life and external contacts. He further argued that the system 'will not work in a stratified society with economically specialized groups, such as modern society [and nowadays it] serves mainly as a symbol of Oromo political ethos and achievement, as well as illustration that there were traditional constitutional limits on the exercise of power.'

In the case of the Sidama, most external influences came through Christian missions, the aid agencies and associated schooling. The expansion of Lutheran, Evangelical and Roman Catholic, and Adventist churches since the 1950s and the 1960s allured a good deal of social groupings to quit their customary duties and to join them instead. The fact that the churches, particularly Catholic and Adventist, were based in the rural areas indicates their keenness to acquire more members by demonstrating their usefulness for the needs of the rural population. In most of the areas this author observed, many of these churches were accompanied by schools and health clinics offering useful educational and health facilities. Nevertheless, while competing with local values, the churches have also played a complementary role.

Some of those churches preached in the Sidama language or translated or wrote books in Sidama. Prominent among them was a Catholic priest who compiled a Sidama-English Dictionary. The priests and the churches faced no insurmountable obstacle, in this regard, since the *halaale* code has messages that reinforce that of the Bible, hence it can be considered complementary to the Bible. But the task of interpreting events shifted from the Sidama elders to those foreign priests who were keen to allure the youth, and through them attract their families. Either way, the end result was to change the world-view of the would-be followers/members who no longer resorted to local norms and practices including ancestral worship.

The work of aid agencies has never been prominent in Sidama until recently. There are different reasons for this fact. Firstly, the self-sufficiency ethos provided by the moral code precludes any tendency to be dependent on external alms. Begging is morally unacceptable and support comes from the community itself when needed. Secondly, aid agencies did not have permission to by-pass the Ethiopian center and carry out their programs in Sidama. Thirdly, there has not been a well-publicized emergency situation worth attracting the attention of food aid as in the northern parts of Ethiopia. Thus, the few development-oriented aid programs present in Sidama had their start through church groups, i.e. Irish Aid in the early 1990s.

EMPIRE STATE INTERVENTION

The impact of the Abyssinian conquest and the imperial domination was reinforced by tumultuous developments in the 1970s and 1980s. The relative backwardness of the imperial era meant that cultural impositions were resisted as much as they were repulsed. For example, Menelik's direct attempts at forced baptism and associated fasting and the shaving of people's hair as material marks were smartly ignored. Concern during Haile Selassie's regime shifted to economic exploitation and gradual consolidation of central power without undue confrontation on the cultural and spiritual arena. In the 1960s, while the government encouraged the short-lived self-help associations to take over local judicial and administrative functions, it actually re-centralized control and eliminated all creative autonomy (Hamer 1996: 548-549).

The *derg* revolution of 1974, in particular, and what en-sued its downfall, had pervasive effects in Sidama cultural and social underpinnings.[6] Given the centrist venture of the *derg*, the 'consensual authority of elders, unless practiced clandestinely, virtually ceased to exist except in conformity with government edicts.' (*Ibid.*) The communist style of sociopolitical organization that spread its tentacles from the center to the villages, and the physical force that accompanied militaristic bureaucracy disturbed the politico-cultural airwaves of the Sidama world. It undermined the social complementarity between elders and youth as well as between genders. At the same time, the consensual authority of elders was transferred from local *songos* to *qebele* (Amharic term) committees. Making life worse and destabilizing the internal mechanisms of survival, the government policies of taxation and marketing controls became more oppressive. The practices of collective farming and villagization coupled with forced conscription of the youth into the army to fight in Eritrea were also devastating.

The regime that replaced the *Derg* in 1991 was less than enthusiastic in supporting elders' councils. Its main fear was that they might undermine its fragile central authority. Also, the TPLF regime introduced pervasive inter-generational conflicts. By a selective and manipulative arming of the youth they disowned the elders of their moral authority. Thus, the TPLF regime has contributed to the polarization of the generation divide. Upon assuming power it promoted a decided minority of youth, not all youth came to be deceived or allowed to be used, with minimal experience of the Abyssinian political machinations at the exclusion of all those with a thorough knowledge and experience. Worse still, the sooner the less experienced youth had gathered the knowledge and started asking the inevitable, they were sacked or imprisoned and replaced by far less experienced younger ones. For the time being, this practice enabled the TPLF regime to manipulate the overall process of governance.

What followed was a social dis-articulation and a lack of moral direction. Sinister motives also came to work with the connivance of the public office holders. For example, politically moti-vated semi-religious fanatic groups covered the ground emptied of the moral code and the direction of elderly authority. Groups such as the Pentecostal, Full Gospel, Hawariat, Animotem ('We don't die') went on taxing the poor while taking the youth away from work and education and away from the protective shields of their parents and elders. Like anywhere else, the youth, seem-ingly freed from the shackles of the elder's authority, roam the countryside attending to any news of a mass congregation. What is happening with the mushrooming of quasi-religious groups has worrying dimensions and no action is forthcoming from the political center to examine the problem lest to worsen it.

In this way, the actions of the subsequent Ethiopian regimes posed a threat to *halaale* and the future of the Sidama. Hamer (1998b: 7) noted this scenario when he wrote,

> Considering the experiences of youth in being removed from the land, impressed into conflicting military organisations, and losing the authority and instruction of the elders, it was not surprising that a condition of cynicism, even nihilism, engulfed much of the young generation (personal communication).

Such a pervasive role of the contemporary state was also noted in the case of the Orma people. There, state interference in produc-tion, marketing and distribution led to a stratification of social life, favoring wealthy individuals, and a decline in the redistri-bution process. Competing interests were no longer negotiated through consensual agreement and the Orma increasingly came to rely on the sanctioning force of the state (Ensminger 1990, 1996, also Hamer 1998b: 10).

EDUCATION, MODERNIZATION AND GLOBALIZATION VERSUS TRADITION

Western style education is another element affecting the authority and the perception of age. The establishment of lit-eracy in garrison towns initially aimed at educating the sons and daughters of the settlers later spread to rural Sidama through mis-sionary schools. With uneven distribution of schools and schooling, the outcome of such literacy was beneficial to the political center and not to Sidama society. Lately those who made it to university education were unable to promote their peoples social and political heritage, and they were taken out of Sidama to work or live in other areas. Some Sidama managed to go abroad and formed the Sidama Diaspora. The progress of the political movements, national awareness, and further studies strengthened social efforts in Sidama itself.[7]

It should be noted that the same education poses a dilemma that exists elsewhere in Africa. Today, an African resides in different cultural worlds. He is the subject of the modern non nation-state whose dominant culture is domination and insecurity. He is the member of an embracing ethnic sociality where his true national identity lies. He is also seduced by the comforts and discomforts of the 'global' fervor. He listens to different types of music coming from different worlds. Like everyone else in the modern world, he is less certain about what is appropriate to his descendants. He lives a life of confusion and improvisation. Compounding the problem is the lack of a guiding and paternalistic authority. The contemporary state does not offer that role any more because in many ways it has become dependent on, almost a servant to, a global capitalist system for its operations. In effect, it has become deleterious to its subjects. Thus, a farmer chief from Lesotho added a government to rats as one of his major problems (Hameso 1997d).

The conflict between a partial entry into a capitalist system and the current dealing with Sidama tradition is not always easy. There is a mistaken perception in the West about non-Western traditions. Going to the days of Walt Rostow's American political economy, not to mention Karl Marx's historical modes of production, there is a theorisation which classifies societies into distinct stages of socioeconomic growth starting from the traditional 'progressing' to the age of mass consumption and beyond (Rostow 1960). In this universalised path, the non-Western, and therefore the non-modern is seen as traditional, in need of change, and often in need of replacement. This went well with Darwin's biological approach that was translated to social change where there is a universal, unidirectional trend in evolution. But then nothing suggests that tradition is generally unyielding. On the contrary, in Africa tradition has served the past fairly well to survive and thrive against internal and external aggression, and against natural disasters. In fact the modernization of Western societies was founded on Western traditions and values reflecting their economic, social, political and scientific development. It is sadly odd to perceive traditions in Africa as immutable and always against change. The real problem is that they have been under constant pressure for change and permanent state of transition to nowhere. It is only the reality and the history surrounding them that presents a state of stagnation. In other words, they did and can play part in change.

The question still remains, does a resort to an exclusive advice from the old help the current generation survive the ever-prying eyes of global capitalism? Does it spare them from the exploitative trans-national and transitional local elite? Or does it help them prevail in the face of a harsh natural and social environment? In other words, is it relevant? These are questions many ask in their daily lives. If the issue becomes one of competition and not of complementarity, one would ask questions like what gives the old the monopoly of authority? The answer lies in the resort to the moral code, the belief system, subjective and personal reference, owning the monopoly of coercion, the severity of the moral sanction, and knowing the Sidama world more than anything and anyone else. But the question now is how this can work with the contemporary influences permeating the Sidama world?

In order to survive and thrive the Sidama need to know. Firstly, they need to know about the Sidama world, which like others is mutable and changing, then they need to know about the ever- changing dynamics of the rest of the world. It is not plausible to assume that the Sidama will remain an agricultural society. Secondly, the Sidama need to be conversant with processes of knowledge creation and acquisition, the development of the media, the influence of formal education and teachers, the enlightenment of parents, the role of literacy within society, the spread of the written word and the spread of nationalism and national consciousness. The question is not whose knowledge is sound and more useful. The question is which notion is more useful to Sidama as the notions of *mzee* (old man) goes hand in hand with *mwalimu* (a teacher or even a father of a nation) as in the Kiswahili cultures.

OTHER ISSUES OF THE MORAL CODE AND PROBLEMS OF GERONTOCRACY

It is the case that age systems may offer an alternative means of organizing society when other ways are ineffective or corrupt under a contemporary post-colonial state. But in such an organization, the gerontocratic ladder is not easy to climb. The mechanisms of social mobility in a structured order are rigid and the waiting period may be long. Neither should there be an illusion to idealize the gerontocratic systems as if the moral code poses no problems. The exertion of the authority of the elders may be inefficient, time consuming, based on the preoccupation of imposing order and social consensus rather than engineering social changes that are essential for collective survival. It is also possible that it turns out to be less creative and less empowering. It may suppress the youthful vigor; it may rely on control of elements of human nature such as greed and jealousy. These may invite an atmosphere for heightened conflict as the existence of periodic rebellions by the youth at inter-clan dances and rituals is aggravated by the fact that the old possess the resources, the organisation and the information at their disposal. As a result, older people demand respect, service and authority while the youth have only the prospect of becoming the respected elders of the future.

The dilemma now is how to reconcile the 'real world' geared towards competition and a moral- code suited to hospitality and the maintenance of peace and order. The preoccupation with order also affects the chances for change and entrepreneurship both essential for socioeconomic production and reproduction.

There is another challenge to *halaale* as a moral code and as an ideology whose practicality may assume the political nationhood and cultural autonomy with the powers to limit the entry of undesirable and external influences. While autonomy and the internal environment remain fluid, it is not clear how it may lessen the pernicious external influences. While the substance of the moral code does suit resource distribution and social justice, the time consuming process of conflict resolution and the subsequent personal arrangements make it less efficient. The production for markets (the cash economy) and stratification of life does not leave sufficient time for prolonged discourse. Hamer (1998: 146) admits that arriving at consensus is invariably a long, tedious process and a waste of time. Therefore the balance between efficiency and equity remains a problem.

No wonder then that with the dynamics of change of rising population growth, emphasis on cash accumulation, and with the introduction of a coffee economy different facets of disharmony have emerged. There is a strong adversary in the form of competition from outside-worlds that undermined the superiority of the wisdom of the Sidama elders. These points indicate the degree of the prevailing contest and uncertainty. But, even if one rejects the negative aspects, there is a need for ways of conserving the useful elements of the moral code including the resort to participatory local administration, public debate, consensus building, and ritual confirmation of collective decisions.

CONCLUSIONS

I have argued that Sidama society had had flamboyant social and political institutions. Despite the lack of written records, the Sidama had well known moral codes, laws, conventions and sanctions with predictable means of enforcement. The elders had powers to legislate, to take administrative actions in order to meet emergencies, to mediate disputes, and to judge and enforce their decisions. Sidama society's certainties and convictions came from reliable and wise advice from a group of gerontocrats.

Through time, changes took place that affected the perceptions of age. Among them, the developments of the late nineteenth and the mid-twentieth century including the conquest, the expansion of a cash crop economy, the expansion of Christianity, the political co-optation of the elders, and the 'Communist' military propaganda and agitation of the seventies. Those periods in history have all helped to undermine the authority of age and age systems in providing respect and service, as ongoing Ethiopian systems forced a political corruption that does not warrant the perception of reliable elders and unreliable youth.

Within this framework, while the Sidama past has helped the survival and the sustenance of the Sidama world as we know it, it may yet need appraisal and modification to see it through the contemporary age. It is highly likely that the elders will continue to have a role mainly in conflict resolution or even in mediation, and the re/interpretation of the moral code and values. They may help opinion farmers, educators and decision-makers to rationalize certain courses of social action from the past and in the present.

In an African setting, reference to traditional values and roles may help the current generations in projecting a historical link with the past that serves as a springboard to direct the future. In the case of the Oromo, Abbink (1998: 163) argued that the 'traditions of political organization, customary law and cultural autonomy provide elements of a value system and a fund of collective memory and identity'. Baxter (1983: 183) is also of the view that the 'values drawn from the past do ... have contemporary relevance and a hold in all our imagination.' For the Sidama, the resort to elders for consultation and sharing of wisdom is vital, but the exultation and exclusion of chronological age for decision-making and leadership cannot be be warranted. Among other things, that will invite, given the current circumstances, despotic and authoritarian tendencies. Neither it will help handle contemporary problems.

Today we are living an era of tumultuous changes and ceaseless pressure. The external dimension of that pressure comes from national imperialism that exerts aggressive campaigns to stamp its economic, social and political control on other worlds. Intended or not, it attacks different societies, their norms, their world-views, and their beliefs. For the aggrieved parties, the mechanism of social survival may require protecting and preserving the moral order and mastering the technical and intellectual side of economic management. The elders are well suited to the former task but the latter is better left to those well versed with the outside world that may be relatively young. Thus, the management of social change in the much-hyped age of 'globalization' requires sophisticated, multi-disciplinary knowledge obtained via a well-structured, formal education of the youth. It is also possible that experience and knowledge have limits; so are the ones obtained from chronological age and the laboratory of living within the boundaries of a nation. Trouble arises when these boundaries are crossed. That is precisely what has happened in many African societies, where the old ways are useful apart from their symbolic importance.

Today, in the age of growing change, that of nationalism and over-zealous imperialism the struggle required to minimize its negative elements emanates from people who know not only of the Sidama world but also about many others. The spontaneous rise and fall of peasant uprisings and protests seen in Sidama in the past can be avoided by a deliberate nationalist program that relies on a written word and not on subjective, personal remembrance of the oral code. Literacy works to reinforce permanence and preservation, notions close to the heart of a nationalist. Thus the aspiring nationalist needs the approval of the elders, he/she requires the symbolic values of the past in order to topple the oppressive structures imposed by another unyielding past.

Public debate and scholarly research might be necessary in order to suggest what to take on board and what to ignore from the past. This may entail controversy and temporary uncertainty, currently the case. The conviction is that out of controversy emerges a new consensus. In every society whether modern or non-modern, the certainties of the past give way to new problems and solutions. During the transition period, the fear of the unknown forces many to embrace what remains of the past whereas the need for change forces acceptance of new interpretations. In doing so, one should not fall into the trap of a common behavior of failing to appreciate what one possesses in aspiring to have what one does not have. In national and cultural terms, the aim would be to maintain positive dimensions and to dispense with elements that are proven to be ineffective and of dubious utility. The critical issue is, therefore, one of balancing the elements of age, wisdom, experience and authority in manners that are socially useful and morally acceptable. While mere copying of Western traditions and values leads to ever more alienation of those involved, its negative effects are more pronounced with those who copy them than they would happen in their original place where the means also exist to deal with them.

Notes

1. The survey carried out by The Sidama Development Programme in 1995 showed that Sidama had 3.7 million people as its population. See The Sidama Development Programme, *A Socioeconomic Profile*, Hawwasa, July 1996; *The Hutchinson Encyclopaedic Dictionary*, London: BCA, (1991: 368); and U.S. Department of State, *Country Profile: Ethiopia*, The Bureau of African Affairs, 4th December 1997.

2. A gap still exists in the knowledge creation about the historiography, about the studies of economic, social and cultural values, and about the importance of local knowledge in offering solutions to local problems. William Shack argued that 'lack of critical scholarship had advertently distorted the human achievement of the conquered peoples … including transformations of their social, cultural and political institutions'. (Shack in Jalata 1997: 95).

3. Coptic Christianity is the main religion of the northern ethnic groups. In the South, the Coptic Church was based in some urban areas and mountainous garrison settlement areas where the majority of settlers spoke Amharic. Braukamper suggests that the orthodoxization campaign failed to go beyond 'the sphere of influence of the military colonists from northern Ethiopia' (Braukamper 1992: 197).

4. See Hoteso (1990: 100-124) for the roles of *murichas, cinanchos,* and elders.

5. See *The Sidama Concern* 2 (1997/1): 6-7 for comparisons. *Gada* is an age-grading and generation system of governance. It is based on consultative decision-making and constitutional limits on the exercise of power. The oral law for Sidama and Oromo draw from the same word, *seeraa,* acting as a social sanction. There is also an assembly system that aims to reach consensus under the shed of a tree (*odaa* in the case of Oromo, *odakoo* for Sidama). This is another aspect shared by both the Sidama (*xadoo*) and the Oromo (*gummi*). Asmarom Legesse provides a classic work on the *Gada* system (Legesse 1973), while Marco Bassi provides a more recent approach (Bassi 1996).

6. We note that in the same year of disturbance, i.e. 1974, a *mogissa* age-set was initiated following the *hirbona* age-set of 1967.

7. Formed in the late 1970s, the Sidama Liberation Movement functioned for most of the last decades from outside Sidama. It joined the TPLF/EPRDF dominated transitional government of Ethiopia in 1991 and it was ousted shortly after. Through its intellectual reflection *The Sidama Concern* continued to contribute towards a national, regional and international awareness of the political situation of Sidama within contemporary Ethiopia.

References

Aguilar, M.I. 1998. 'Gerontocratic, Aesthetic and Political Models of age', in M.I. Aguilar ed., *The Politics of Age and Gerontocracy in Africa: Ethnographies of the Past and Memories of the Present.* Trenton, N.J. and Asmara, Eritrea: Africa World Press.

Bassi, M. 1996. 'Power's Ambiguity or the Political Significance of Gada', in P.T.W. Baxter, J. Hultin, J. and A. Triulzi. eds. *Being and Becoming Oromo: Historical and Anthropological Enquiries.* Lawrenceville, N.J.: The Red Sea Press.

Baxter, P.T.W. 1994. 'The Creation and Constitution of Oromo Nationality', in K. Fukui and J. Markakis eds., *Ethnicity and Ethnic Conflict in the Horn of Africa*. London: James Currey.

———, J. Hultin, and A. Triulzi eds.1996. *Being and Becoming Oromo: Historical and Anthropological Enquiries*. Lawrenceville, N.J.: The Red Sea Press.

Bulcha, M. 1997. 'Conquest and Forced Migration: An Assessment of Oromo Experience', in S. Hameso, T. Trueman and T. Erena, eds., *Ethiopia: Conquest and Quest for Freedom and Democracy*. London: TSC Publications.

Braukamper, U. 1992. 'Aspects of Religious Syncretism in Southern Ethiopia', *Journal of Religion in Africa*, 22 (3): 194-207.

Brogger, J. 1986. *Belief and Experience among the Sidamo: A Case Study Towards an Anthropology of Knowledge*. Oslo: Norwegian University Press.

Ensminger, J. 1990. 'Co-opting the Elders: The Political Economy of State Incorporation in Africa', *American Anthropologist* 92: 662-675.

———. 1996. *Making a Market: The Institutional Transformation of an African Society*. Cambridge University Press.

Hamer, J. 1970. 'Sidamo Generational Class Cycles: A Political Gerontocracy', *Africa* 40: 50-70.

———. 1994. 'Commensality, Process and the Moral Order: An Example from Southern Ethiopia', *Africa* 64 (1): 126-144.

———. 1996. 'Inculcation of Ideology among the Sidama of Ethiopia', *Africa* 66 (4): 526-551.

———. 1998a. 'The Sidama of Ethiopia and Rational Communication: Action in Policy and Dispute Settlement', *Anthropos* 93: 137-153.

———. 1998b. 'Gerontocracy as a Tradition and a Mirror for the Future', *The Sidama Concern* 3 (3): 5-11.

——— and I. Hamer. 1994. 'Impact of Cash Economy on Complimentary Relations among the Sidama of Ethiopia', *Anthropological Quarterly* 67: 187-202.

Hameso, S. 1997a. *Ethnicity in Africa: Towards a Positive Approach*. London: TSC Publications.

———. 1997b. 'The Language of Education in Africa: The Key Issues', *Language, Culture and Curriculum* 10 (1): 1-13.

———. 1997c. *Ethnicity and Nationalism in Africa*. New York: Nova Science Publishers.

Hameso, S. 1997d. *State and Society: An Assessment of African Experience*. London: TSC Publications.

Hameso, S. 1998. 'The Coalition of Colonised Nations: The Sidama Perspective', *The Journal of Oromo Studies*. 5 (1&2): 105-132.

———, T. Trueman and Erena, T. eds. 1997. *Ethiopia: Conquest and Quest for freedom and Democracy*. London: TSC publications.

Hoteso, B. 1990. *Sidama: Its People and Its Culture*. Addis Ababa: Bole Printing Press. [in Amharic].

Jalata, A. 1997. 'The Struggle for Knowledge: The Case of Emergent Oromo Studies', *African Studies Review*. 39 (2): 95-123.

Keller, E. 1987. *Revolutionary Ethiopia: From Empire to People's Republic*. Bloomington and Indianapolis: Indiana University Press.

Kertzer, D.I. and Madison, O. B. 1981. 'Women's Age-Set Systems in Africa: The Lutuka of Southern Sudan', in C.L. Fry, *et al. Dimensions: Aging and, Culture, and Health*. New York: Preager.

Kurimto, E. and Simonse, S. eds. 1998. *Conflict, Age and Power: Age systems in Transition*. James Currey: Oxford.

Legesse, A. 1973. *Gada: Three Approaches to the Study of African society*, New York: Free Press.

Rostow, W. 1960. *Stages of Economic Growth*. New York: Cambridge University Press.

Spencer, P. 1965. *The Samburu: A Study of Gerontocracy in a Nomadic Tribe*. Berkeley: University of California Press.

Stanley, S. 1966. 'The Political System of the Sidama', in *The proceedings of the Third International Conference of Ethiopian Studies*. Addis Ababa. Vol. III.

——— and Karsten, D. 1968. 'The Luwa System of the Garbicco Sub-Tribe of the Sidama (Southern Ethiopia) as a Special Case of an Age Set System', *Paideuma* 14: 93-102.

wa Thiongo, N. 1986. *Decolonising the Mind: The Politics of Language and African Cultural Literature*. London: James Currey.

Chapter 7

CHANGING ROLES OF THE IGBO ELDERLY: A RESPONSE TO NIGERIAN MODERNIZATION

Stella Herzog

Miss not the discourse of the elders (The Apocrypha 8:9)

INTRODUCTION

I was involved in research among the Nnewi Igbo of Nigeria for just a short time. Whenever I asked a question the ways employed to respond were more intriguing than the answer. My question was presented to an elder during a weekly family meeting. At this meeting men of the family sit in a horseshoe arrangement in the center of the compound. Women stand and sit at the back of this horseshoe, making occasional comments. Instead of being answered, my question was forwarded to the next higher level of elders. I waited another week. This process was repeated at least four times. At the ultimate meeting there were 8 to 10 men present (no women), all white hared and obviously quite elderly. They sat in the traditional horseshoe and discussed my question. I soon received the answer. Not any answer would do. The answer had to be one of truth.

The Igbo custom is that to find such truth one must proceed to the elders. As to ensure their honesty individuals must achieve the title of Ozo. When this title is conferred upon them they are given the ofo, a small stick of 4 to 5 inches taken from a special tree),[1] which when struck on the ground by the title-holder it guarantees the verity of their declarations. It acts much like a judge's gavel. It is believed that when somebody reaches a late stage in life he should receive this emblem of honesty since telling anything but the truth would not be to his advantage. Obviously I learned from this experience that for questions of historical culture elders still remained the encyclopedic source.

In this chapter I will examine various roles elders perform for their society and discuss how those roles have been altered from pre-colonial, to colonial and post-colonial periods.

Pre-colonial African elders, in societies like the Igbo, had centralized power. It was the introduction of a new livelihood, in this case transport commerce, that impacted two significant aspects of socio-cultural life among the Nnewi Igbo, altering the type of power elders wielded. These aspects include (1) migration and (2) education.

New forms of transport introduced in the colonial period increased levels of migration from Nnewi, whose people opened transport businesses all over Nigeria. For the first time large numbers of families lived far away from the elders' authority.

Nnewi people engaged in new forms of education through Church and Government Schools. School attendance was encouraged to enhance Math and English skills for trade activity. In addition transport apprenticeship began and the number of young men away from Nnewi vastly increased. The new informational base of Nnewi People undermined the elders' authority, and made communication with them more difficult.

During the colonial period, restricted trade with countries specified by the colonial masters was the norm. However, after the colonial period African countries initiated trade with countries of their own choice. This multiplied their international connections. Migration to many new countries for education and entrepreneurial activity increased. Expertise grew in the new economic realm of transport. As a result the quantity of international connections increased. Such radical changes to the economic base of the community resulted in turbulence within the family system. Nnewi people responded by creatively assigning new roles to the elderly. Thus, Nnewi and particularly the elders remaining at home provide a continuing home base for the Nnewi business Diaspora. The growing elder population contributes to Nnewi's expanding economic base by adaptively taking on new familial roles.

Before describing those historical developments, a few terms and their usage within this chapter need some explanation and description.

TRADITIONAL AND MODERN

The words traditional and modern as well as historical periods designated in this chapter are used only as heuristic devices for discussion. In real life the timelessness of culture, like the timelessness of the psyche often prevails. The following anecdote should explicate this. In the late 1970s an employee of a large Nigerian transport company complained about his salary to his payroll manager. He stated that the company had skipped one of his past salaries. The comptroller confirmed that 'the man is Eze[2] Ozu** – a man with such a title must tell the truth'. Backed by his cultural beliefs the comptroller gave the employee his back salary. Traditional beliefs and practices hold important sway in the modern practice of business.

THE ELDERLY

In this chapter I discuss three groups of elders: (1) Those 'traditional' elders heard about by the researcher who were over 60 before 1970 (2) those 'present' elders of 60 and over in the 1970s and (3) those 'future' elders who will be so during the 21st Century.

ELDERLY AND FAMILY SYSTEMS

One cannot understand or discuss roles and status of one family member, in this case the elderly, without considering how a change in the role of any one family member may significantly modify others (Okonjo 1970:38). That is why in this chapter I discuss children and middle aged people and their systemic relationships to elders.

MIGRATION

Migration, as understood in this chapter, is of several types. The Igbo attend universities and boarding schools all over the world. After their schooling ends they often remain near the school, taking up jobs for many years, sometimes 12 or even 20 years. Eventually, a majority return to Nigeria after having learned a great deal from those experiences abroad. Many Nnewi Igbos move to other places in Nigeria but keep attachments to Nnewi, perhaps even maintain a second household there.

EDUCATION

The word education takes on a variety of meanings in the context of this chapter. There is 'traditional education' that includes the use of example, explanation, and formal institutions, as well as apprenticeship in numerous traditional crafts and professions and also age appropriate schools or 'bush schools.' Moreover, there was traditionally the placement of aristocratic boys to live in other kingdoms for educative purposes. I also discuss formal schools and apprenticeship systems that introduced western methods of education. The Church is also viewed as an educative institution, since it alters ideology, as well as it initiates the building of academic institutions.

PRE-COLONIAL PERIOD

Although specific powers traditionally were and until the present day are assigned dynastically and occupationally, generalized control over much of the society during the pre colonial period was based on age. The relationship between the young and old is like the interaction of two classes. The elders are the owner and managerial class while younger adults and children represent the working class (Shelton 1972: 209). While elders 'own' the lineage, land and rights of people, younger people work the land and turn over their proceeds to the elders. The elders command the labor of the young and direct their movements within the context of marriage and work.

Power and authority based on age followed an organization of geo-kinship.[3] Nnewi town was divided into four quarters, each of which was named after an ancestor, all of them siblings. The sibling's relationship, as the quarters, was based on seniority. Each quarter was then divided into descendants of each of these four siblings, and their descendants. Problems and claims by community members were resolved and judged by elders who were connected through the kinship system that was isomorphic with land holdings. Elders mediated economic disputes such as who owned what commodities, trees, land, etc. Their responsibility extended as well to decision making between their own town and others. For example, in Nnewi, there was a negotiation for the buying of a dance from another town. The proceedings began with messengers carrying requests between elders of both towns. The final contract, however, was agreed through direct interaction of both towns' elders.

In such situation, esteem for the individual grows in relation to the amount of power one gains over the society as one grows older or moves into the 'upper class'. The contingency of this respect is based on the alertness of mind and legislative ability for the upper class and the greater skills of physical strength needed for physical labor carried out by the lower class (Ibid.). Overlaying kinship organization where power is based on age finds individuality recognized in the Nnewi Igbo title system. This status hierarchy expresses degrees of personal prestige, political and economic power. This title system although not based on an aging hierarchy mirrors it. Hoben (1970: 204) found this for the Amhara and I found it for the Nnewi Igbo.

Apart from the above duties assigned to elders they were also responsible for the religious life of the community. Because of their age they were on the cusp between the ancestors and the living, and therefore culture brokers between the two. They said daily prayers for the family offering sacrifices in their own compounds. They often led political rituals where religious roles aided in the organization of festivals, ceremonies and other events.

COLONIAL PERIOD

There were two significant revolutions that occurred among the Igbo along with the arrival of the colonials. These were (1) changes in educational form both (a) Western-style schools, and

(b) apprenticeship programs as well as (2) migrations of middle aged and young adults from rural to urban areas for entrepreneurial activity. These transformations in life style took place gradually. They mirrored somewhat the colonials who came. The colonials were of two types, church leaders, and businessmen adventurers. The churches brought western education, and the businesses brought entrepreneurship that often required movement of goods and people. Initial reaction to westerners was often antagonistic. The general trend was to covet the Igbo culture. I was told a story by an informant who said her mother used to sneak to the edge of Nnewi to sell her palm wine. She had to hide her behavior because commoditizing this product was generally frowned upon. There was later great resistance to the manufacture of palm wine, which in fact remains a home based industry to this day. Those most dissatisfied with Igbo culture were often first to join the church and send their children to church schools.

Education

A positive belief in modern education took fire in Igboland. Demand grew for the church to build schools. Education as a ladder for elevating one's status became deep rooted among Igbos, and continues to be a central focus for change. The introduction of western type schools, and strategies for obtaining education through national and global connections (initially in correspondence schools), had a huge impact on the Igbo family economic system. The desire for education required a major financial investment. School fees, books, and uniforms needed to be paid for. Boarding schools required tuition and board. Resources traditionally controlled by elders, due to their position of authority in the family were then controlled by those in more pivotal economic positions – mostly middle aged businessmen. Consequently funds were more likely to be directed toward education of younger people than to services for the elderly. Values were altered in such a way as to influence the direction of economic flow.

Western education was introduced into Nigeria by the churches. During the colonial period school attendance (schools and supply fees) was prohibitively expensive. Therefore most people who could garner resources and manage to obtain even a partial primary school education were twenty to thirty years of age by the time it was completed. Younger teenagers and children still performed farm and household tasks, including helping elders. Gradually school attendance began to start at an earlier age. However, schools followed the British tradition and became boarding schools that took the students away from home. Except for vacation these teenagers, in greater numbers, were unavailable to compound life.

Youngsters, who did not attend secondary schools were usually engaged in vocational training. In Nnewi, for boys, this took the form of 3 to 5 year apprenticeships to skilled mechanics, auto parts tradesmen, or other like businesses. Many were sent to live in other places in Nigeria. Girls training to be seamstresses were more likely to stay home.

Youngsters who remained in town were children (1) under six, (2) six to twelve and high-school youngsters who attended local day schools, and (3) those apprenticed in the Nnewi markets. Another group at home included older students who stayed in the villages but took correspondence courses.

Remaining in town during this time one finds older people, children, and the fewer adults who continued to stay. Children and elders constructed an alliance of dependency. Because there were not as many adults in the villages this dyadic alliance increasingly monopolized the greater part of a child's compound work time during these years. At the same time the gradual drawing of the children away from the home milieu in schools lessened the relaxed substantive interaction between young and old.

The blessing of having children, a value inculcated in Igbo society, mirrored the helpful services performed by children for elders. Offspring were a major form of social security for the help-lessness that comes with aging (Ramphal 1979: 155-156). The elderly were historically dependent upon young children to help them. Often a child was assigned to a grandparent for the specific purpose of 'grandparent aid'. The rights and duties traditionally exchanged between children and grandparents were as varied as, (1) carrying messages, (2) marketing, (3) transporting goods,

(4) cooking, (5) sweeping the compounds, (6) giving physical support, a helping hand, (7) offering psychological support through respect and companionship, and most importantly (8) through stories and direct edification receiving education necessary to carry on cultural traditions. In return for the above activities' grandparents as elders (1) brought order to the community at large, (2) provided significant role models, (3) helped educate and socialize children, and supplied affection not as consistently available from hard working parents. The gradual change in this relationship required new role replacements. These changes ruptured the relationship between old and young. The number of children available for these services declined over the years.

Children were not only unavailable during school hours but spent off school hour's doing homework. They were much less available for compound life. These many hours directed toward themselves reduced their presence to grandparents. Osumane Sambene, describes a scene between grandmother and grandchild in a God's Bit of Wood,

> Old Niakoro called her grandchild...no reply.
> 'She is doing her school work,' said Assitan,
> walking over from the group of women. 'What
> did you want, m'ba?' 'Put the iron in the fire for
> me,' NMiakora replied (Sembene 1970: 36).

The grandchild's inability to help her grandmother because she is concentrating on her homework threatens their relationship. The cultural responsibility of the elderly to educate the young is stripped of its essence. This is poignantly emphasized when Old Niakoro,

> Demands with mockery and sadness in her voice,
> 'Learning what?' 'If I call you I am told not to disturb
> you – and why?' Because you are learning the white
> man's language. What use is the white man's language
> to a woman? To be a good mother you have no need
> of that. Among my people, who are your father's
> people, too, no one speaks the white man's language,
> and no one has died of it! Ever since I was born – and
> God knows that was a long time ago – I have never

> heard of a white man who had learned to speak
> Bambara, or any other language of this country. But
> you rootless people think only of learning his, while
> our language dies'. (Ibid.: 27)

The grandparent's response in this case is direct hostility. Although the reactions of elders differ, e.g., withdrawal, dismay, hostility. They all feel a deep loss. It is a double loss. They fail in their immediate role as grandparent, and in their responsibility to replicate their culture.

At this time there was a deep rupture in family and cultural behavior due to new forms of education on the African continent. Schooling was seen as rendering what African Identity there was (Achebe 1961, 1966).

Christianity introduced new ideas through the church as well as school venues. Consequences of religious conversion to Christianity largely altered ritual performed by elders. In most compounds traditional daily religious prayers began to wane, since most members of the compound were now Christian. Moreover, there were an entirely new constellation of religious, economic and political rituals requiring representation by much younger elites of the community. For example the opening of a bank is an event that while using traditional cultural symbols such as breaking kola nuts, and drinking palm wine, dispense with the elders and employ modern elites such as doctors, lawyers, professors, and bankers to do the honors. However, during the colonial period elders were required for those ceremonies significant to the community's traditional life.

Due to educational change there is a real difference in class composition (Shelton Ibid.). Before the appearance of colonialism in the early 1900s significant community decisions were made by the Igwe, the Obi's of the other three quarters of Nnewi, and elder representatives from the large families of Nnewi. However, pressure for decisions by British indirect rule made it incumbent upon the Igwe of Nnewi to draw on new individual sources and new kinds of information. Therefore, the Royal Nnewi Court was instituted and composed by the power elite of Nnewi. Its members draw from the highly educated and wealthy businessmen of the area. By the late 1970s the court had about 50 members. Its purpose was to consider problems evinced by changes impinging on Nnewi and it's citizenry. The Court appointed action committees to investigate problems and give their analysis and recommendations to the court.

Types of problems included community issues of development and family conflicts. For example, the court's concerns included the building of roads, schools, hospitals, and the installation of electricity and telephones. Court's members were chosen because of their expertise, which is now obtained at an earlier age than ever before. For instance the present market was planned by architects and urban planners, who have professional degrees, as well as by wealthy businessmen, who have extensive marketing experience. These individuals were either Royal Court members or selected by the court to make recommendations. Merely being an elder, or owning a title is no longer sufficient for the needs and processes required in these types of decisions.

After these changes there is a new managerial and administrative class of the town, and the court is not composed of elders making decisions. However this new institution of the Royal Court, powered by younger men, is not necessarily in conflict with the position of the elderly. Igbo people wish to obtain change and keep continuity therefore they effectively mesh their institutions. The Royal Nnewi Court reports to the Igwe. He also plays an important role in the activities of the elderly through the Nnewi Kin system discussed earlier in this paper. As long as those supplying financial backing for community development are citizens of the local area the above court should be composed of the same members. However if federal and state moneys begin to flow into the community for development purposes other people might obtain greater decision making power.

Migration

Third World migration is visualized as a movement into African cities. However, since most Nnewi Igbos who moved did so for business reasons they migrated to different sized population areas. The size of places varied from crossroads to huge urban areas. They relocated where transport and spare-parts were needed. Although urban areas were an obvious place for centralized distribution, small towns displayed a growing requirement for auto parts, consequently retail stores were erected.

Migration for work created an imbalance of peer groups between those away from the Nnewi home-towns and those remaining. One begins to get a picture that is common throughout Africa where modernization and urbanization are taking place. It was the older people, the children, and the few adults who remained in the towns in rural areas.[4] The absence of young and middle-aged adults from rural towns in southeastern Nigeria exacerbated difficulties for the aged. The support system for this group was now long-distance and intermittent. Those settled away from home traveled home only for holidays, and vacations. They remitted money home by messengers or mail. Those middle-aged adults who remained home were more often women, since more men than women leave towns. As a result there was a greater number of adult women than adult men in the towns at that time. This contributed more to the needed care of elders than would have been available if they left in the same numbers as men.

One response by the elderly to being more alone in their town was to take greater responsibility to provide for themselves, and even others. Older women continued cooking, not only for themselves and the elderly men, but for those youngsters left in their family compounds. Men are usually economically responsible for their mothers during their elderly years, as found throughout African patrilineal societies (Le Vine 1965). Often men with low incomes are in reality unable to take care of their obligations. As a result older women particularly a widow of such sons must be self-sufficient (see Guyer on Beti widows 1979: 13).

Migration Travel Education and Enlightenment

Many Igbos served in the British forces in World War II. They ended up traveling far from home and staying away for long periods of time. This experience gave them a very different and broader perspective of the world and of travel. The experience of having traveled so far boosted their prestige at home. This both challenged the elder's experience and brought new skills to the elders to use in community decision making. Igbos now had individual contacts not only with people in Great Britain but with Britain's allies as well.

Both migration and education have effected traditional marriage customs. In Pre-Colonial times it was prescribed for a man to marry someone from his mother's village in Nnewi. This meant that a woman would be near her own female relatives, and that harmony would prevail around the cooking pot. Many men moved to new towns and cities for business purposes. They had neighbors not from their mother's village. Nnewi Igbos living in for example Madugiri, Kano, or Lagos, lived together in enclaves near their businesses. They had greater interaction with Nnewians from different quarters. In small towns with few Nnewi business-men, the interaction of young males with other Igbos, and people from other ethnic groups was more possible. In addition when boarding schools became more prominent youngster's from all Nigerian ethnic groups in these situations became friends. New friendship bonds led people to bring home friends for school vacation, and closer relationships ensued. Marriage possibilities broadened as a result of migration and education. This made the job of elders who arranged and/or agreed to these marriages more complex, as information about a family was more difficult to obtain. Required marriage ceremonies, which span over many years and involve both sides of the family, were more difficult to organize.

1960 INDEPENDENCE AND POST-COLONIAL PERIOD

Nigerian Independence brought one economic revolution to the country that greatly effected Nnewi. Nigerians by law could do business with anyone in the world, and were no longer locked into economic relationships with Britain and her former colonies. Although Britain remains Nigeria's major economic partner, Igbos after Independence began to travel to new parts of the world, and to send their children to study in countries they never had been to before. Again, new arenas of education and long absences turning into short-term migrations began to steam roll family members into new relationships.

Education

Judges and lawyers educated in England competed with the authority of elders. The political and economic power of elders lessened. In reality an individual can choose which system (traditional or Nigerian) would be more advantageous to the outcome of their own interests. Individual choice also threatened the authority of elders that was ultimately lessened by this more complex plura-legal system.

Even though individuals siphoned off the power of the elders by taking their litigations to court, elders are still kept busy. Many individuals still work out their differences through the courts of the elders. Some litigants begin with the elders even though they may switch to the courts if they don't agree with the community based decisions. In addition, elders, due to their age, have a thorough knowledge of the laws, values, and ethics of Nnewi. They know the litigants in the case extremely well, and can read their innocence and guilt through their responses to inordinately skillful questions posed to them. Thus the elder's role in assessing and alleviating community problems still is an essential factor in the continued salience of community life.

As a result of the 1976 Nigerian law of Universal Primary Education almost all Igbo children began to attend school for at least the primary six grades, beginning at age six. The numbers of children attending school until 12 years of age dramatically increased. This removed children age six to twelve from the compound, making them unavailable for farm and household duties for an important part of the day. The historical relationship of being near each other for much of the day altered.

Control over labor by the youth lessens in response to new vocations available to youngsters. Elders lack the needed education and experience required to make appropriate decisions. Elders do not understand the training required to become a engineer, sociologist, etc. However, general requirements for such careers are fathomable by elders. The wisdom of the elders on the psychology and intelligence of youngsters has always been honored. Families asked elders whether the prospective person is responsible, bright, creative, or independent enough, to enter specific trades, studies, or careers and to travel and live far away and for long periods of time. When the future of youngsters are planned at family meetings, elders' opinions are respected.

The pressure to reclaim Igbo history and culture was subsequently generated by (1) Nigerian Independence in 1960, (2) the world wide pop culture movement to 'do your own thing' in the 1960s and (3) the American Civil Rights Movement. Returning to Africa in the 1970s African students educated abroad gained a new respect for their own identity. Elders became more dependent on emissaries bringing new information for community decision making. At the same time the reclamation of African identity depended on obtaining details from elders. Their role used to be essential for the total survival of their people; it is now necessary for the preservation of cultural identity.

The elder's traditional role 'to educate' has continued, albeit in newer mediums. For example, in Nnewi traditional dances are being taught to youngsters in the school system, as part of the curriculum, just like Physical Education. Community elders teach dances to school-teachers who then instruct their students in school. One also finds evidence of elders input at the University level. It is the responsibility of each college-student to do a thesis in their senior year. Those in the social sciences require investigation and research conducted in the home-towns. Information for those theses is obtained from interviews with elders. The appeal of preserving Igbo Culture exists not only in formal schools, but beyond schools as well. Alerted to the possibilities of a dying culture, by such artists as Achebe (1960: 1974), who depict the way in which involvement in western culture has turned Igbos away from their own tradition, action is now being taken to reverse the course of this trend. This cultural resurgence arose all over Igboland, not only in Nnewi. There is a journalistic push to resuscitate the Igbo language itself through newspapers, proverbs, wisdom's and stories being published in this language.

Professionals interested in indigenous African activities related to their own field are beginning to do research on parallel fields. Some doctors are initiating research on traditional cultural health practices and certain individuals provide expenses for historical research and awards for continuation of specific cultural practices. In Nnewi, there is an annual award for the best woman's dance. National interest in indigenous legal practices required consultations with elders in order to add relevant information for the formation of a national constitution, exercise that took place in the late 1970s. At that time there was a feeling of excitement about creating a set of laws that included African Culture. Although the general plan was to follow the American constitution it was also to include African cultural traditions. This type of activity required help from the elders.

Another form of identity growing is one's identification with family and ethnic group portrayed in attitudes towards land. Power over land follows traditional rules arbitrated by elders. Most land is farmland, however its economic power however diminishes in comparison with the greater financial sustenance derived from business. Nonetheless, the economic value of the land has grown as its significance to cultural identity has increased, as land has become scarcer due to population growth. Elders' control over this resource is still important but of a different nature than ever before.

Christian education was often negative toward African ways. However, Western educated Africans swept by the 1960's pride on Africa began steeping themselves in traditional dress and behaviors. One ceremony resuscitated by the Nnewi Igbo, that directly affects elders is that of ikujenwa, i.e. the presentation of a child to his or her grandfather's compound. It is a large ceremony involving the entire extended family of both parents, and it legalizes the child in his mother's father's compound and gives the child rights in the family. It is such an important ceremony that a child may not marry until her mother has performed the ceremony for herself. Although these ceremonies generally happen when a child is young adults may also be part of it. Igbos are now availing themselves of this opportunity.

Igbos enjoy change, and it is through this venue that they continue to discard and embroider their own traditions. What they discard from use they retain in text form through novels, theses, academic publications, and general journalism. Older cultural traits are blossoming in new ways; as people put on African forms of dress they also dress their lives with rejuvenated cultural ceremonies.

Immigration and Its Results

When historical and geographical particulars are unknown the general assumption that country migration patterns push men to urban areas and keep women in towns makes sense. However, when we examine historical particulars other patterns become obvious. Until the outbreak of the Nigerian Civil War there was an exacerbation of the processes leading to a rural/urban dichotomy. In Nnewi, as a result of Civil War rehabilitation efforts in the 1970's separation of the men away, women at home has decelerated. The Civil War forced the return of Igbos to their home areas. Many returnees referred to themselves as 'refugees in our own towns'. Confronted with the lack of amenities in their own homes their immediate wish to remedy this situation lagged until rehabilitation began in the 70s. Exhaustion after the war motivated many to remain at home in Nnewi after the Civil War. Their interest guided the building of a Central Market that supported their prewar investments. By 1978 over 1,000 new businesses in transport spare parts opened in Nnewi. A small city became a central distribution point for auto spare parts in Nigeria. Many men over fifty started these businesses and it was younger Nnewi men who returned in order to restart those stores for spare parts found throughout Nigeria.[5] The presence of so many men in Nnewi brought back to the community a wealth of more direct financial, administrative and psychological support.

The presence of more businessmen in Nnewi also accelerated Community development. The number of development drives multiplied, while philanthropic values were forceful and successful. The building of schools and hospitals increased, and as a result there was an increase in children who remained at home rather than attended boarding schools. More people lived longer due to the building of new hospitals and the provision of better medical care. This infusion of more people and finances in particular created a much more comfortable environment for the elderly.

Businessmen at home improved their own property thus providing more amenities for the elderly, i.e., transportation, electricity and water. Differences between the town and urban areas lessened. The physical presence of so many businessmen meant that money needed by the elderly was immediately available. They no longer had to wait for messengers, or post for economic support. Businesses located in Nnewi meant that more youngsters apprenticed at home and became available to their families. As a result more teenage males remained at home in the community and were therefore more available to grandparents.

After the Civil War, economic investment exploded at home joined in by those living away, as well as those at home. The construction of more and larger private homes fulfilled several purposes: (1) Retirement motivated by the construction of many buildings, (2) The majority of these modern homes had apartments for parents, or were built immediately next to parent's homes, (3) The homes were enjoyed during holidays and by visitors, (4) Building a home in one's home town accrued prestige to self and family. Thus, many elders lived in newer housing and took care of the establishments for their adult children. These homes satisfied the cultural requirement to care for the elderly, and as a result many elderly people lived in finer housing than ever before. There was a correlation of new housing with the wealth of their children (see Peil's on Ghanaian factory workers, 1972: 209).

Homes, however, unlike elite housing in the West, that segregates the wealthy from the poor, reside on one's own family's territory. Therefore elders remain as they have always been in proximity to their families. Their farm surrounds them. Elderly women continue to perform their farm and trading activities out of habit as well as necessity, while men continue to meet and make family and community decisions.

One form of elite behavior in Nnewi has always been a system of title taking. The return to community and ethnic identity have bolstered this cultural system. Title taking is one form of outwardly designating one's status within Igbo communities. Titles cost a great deal of money, and require hard work to obtain them. A person trains in a significant amount of ritual and then set apart from the rest of the people by certain symbolic behaviors (rights and duties). However the title brings with it social benefits. In Nnewi there are several titles for men, and one for women. By 1980 the highest title cost about $45,000.00. In two quarters of Nnewi, Uruagu and Nnewichi, title taking is possible as low as age forty and fifty. In the two other quarters of Nnewi, Otolo and Umudim, one must be sixty or older to obtain a title. The women's title Ekwe, has no real age barrier, and hasn't been taken since Independence, although there are presently many older women who retain this title. People come to these titled individuals for their cultural repository of knowledge. They participate in festivals, ceremonies, and community affairs. The elderly held such high status historically. However, due to urbanization, industrialization, and expanded markets, the Igbo title system in the form of a cultural template, is adopted by men who although younger are wealthy enough to afford such titles. They imposed a renamed title system on the business status hierarchy they are creating. Thus the title taking tradition continues within a younger group of men.

CONCLUSION

In the early 1900s many Igbos wished to retain all the trappings of their culture. In response to their broadening education and world wide migration they became enamored with change. This ethnic group takes from the global market of commerce and education that which helps them adapt better to the changing world. They stop using that part of their culture that is no longer amenable to a changing world while preserving it in text form. Elders are integral to this process as they provide information, and roll models for the future.

In this chapter I have discussed several historical factors that nurtured the direction of change these roles took from the colonial period to the present. Future directions will depend very much on how Nigeria integrates into the global society in the future.

Although historical changes influenced the direction of how the role and status of Igbo elders changed, the two most general inducements included western styled schools and changing migration patterns. These two factors had the greatest impact on the family constellation, and therefore the role and status of elders.

Igbo elders play, even in today's society, a significant role in decision making. This role is one of psychologist, lawyer, and hallooed historian and philosopher. Although the resources they control have greatly altered, lessening, gaining, and varying in dimension, elders have not lost their access to a decision making body, which is a very significant resource in itself (Leeds 1973: 29).

Much younger men employ Igbo cultural templates traditionally used by the elderly to rule and administrate, to bolster their own business activities and to create a new status hierarchy. Thus, the importance of the elderly situated at the apex of the living family is of great significance. The Igbo continue to enjoy counting generations and orienting themselves with relative ease inside a family of eleven to thirteen generations. The position of the elders in this matrix, and their ability to immediately portray it, is in itself a feat requiring respect.

ACKNOWLEDGEMENT

I am most grateful to Carol Holzberg for including me on her panels on Aging at the Northeastern Anthropological Meetings, 1980, Amherst, Mass. and at the Canadian Ethnological Society Meetings, 1981, Ottawa, Canada. I would also like to thank Sara Berry, Jane Guyer and Jean Hay for their interesting comments.

Notes

1. *Ofo* ownership is not a monopoly of men, women own it, although it is of little importance to them (Alutu 1963: 188).

2. Eze signifies a title such as doctor, which is followed by the kind of knowledge (philosophy), in this case Ozu. It is usually elders who are wealthy enough to obtain such titles.

3. Geo-kinship is a word I coined to mean the isomorphic relationship between land ownership and kinship groups.

4. African communities, due to factors of out-migration, have become almost homogeneous for two age-groups. They do in fact behave as retirement communities. The middle age adult population migrates and returns in time to retire in their hometown communities. For further discussion about the retirement community, see Legesse (1979: 61).

5. However, this was not always the case. I observed several men over fifty in large cities such as Kano. In these cities there were usually several families of up to three generations of Nnewi Igbos who had settled. They still considered themselves from Nnewi, and they were considered Newians, even though they had made their life so to speak 'abroad'. Nevertheless, to find a person who would be in the category of elder still residing in the city was truly rare. Most men in their seventies had by that time returned to Nnewi to live.

References

Achebe, Chinua. 1960. *No Longer at Ease*. Connecticut: Fawcett Books.

———, 1974. *Things Fall Apart*. Connecticut: Fawcett Publications.

Arth, Malcolm J. 1968. 'An Interdisciplinary View of the Aged in Ibo Culture: Journal of Geriatric Psychiatry, Ideals & Behavior: A Comment on Ibo Respect Patterns', *Gerontologist* 8 (4): 242-244.

Benedict, Ruth.1967. *The Chrysanthemum and the Sword*. New York: Cleveland.

Cox, Frances M, and Ndung'u Mberia. 1977. *Aging in a Changing Village Society: A Kenyan Experience*. Washington, DC: The International Federation on Aging.

Daily Star. 1979a. 'Federal Government Tackles Erosion'.

———. 1979b. 'Agulu/NManka Erosion Menace: First Attack Begins', 12/19, 14.

Delaney, William Phillip. 1977. Socio-Cultural Aspects of Aging in Buddhist Northern Thailand. Ph.D. Dissertation, University of Illinois.

Du Toit, Brian M. 1968. *Cultural Continuity and African Urbanization, Urban Anthropology*. Elizabeth M. Eddy, Ed. Athens: University of Georgia Press, 58-74.

Fuller, Charles E. 1972. 'Aging among Southern African Bantu'. In *Aging & Modernization*. D.O. Cowgill and L.D.Holmes, eds., 51-72. New York: Meredith Corporation.

Hoben, Allan. 1970. 'Social Stratification in Traditional Amhara Society', in *Social Stratification in Africa*, Arthur Tuden and L. Plotnicov, eds, 187-224. New York: Free Press.

Holzberg, Carol. 1979. Review of *Number Our Days*, Barbara Myherhoff, New York: E.P. Dutton.

Holzberg, Carol. 1980. Cultural Gerontology: Towads an Understanding of Ethnicity and Ageing. MS. University of Mass.

Korieh, Chima Jacob. 1996. Widowhood Among the Igbo of Eastern Nigeria. Thesis. University of Bergen, Norway.

Lareau, Leslie Spencer. 1977. Widowhood in a Rural Environment: Adaptation as Role Modification. Ph.D. Dissertation. University of Illinois at Urbana-Champaign.

Leeds, Anthony.1973. 'Locality Power in Relation to Supralocal Power Institutions', in *Urban Anthropology: Cross- Cultural Studies of Urbanization*, A. Southall ed., 15-42. New York: Oxford University Press.

Legesse, Asmarom. 1979. 'Age Sets and Retirement Communities: Comparison and Comment', *Anthropology Quarterly* 42: 61-9.

Le Vine, Robert A. 1965. *Intergenerational Tensions and Extended Family*. Englewood Cliffs, NJ: Prentice Hall.

Ludwig, F.C. 1980. 'What to Expect from Gerontological Research', *Science* 209 (4461): 1071.

Maxwell, R.J., E. Krassen-Maxwell, and Q. Silverman. 1978. *The Cross-Cultural Study of Aging: A Manual for Coders*. New Haven: HRAFlex Books.

Maxwell, Eleanor Krassen and Robert J. 1980. 'Contempt for the Elderly: A Cross-cultural Analaysis', *Current Anthropology* 21 (4): 569-570.

Mead, Margaret and Rhoda Metraux, eds. 1953. *The Study of Culture at a Distance*. Chicago: University of Chicago Press.

McCall, Daniel F. 1969. *Africa in Time-Perspective*. New York: Oxford University Press.

Meltzer, Michael William. 1978. Psychosocial Activity among Elderly Members of the Legal Profession, Ph.D Dissertation. University of California Press at San Diego.

Myerhoff, Barbara. 1978. *Number Our Days*. New York: E.P. Dutton.

Ofomata, G.E.K. 1975. 'Soil Erosion' in *Nigeria in Maps: Eastern States*. G.E.K. Ofomata ed., 43-45. Benin City, Nigeria; Ethiope Publishing House.

Okonjo, Unokanma. 1970. The Impact of Urbanization on the Ibo Family Structure. Germany: Gerhard Offsetdruck. Dissertation.

Ottenberg, Simon. 1959. 'Ibo Receptivity to Change', in *Continuity and Change in African Cultures*, W.R.Bascom and M.J.Herskovits, eds., 130-143. Chicago: The University of Chicago Press.

Peil, Margaret. 1972. *Studies in Rural Capitalism in West Africa*. Cambridge: University Press.

Pitt, David C. 1970. *Tradition and Economic Progress in Samoa*. Oxford: Clarendon Press.

———, 1976. *Development from Below: Anthropologists and Development Situations*. The Hague, Paris: Mouton Publishers.

Pollack, O. 1980. 'Shadow of Death over Aging', *Science* 207 (4438): 1071.

Ramphal, Shridath S. 1979. 'International Cooperation and Development: The Role of Universities', *The Journal of Modern African Studies* 17 (2): 183-198.

Sembene, Ousmane. 1970 [1962]. *God's Bits of Wood*. New York: Doubleday.

Shelton, Austin J. 1965. 'Ibo Aging and Eldership: Notes for Gerontologists and Gerontologists', *Gerontolist* 5 (1): 20-24.

———, 1968. 'Igbo Childraising, Eldership, and Dependency: Further Notes for Gerontologists and Others', *Gerontologist* 8 (4): 236-241.

———, 1972. 'The Aged and Eldership among the Igbo' in *Aging and Modernization*, D.O. Cowgill and L.D. Holmes, eds., 31-49. New York: Meredith Corporation.

Sohngen, Mary. 1977. 'The Experience of Old Age as Depicted in Contemporary Novels', *Gerontologist* 17 (1): 70-87.

Spradley, J.P. and McDonough, G.E. 1973. *Anthropology through Literature*. Boston: Little Brown.

Uchendu, Victor C. 1965. *The Igbo of Southeast Nigeria*. New York: Holt, Rinehart and Winston.

Uzoaru, C. Onyegbule. 1979. 'The Way We Are', Special Issue, *Quarterly Journal of Africanist Opinion* 9 (4): 56.

Chapter 8

ANCESTRALITY AND AGE CONFLICTS IN BLACK-AFRICAN SOCIETIES[1]

Theophilos Rifiotis

To Ierece

There is only one method in social anthropology, the comparative method - and that's impossible.

E.E. Evans-Pritchard

Old age presents itself as a sphinx for the end of our century. The more rapidly studies advance on the biological and psycho-social foundations of the aging process and longevity increases, the greater seems to be our questioning about the conditions of sociability during the 'final stage of life'. The notion of 'final stage of life' is so naturally equated to chronological old age that it appears as a biological and universal given: the final point to which all mortals inescapably tend. It is precisely around the complex phenomenon contained in the acceptance of the notion of life stages as a biological as well as a logical truth, that I orient the present essay.

The results of my research on elders and age dynamics in Bantu-speaking societies[2] could be summarized by the expression "The Life Cycle Completed", the title of a well-known work by E.H. Erikson (1990). Starting from the analysis of their oral literature and other ethnographic data I will show how these societies develop a notion of aging dynamics that involves a stage beyond death. In fact, this notion is important for the definition of the sociability structures between age groups as well as fundamental for a definition of old age as a condition.

The material analyzed here points out to the difficulties in generalizing about the condition of the aged in traditional societies and the need for interpretations according to a specific social-cultural system which render proper meaning to this stage of life. However, I believe that the analysis of specific cultural systems can be useful for comparative purposes. Therefore, in this chapter, I also intend to point out to certain aspects regarding aging which will allow us to reflect in general about the basic conditions of sociability during the latter period of the vital cycle in particular. Ideas will cover the reciprocal relationship between age groups and notions of family, birth and death.

My research began as a question that can be summarized as follows: in Black-African societies, where orality is the privileged way of transmission and of maintenance of knowledge, how is the figure of its guardian, the elder, represented? It is easy to notice that such a question is equivalent to a type of truism; that is, if oral manifestations, such as oral literature, are transmitted by the elders, what could be found in them but a reaffirmation of the values of elderliness? It should be remembered that the narratives analyzed here were obtained from non-urban populations which live in villages in the interior of the African continent and, as such, express a specific cultural configuration aiming to build a particular type of person and citizen. In Black-African societies, stories do not have only a didactic function, limited to the 'morals of history', but they also communicate a discourse that promotes thinking and produces awareness and 'maturation' (Calame-Griaule 1965).

It is from this perspective that my research of stories and legends, or better, of narratives, led me to identify a narrative motif type that relates conflict situations between the youth groups and those of the elders. The narratives treated in this research constitute a *corpus* that suggests a Bantu vision of elderliness tied to the dynamics of age groups and to the conflicts between them. They relate situations in which those conflicts culminate with a generalized assassination of the elders. Through the examination of these narratives, I will try to show that they can be understood as containing a double message. On the one hand the young should recognize the wisdom of elders, and, on the other, the elders must prepare for the next stage of the vital cycle, that is, to become ancestors.

THE *CORPUS* OF THE NARRATIVES

'May the old ones die!' This *motto* of the youth marks the initial dis-equilibrium, the rupture of the social contract that thus establishes the basis of the main narrative sequence in each of the narratives analyzed in this work. Beginning with a situation of chaos and death, the narratives relate the vicissitudes of the young boys, who, upon assassinating the elders, including their own relatives, create their own villages, the 'young boys' villages'. Starting from this initial disjunction, present in each of the narratives, a narrative sequence is formed by the difficulties and tests to which the youth are submitted. The resolution of these tests demands the presence of an elder who has been saved and hidden, generally by his nephew or son. In the development of the narratives, which we are trying to characterize in a concise manner, the solution of the test to which the youths are submitted depends on this elder/relative. He must transmit the necessary knowledge that enables the young boys to overcome the test and, finally, to recognize the elder's value.

Space limitations here do not permit the complete presentation of the texts. The material pertaining to the Bantu societies selected for this work is composed of six variants of the narrative summarized above. They were collected by various researchers (Rifiotis 1994: 152f.), and come from the Makonde (Mozambique)[3], Mbala (Democratic Republic of Congo)[4], Tumbuka-Kamanga (Malawi),[5] Tshokwe (Angola)[6] and Luba (Democratic Republic of Congo) ethnic groups. Two variants of the Luba ethnic group are included and are referred to as Luba[7] and 'Molenda' (name of the region in which the latter variant was collected).[8]

To facilitate our discussion and compensate for the absence of the full texts, I have constructed the following synoptic chart in which the narratives are presented according to the sequences identified by our structural analysis (Rifiotis 1994) based on the complete texts. In the aforementioned analysis, the Makonde (Mozambique) variant was used as the reference narrative; it was translated from the original language and then analyzed using ethnographic data.

Bantu-speaking narratives							
N.	NARRATIVE SEQUENCE	MAKONDE	MBALA	TUMBUKA	TSHOKWE	LUBA	"MOLENDA"
1	*PLOT BY THE YOUTHS AGAINST THE AGED*	YES	YES	YES	YES	YES	YES
1	*YOUTH DECIDE TO KILL THE AGED*	YES	YES	YES	YES	YES	YES
1	*YOUTHS KILL THE AGED AFTER THE PLOT*	YES	YES	YES	YES	YES	YES
2	An aged/relative survives	YES	YES	YES	YES	YES	YES
2	*KINSHIP RELATION BETWEEN SURVIVOR AND SAVIOR*	Maternal-Uncle	*MATER-NAL-UNCLE*	*PARENTS*	*MATER-NAL-UNCLE*	*FATHER*	*PARENTS*
2	*PLACE WHERE THE ELDER WAS HIDDEN*	Forest	*SPRING*	*CAVE*	*FOREST*	*FOREST*	*FOREST*
3	an enigma is presented	YES	YES	YES	YES	YES	YES
3	type of problem	*SNAKE*	*MEANING*	*SNAKE*	*SNAKE*	*SOURCE*	*SNAKE*
3	*YOUTH DO NOT KNOW THE SOLUTION*	YES	YES	YES	YES	YES	YES
4	*THE PROBLEM IS COMMUNICATED TO THE ELDER*	YES	YES	YES	YES	YES	YES
4	*ELDER HAS THE SOLUTION*	YES	YES	YES	YES	YES	YES
5	*ELDER COM-MUNICATES THE SOLUTION*	YES	YES	YES	YES	YES	YES
5	type of solution	MOUSE	*KNOWL-EDGE*	*GRASS-HOPPER*	*GRASS-HOPPER*	*QUES-TION*	*GRASS-HOPPER*
6	transmitter of solution	mother	elder	*YOUNG BOY*	*YOUNG BOY*	*YOUNG BOY*	*YOUNG BOY*
7	*INQUIRY ABOUT THE ORIGIN OF SOLUTION*	NO	NO	YES	YES	NO	YES
7	*VALUE OF THE ELDERS IS RECOGNISED*	YES	YES	YES	YES	YES	YES

THE NARRATIVE SEQUENCES

The description of the narratives' sequences presented in the chart above is fundamental for the understanding of the internal logic of the discourse found in this material, and, as I will show later, for the understanding of seniority and of the notion of the 'final stage of life'. In this presentation of the material analyzed, I follow the order of the narrative sequence in each of the variants, trying to show through this procedure the narrative development and, at the same time, the variations presented by each one. After this descriptive stage, I systematize the themes evidenced in the sequences for a deeper analysis in search of the significant structure of this *corpus*.

Sequence 1:

In the first sequence all the narratives present the following elements: the young boys' conspiracy, their criticism of the elders' rule, the decision to kill them and the ensuing widespread gerontocide.

The opposition between young and old generically expresses a generational polarity. The linguistic study of Makonde (Mozambique) variant shows that the youth are in the social category of *vanemba*, that is, boys who have just completed the initiation rituals and who are yet unmarried. The elders are designated by the term *vananolo*, which is equivalent to 'respectable' person without a necessary reference to age (Rifiotis 1994, 1999).

The criticism of the elders is vague, or may not even appear in the text, as in the Tumbuka version. We could summarize this firstly as a sequence of the construction of new rules for the governing of the villages. In the 'olenda' variant, we have an intermediary passage in which the narrative reports the young boys' revolt: they refuse to contribute to agricultural work. This functions as an auxiliary sequence that reinforces the youths' complaints and dissatisfaction. Gerontocide is practiced in a widespread manner, allowing the youths to govern in their own way, as they intended when they plotted the conspiracy. This sequence can be considered as a rupture of the contract. It is this function that launches the narrative and that facilitates the creation of the youth' rule. In terms of structural analysis it is the first cardinal function of the narrative.[9]

Thus, the first movement of the narratives is a separation between *elders* and *youth*, which creates the conditions for a social life without the external restrictions set by the elders. This opens up the logical possibility of a test for the new rules, leaving their viability pending. However, indications in the narratives point to the failure of these rules due to the infantile character, we could say, of the re-vindications and complaints: 'the old ones bother us'; 'they force us to plant and to harvest'.

The beginning of the narratives is dominated by the idea of a contract, which implies, in logical terms, four elements that catalyze the narrative development: order, acceptance of rules, prohibition and violation. Note that the first two elements refer to the establishment of the contract, whereas the second two are related to its rupture. We can consider that in the narratives there is a rupture of the contract presupposed between *young* and *old*, and that a new contract is created upon the rupture of the first. The death of the elders and of their rules is equivalent to a renewal, the installation of new values and rules. 'Let's build our own villages' say the youth in the Makonde variant, as if they were reviving the primordial experience of the creation of their own society.

Sequence 2:

In this sequence we have the information that all the elders were murdered, except for one, who in most cases is a maternal-uncle of the young boys, but (as in the Luba case) he can be the father.[10] This kin relation with the elder who is hidden appears in all the variants.

The elder is hidden by the sister (Makonde), by a nephew or by his son (remaining variants). The hiding place is, in most cases, the forest, but it can be a spring or a cave. The place where the elder hides not only carries information that gives authenticity to the narratives, but it also qualifies this place. Let us explain: the forest, the spring, or even the cave, are not places associated with the youth' group, in the same way that the solution of the problem put before them in sequence 3 lies beyond their domain.

The function of this sequence is key for the continuity of the narratives, since even though the rupture between generations is set in action, the existence of a representative of the previous contract provides the possibility of reversal. The index given by this sequence is that the elder who escaped is a kin of the young boys. Although some of the narratives are explicit about the fact that the youths slay their parents, most of them emphasize the undifferentiated treatment that the elders suffer in the hands of the youth. The passage of an opposition expressed between generations to one of consanguine relations is a significant semantic investment.

Sequence 3:

In all the variants, the youth face a test whose solution is beyond their reach. This test generally involves a snake in various situations: most frequently it coils around the chief's neck, but also appears in the elder's son's navel or as a strange hunting prey without a head or paws. It is an uncommon situation, an enigma for which the youths have no answer.[11] They do not know how to eliminate the snake without hurting the child or killing their chief, or they do not know the meaning of the animal (Mbala). In the Luba case, the parents of the girl betrothed to the youth' chief demand that he make a jug of smoke to transport water from a spring.

In the Makonde case, the youth's child is born with a snake in the navel; this puts the child's life in check and, in a general sense, the reproduction of the group itself. The problems that the young boys must face have, therefore, broader implications than what the narratives show in a first reading.

The problem that has no apparent solution is a kind of test to which the new social contract is submitted. It should be kept in mind that the rupture of the original contract, in terms of the narrative's logic, does not require a test, although it can be present. In reality, the test constitutes a certain liberty, given by the organization of the narrative, in order for the young boys to attempt to resolve it, even though that is impossible. Thus, the test acts as an affirmation of the young boys' freedom, and its resolution qualifies them to assume rule of the villages.

In order to surmount the problem a helper is called upon: either one of the young boy's or the mother (Makonde), who serves as an intermediary in order that the real helper, the surviving elder, can communicate the necessary knowledge.

Sequence 4:

Without the solution for the problem, the young boy who hid the elder/relative goes to him and asks for advice. In the Makonde case, the group of young boys asks their mother for help. She goes to see her brother and asks him how to save the child that was born with a snake around the navel. However, in general, it is the youth that hid the elder who looks for the solution and acts as mediator between the youth' group and that of the elders. The responsibility rests on him to communicate the necessary knowledge.

Thus, the plea is made by someone singled out among all the boys for having saved his elder/relative. It is worth noting that this youth is never the one chosen by the boys to be chief, even when he is selected from those who carried out the rebellion (Tumbuka and 'Molenda'). In the four variants in which there is a young chief (Tumbuka, Tshokwe, Luba and 'Molenda'), the problems' solution generally is far beyond his reach. There are narrative indexes of the chief's impotence, because, besides ignoring the solution, he made himself a target for the snake.[12]

Sequence 5:

In this sequence the surviving elder, without imposing any conditions, provides the answer for the test. This point is particularly significant if we take into consideration that the elder could use his knowledge to subjugate the youths. In fact, as we will see later, the knowledge could be manipulated as a dominance mechanism; however, the discourse contained in the narratives points in another direction: the knowledge should serve others, it should be shared and effective. In fact, the analysis of an equivalent *corpus* collected in non-Bantu cultures suggests that this a distinctive characteristic of the Bantu (Rifiotis 1994).

The elder tells the youth to use mice or crickets to attract the snake and then kill it. In the Mbala case, the maternal-uncle goes to the village, he recognizes the strange animal and he suggests that it be decapitated. In the Luba version, the young chief solves the test by asking, in return, to borrow the parents' jug for transporting the water.

In most of the variants, we have the affirmation that the solution is easy and it is immediately given. In the Mbala case, the maternal-uncle asks to see the prey and identifies it as a manifestation of the ancestors. The Luba variant mentions also the practice of a ritual for the ancestors.

Sequence 6:

The youth, or the mother in the Makonde case, communicates the teachings of the elder to the others. Following the elder's advice, the serpent leaves the child's navel to devour the mice or crickets or uncoils from the chief's neck and is killed with a machete. In the Mbala case, the elder identifies the animal and asks that it be sacrificed in order to give happiness. In the Luba variant, the parents of the bride-to-be recognize the suitor's wisdom and permit the marriage.

The adoption of the procedures communicated by the elder relative, which results in the serpent's elimination, signals an integration between the new and the old order. Some narratives make this integration explicit in the surviving elder's speech itself, when he affirms in sequence 5 that the massacre of the elders 'is not important' (Makonde) or that 'the elders are evil' (Tshokwe). In the Mbala variant, a voice is heard after the animal is identified proclaiming that the blood of the animal saves the men, and a reconciliation of the generations takes place through sacrifice.

The adoption of these procedures is equal to the redress of the initial fault committed by the youth, and, consequently, to a restoration of the contract that was broken in the beginning of the narrative.

Sequence 7:

This sequence is characterized by the integration of the surviving elder into the young boys' village. The success of resolving the enigma legitimizes the youth' passage to another status: to marry, to have children, etc. The recognition itself of the importance of the elders and the demand that they live together explicitly marks this change of social roles.

This sequence encompasses the recognition that without the elder the problem would not have been solved. The restoration of the equilibrium through redress of the initial fault, presented in sequence 6, demands the recognition of the elder's importance. Sequence 7 can be viewed as supplementary to the previous one. However, given the pedagogic character of the narratives, the recognition appears in an explicit and even redundant manner.

The value of the elder/relative is evidenced with the transfer of knowledge to the youths. Through this transfer they become qualified to govern the villages. Recognition of this is emphasised in the request that the surviving elder reintegrate into the village. Only in the Makonde case does the maternal uncle refuse to return, declaring 'I will remain alone without those of my age group who died'.

THE NARRATIVE CYCLE

The identification of the narrative sequences allows us to characterize the narrative cycle in terms of the general transformation that operates at the level of discourse. In other words, we are trying to identify the elements that produce the transformation of the initial situation, marked by rupture, to the final one: the narrative cycle. These elements have the function of selecting potentially available contents of the initial situation that will be present in the composition of the final one.

It should be kept in mind that the initial situation does not necessarily correspond to the first narrative sequence and even less to the first sentences of the narrative, nor does the last situation correspond to the final sequence. The identification of these situations cannot, therefore, be lineal. On the contrary, it is from the final situation, with the elements selected by the narrative itself, that we can retrospectively characterize the initial one. For this reason, we will first identify the final situation of the narrative, and only afterwards the initial one. This will allow us to characterize the process of the selection of contents operating in the narrative discourse.

THE FINAL SITUATION

The final situation updating the contents of the narratives is marked by cardinal functions, which in structural analysis represent the dynamics of the narratives. Everything that was possible in the text is achieved in the final situation, which is equivalent to a return to the contract broken by the young boys' actions. In the variants analyzed, this situation corresponds to sequence 6, in which the test is solved. The resolution involves a communicating agent, the one who hid the elder/relative, and it is through his acts that the elder re-approaches the young boys. To re-establish the contract, the young boys must do something determined by him. Thus, the death of the snake is central to the resolution of the problem and it lies at the center of the entire system of relations between elders and novices.[13]

The final situation is primarily characterized by practical application of the knowledge that the elder possessed rather than by the recognition of that knowledge. Recognition results from the demonstration of the efficacy of the recommended 'remedy', and this confers the privileges of elderliness, such as those we found in the narratives: respect, authority, economic privileges, etc. In terms of age groups, the existing opposition between old and young is treated in terms of power, or better, in terms of authority. In the cases where the massacre is organized and led by the village chief himself, the chief loses the capability to fulfill his role. For example, in the Tshokwe case, he loses his voice, the gift of speech; or in the Tumbuka and 'Molenda' variants, the chief becomes immobilized, rendering impossible his exercise of office.

Power must be based on the highest principles, since it should be related to knowledge acquired through merit or social recognition. Naturally, routine or daily practices do not always reflect these principles. Not always there is respect on the part of the youths, and not all the elders are worthy of the power and privileges of elderliness. Thus in moments of conflicts, domination is frequently maintained by the threat of evoking the ancestral spirits to punish the disobedient.[14] The evocation of the ancestral spirits and any contact with them is exclusively an attribute of the elders, which implies that the relations between the generations should correspond to the relations with the ancestors.

Elderliness is understood as a coming to be, as an improving of the person. It is through the transmission of knowledge and laws by memory that associates elderliness with power. On the other hand, elderliness and ancestrality are closely tied and mutually reinforce each other. However, the fundamental principle is of ancestrality,[15] which confers the sacred basis to elderliness. The very authority that elderliness can confer depends on the prevailing notion of ancestrality present in a given society. Hence, the opposition relative to the age-grade criteria is subordinated to ancestrality, which in turn propagates through the generations, re-combining itself with the relations of elderliness. Literature on age-group conflicts and the superposition of generational solidarity in relation to kin solidarity do not account for this phenomenon (Rifiotis 1995).

The variants show that in a black-African context the conflict between generational and kin solidarity is trans-versed by the question of ancestrality. It is important to remember that, in sequence 5, the elder who solves the enigma and saves the village is always a relative. I.e., he, who besides the age principle, is in the closest position to the ancestor-founder of the lineage or of the village, in the case of those composed of extended families.

Thus, taking into account the order of development of the narratives, we have, in the beginning, the strengthening of solidarity within the age group, in opposition to the familial group, the elders being the generic equivalent. This opposition leads to the rupture of the contract between the young and the elders, which is re-established through an act that involves a snake. The way through which the contract is retaken is particularly interesting and will be treated below in the analysis of the transformation from the initial to the final situation.

THE INITIAL SITUATION

What I intuitively call the initial situation is the revolt of the youth against the elders, which results in their assassination and the establishment of new social rules. There is not doubt that, among the various contents present in the discourse, there is the revolt as well as the succession of power. Even when several contents are found at the start of the variants, it is clear that those selected are specifically related to the means of guaranteeing social order.

The initial situation is characterized, then, by the need to prove that a legitimacy of power comes not only from age, but also from the effective demonstration of the attributes associated with it. An elder is not necessarily a wise person; he must prove his wisdom. In other words, the narratives are not just about the youth and, let's say their rebelliousness; the narratives present a criterion for seniority, which limits access to this status. It is this criterion that is tested, and not age as something abstract.

On the other hand, the narratives emphasize the fact that the elder, in reality, escapes because he is a relative of the youth who hid him. This proximity in kinship places shows two social orientations: one that demands intra-family solidarity and the other that demands solidarity within the age group.

The problem placed by the narratives could be formulated in terms of the perplexity that recently initiated young males experience as they confront different social demands linked to their status as members of an age group, on the one hand, and membership of a kin group, on the other. The fixed position of the son or nephew enters in conflict with their change of status, that is, the youth's passage to adult status.

THE TRANSFORMATION

The characterization of the initial and final situations leads us to consider the ways in which the game of opposition between age and family solidarity is given. These ways are built starting from the selection of certain possibilities given in the narrative that allow the re-establishment and reconstruction of the initially broken contract.

We can consider, always following the texts, that the transformation from a situation of rupture to that of restoration of the contract involves the death of an animal, generally a serpent. Examining this death in full detail, we observe that the serpent is attached to a human body, that of a child or a chief, and, in order to remove it, the necessary remedy must be found. This remedy, which attracts the serpent away from the body in order to be killed, can be a mouse or a cricket. The narratives emphasize that the snake cannot stop devouring these two animals, affirming the automatism of its reaction. In this way, these animals are used to distract the attention of the serpent so that it leaves the inconvenient position, around the neck of the chief, for example, to be killed by the youths without harming its victim. The Luba case is also concerned with astuteness, or, we could say, with counter astuteness, to solve the problem placed by the bride's parents of transporting a spring to them. In all cases the possession of effective knowledge is fundamental to overcome the test.

The figure of the serpent occupies, therefore, a central position in the narrative's discourse. For this reason it will be the object of detailed examination here. I will try to demonstrate that the serpent is essential for understanding that the narratives refer to a posterior stage for which the elders should prepare. I hope to show, through the study of the symbolism of the serpent in Bantu societies and of the role that it plays in the narratives, that it is not possible to understand eldership isolated from ancestrality. Moreover, these narratives allow us to consider that the youth should take the place of the elders, who should, in turn, prepare to attain the condition of ancestor.

The snake appears soon after the rupture of the contract and the solution to the test facing the youths depends upon its death. Concretely, it appears firstly as a wound around the chief's neck (Makonde, Tumbuka, Tshokwe and "Molenda" cases), which denotes a serious mistake for a hunter. At the same time, we should keep in mind that the serpent represents a link between the living and the ancestors. In this way, the serpent represents the chief's limitations and his submission before the ancestors. Entwined by the serpent, the chief cannot speak, cannot eat, and faces possible death. It is necessary to remove the serpent before this happens, which could result in the death of all. Symbolically, it is necessary to re-establish order, to recuperate power, and to recuperate the capacity of speech. Power and the symbols that embody it are equivalent, as we have shown in a revision of the theories linked to regicide and the figure of the 'divine king'.[16]

In addition, the possession of power symbols implies ownership of the kingdom. Luc de Heusch (Heusch 1982: 14) in his analysis of the symbolism of the serpent in Central Africa, shows that it is possible to find a 'common symbolic language', considering the probable common origin of the several ethnic groups and their history of migrations and wars. A myth of the royal cycle of Rwanda, analyzed by de Heusch (Heusch 1982: 61ff.) deals with the conquest of the drum called *Gihanga*, supreme symbol of royal power, around which a serpent is coiled. In this myth the warrior king *Ruganzu Ndori* decides to face the serpent, and he chooses astuteness as the best weapon; he offers to the animal-spirit drink and meat, which attract it to be killed by his soldiers, and the drum is recovered. Thus, following this specialist of Bantu societies, we could say that *Ruganzu Ndori's* fight against the serpent is comparable to the fight related to the origins of Luba society.[17]

According to de Heuch's analysis, the serpent coiled around the drum takes the role of mediator between the disastrous past and a prosperous future. Through his historical reconstruction, he shows that the king *Ruganzu Ndori* must kill the serpent, once satiated with drink and food, in order to legitimize his kingdom (Heusch 1982: 83). Assuming the idea of a common symbolic language among these culturally related groups, there is an apparent parallelism between the myth of the royal cycle of Rwanda and the *corpus* of narratives analyzed by us in that they both refer to leadership and the coiled serpent. The serpent is, therefore, associated with the ancestors and power, and, in a more general way, with fertility itself, as it is explicitly affirmed in the Tshokwe case (Lima 1971: 377). The serpent coiled around the chief's neck can kill at any moment; however, it only immobilizes the chief until he finds a way of saving himself and attacking it. In other words, power is controlled both socially and ancestrally.

The serpent can be a messenger of the ancestors, as in the Makonde case. In several occasions in his discussion on sacrifice in African religions, de Heusch refers to the symbolic relation between ancestrality and serpents (Heusch 1982: 83, 92). This social representation is common among the Bantu, and it is always related to deviations from the norm. It is possible to affirm that observance of the norms and of the political unit is founded more in a consciousness of the importance of the unit and the interdependence than on a submission to a central authority. The discussion about the norms is linked to these forms of consciousness, and the rupture of this consciousness results in disorder, in the unknown, generally associated with a punishment by the ancestors (Wagner 1981: 354).

Returning to seniority, we are reminded that seniority is always associated with relationships between age groups and it is invoked when the immediate order is in question, whereas invocation to the ancestors only occurs when society itself is in danger, as in the case of the narratives examined here. The test put before the youth' village does not mean necessarily a negation of the village. The formation of new villages in the whole Bantu-speaking area is quite common and results from a division of other villages.[18] The serpent as a test for the youth's new village raises a question: if ancestrality manifests itself through the serpent in order to question the youth's actions, how do we explain that it must be killed in order to solve the problem? What, then, is the sense in affirming, as the narratives appear to do, that the serpent places in check the continuity of society?

Serpents represent a kind of mastery of life and death. They kill with their bite, but they have the 'remedy' to restore life (Paulme & Seydou 1972). The snake occupies a central position in the analyzed *corpus*; it is directly related to the test the youth are submitted to (sequence 3). The test's solution depends on the elders ingenuity: to place mice or crickets near the snake so that it leaves the youths chief's neck (Tshokwe, Tumbuka and 'Molenda') or the child's navel (Makonde). The snake is then decapitated. This appears to represent knowledge of ritual, such as cutting the umbilical cord or circumcising, unknown to the youth. Thus in this case, not knowing how to cut the serpent is similar to not knowing how to circumcise.[19] On the other hand, among the Tshokwe, there is an association of the serpent with birth, which can provoke the germination of a child in the woman's body (Baumann & Westmann 1948: 166). Thus, we can identify it with a return of the ancestor through the birth of the youth's son, and, at the same time, with the ancestors' manifestation regarding the youths' villages.

Furthermore, if we consider the parallel between the umbilical cord of the recently born child and the serpent in the Makonde variant, we will also be in the same universe of meaning, that is to say, that of the passage to a social context. The child can enter the social world only when separated from its connections to his previous milieu; concretely, this means separation from the mother. The child separated from this 'previous world' becomes a social being. Among the Tumbuka, for example, the child belongs to the lineage, to society, and is treated this way from birth: he is kept at home and must not be seen by others until the umbilical cord completely falls. During this liminal period the mother herself is considered dangerous (Young 1931: 15, 41). J. Roumeguère-Erbehardt (Roumeguère-Erbehardt 1986: 27) explains the same point with respect to the notion of life among the Venda (north of Transvaal), in which the celebration of a child's birth must await until the umbilical cord is completely dry:

> [...] then the grandmother of the new born prepares
> a party in which she dances saying: 'My pot tolerated
> the cooking', and also: 'The village now has roots'.

Birth and death, understood like this, are not merely matters of physical phenomenon, but are also a matter of social interest; both are tied to the domain of rebirth. The umbilical cord links the child with the 'previous world'. This connection is also evident in the analogy of the serpent, which is an animal related to the origins (Roumeguère-Erbehardt 1986: 13-24). Birth is a moment of entrance into social life, such that if the child dies before this moment he cannot be cried over, his death cannot be mourned. In the Makonde variant, the serpent around the child's umbilical cord serpent signifies that the child's social life must be sanctioned, which the youth cannot do because they do not know how. On another level, the crisis around the new-born is equal to the inability of the youths to perform the circumcision to which they themselves were just submitted.

The analogy between the serpents that are decapitated and circumcision can be further be observed in the symbolism of being cut in pieces, which means to be separated from the previous social group. This can only occur after the offer of mice or crickets to the serpent. The offering, which could be a tribute paid for the breaking of the contract, acts also as bait to eliminate or draw away the serpent.

In the Mbala variant the unknown beast without head or feet is the animal of happiness. The maternal-uncle reveals the animal's meaning, recommending that it be decapitated. Mushrooms flourish from the body of this animal and are eaten by all. It seems plausible, from the way that the animal is described, to consider that it is similar to a serpent, but we lack sufficient elements for a definitive conclusion. It is interesting to note that according to the specialists of the Mbala region (Hochegger 1975: V), the lack of feet means that the beast is separated from the maternal-uncle; the lack of a head would represent separation from the father. I found an additional interpretation in the work of D. Zahan, who associates the legs with social relationships, particularly with the uterine kin, and, among the Bambara, he relates them also to the organs of sex and speech, organs which construct and de-construct the society (Zahan 1960: 82, 173). This interpretation is particularly interesting because in the Tumbuka variant, a cricket is offered to the serpent; however, in contrast to the Tshokwe and "Molenda" cases, the cricket's legs are severed (sequence 5). In fact, the variant insists that only the legs should be cut and not the wings, which perhaps could be associated with the superior part of the body - the head.

The serpent's death as a sacrifice is a collective action and therefore a sacrificial action, since any sacrificial act can only be taken collectively. This is the case of the previously cited myth about the king who regains power by distracting the serpent to release the drum and be killed by the soldiers. In our case, a young boy brings the astute solution of the elder/relative, which permits the youths to resolve the test, and they jointly kill the serpent. It is important that it is done collectively in order to legitimize their power. In so far as it deals with communication with the ancestors, the following seems to be valid:

> The ancestors are there speaking among themselves;
> for this reason it is also necessary that we are many in
> order to speak with them (Vincent 1976: 190).

The death of the serpent should be accomplished according to the ritual prescription of the elder/relative and not by other means. If the youth tried to kill the serpent in a way different from that taught by the elder, they would kill the chief or the child. By killing the serpent in the appropriate way,[20] it is possible to overcome the test, or to obtain the mushrooms of happiness, as in the Mbala case. In this case, the soil is fertilized where the blood of the decapitated is serpent-like animal gushed. Both the name and the meaning of the animal hunted by the youth are 'happiness', from which the mushrooms flourish. In the sequence, a voice is heard in the village that explains that the flesh of the serpent and its spilled blood caused the mushrooms to sprout. As a result it saved the village.[21] Therefore, we can refer to this sequence as a sacrifice. However, what meaning should be attributed to such sacrifice?

Assuming a parallel with the sacrificial scene, our narratives would have the maternal-uncle as the main officiant of this sacrifice and the nephew as his helper. The relationship that appears between the maternal-maternal, the nephew and the serpent demands a study apart, because it seems to synthesize, at least for the Makonde variant, the relationship that is at the base of the re-establishment of the contract broken by the youth's revolt.

Finally, to expand the symbolic context, it would be interesting to remember the words recorded by M. Griaule from Ogotemmêli, a Dogon elder (Mali), and published in *Dieu d'Eau* (Griaule 1966: 158ff.). Ogotemmêli tells that the invention of death originated from a succession of transgressions. They said nothing to the eldest man, thus breaking with the tradition of respect and submission before the 'natural' chief. When this elder was at the end of his life, following the norm, he took the form of a serpent before rising to the sky. In this form he encounters the youths, and having discovered what had happened, he reprehends them speaking the language of the living. This caused his death. Before this fact the youth go to the village and bring the elders to see the body of the serpent.

The series of ruptures told in *Dieu d'Eau* marks the origin of death. Even so, nothing indicates that for Ogotemmêli this series is evaluated negatively. On the contrary, we have the establishment of a new order where the groups and the individuals come to have new roles to perform. Death becomes part of the human's world, demanding of them transformations. The sequence seems to indicate that death is a human construction, and that the figure of the serpent is a road that the living must travel; always reminding the youths of their mortal condition and the elders of their necessity to become ancestors.

In summary, this digression about the serpent allows us to affirm that the group of narratives indicates the need of a sacrifice offered to the ancestors as an operator of transformation from the initial situation of rupture of the social contract to the situation of its re-establishment. The sacrifice is a form of rescuing the broken contract, or better, re-actualizing it. However, as I pointed out in this part of the discussion, I did not find, contrary to expectation, the idea that the youth had a fault that must be expiated. What we found was a sacrifice that is registered in the narrative as the closing of a cycle that renews the contract between the age groups.

FINAL CONSIDERATIONS

I began this work affirming that old age, in the current tendency of the prolongation of longevity, is a phenomenon that calls up or questions about the conditions of sociability linked to the age groups. I highlighted the idea that the 'last stage of life' as linked to old age has been naturalized in our society. We do not consider the cultural possibility of existence after biological death, such as the Bantu-speaking societies do, and where the cult of the ancestors exits. In order to reflect on these phenomena, I have identified a series of stories and legends collected in Bantu-speaking societies that permitted a reflection about the basic conditions of sociability of the aged in those societies. Basically, I showed the importance of ancestrality for the dynamics of the age groups.

The material analyzed suggests the existence of a conception about the relationships between age groups, one in which respect accorded to the elders is intimately linked to the demand for a proper exercise of the attributes of seniority. It may seem paradoxical, but the youths' rebellion and the establishment of their villages place the elders' power in check. In fact, the narratives show that the elders also have something to lose if they view the cycle of the generations, the new established order, only as the end of their rule, their own end, and not as the beginning of one more passage in life. It is as if we are standing before a game of mirrors, in which the projection of the youths' image as rebels reflects an image of the elders questioning their own status. Everything occurs as if, when questioning the regime imposed by the elders with the objective of destroying it, the youth pass from the condition of unsatisfied rebels to socially valuable reformers. In other words, the figure of youth becomes assimilated to the figure of a mythical founder of society. In this group of narratives the youth appear as agents of the revitalization of the social order.

Thus, I understood that the first question linked to the narratives is that of growth, of individual maturation, whose crucial moment is the separation, the rupture. The symbolism of this rupture calls up on the idea of a crossroads between the general idea of separation, (abandonment, loss, circumcision), and the death of the serpent (renewal, installation of a new order, of a new age group). In this way, the ideas of separation and renewal meet and have, as a consequence, the surpassing of the *Other*, the death of the *Other*, which introduces us to the extremely complex vision of the aging process in Bantu-speaking societies. Instead of finding in these materials an abstract apology for the importance of the elders, I found a reflection on the passage of the elder to the stage of ancestor and the preparation that is demanded of him. The image of the wise elder, i.e. he who accepts the transcendence of the young, is of a 'ghost' that haunts the denial of aging and death.[22]

The old must accept this condition of withdrawal, of isolation, as catalyst of animosities, and as donors. This makes us think about other historical and cultural contexts, such as the practices of abandoning the aged known as the 'abandonment of the seventy' in the Ballad of Narayama or the well known words of Cicero:

> To be applauded, an actor doesn't have need to act in the whole play; it is enough that he pleases in any act that he appears, in the same way that a wise person doesn't have to stay on stage until the final fall of the curtain (Cicero 1928: 110).

I understand that a comparative approach will allow us to accumulate information for a more ample reflection on the problems of aging. For example, those problems implied in the recent statement that the growing number of seniors in our own society represents more a mass of the aged than an elite of elders (Erikson 1990: 11).

Returning to the cultural context of the Bantu, we can say that everything happens in the narratives as if the elder prepares to transcend his own condition and reach that of ancestor. As I suggested previously, the beginning of seniority is a becoming, whose final-end and source of meaning is ancestrality.

The crisis of authority by senior citizens in post-figurative societies, in the terminology of Margaret Mead (Mead 1979), is present in a generalized way in all cultures. This process has been developing throughout the most varied areas of the African continent for some time. On the other hand, power, as always related to legitimacy linked to ancestrality, makes possible that the internal conditions of resistance are present in Black-African society. However, the sources of interference are not always as direct as political oppression, e.g. a colonial system. Currently, it seems that these societies are going in the direction of transforming themselves into co-figurative units (Mead 1979), with clear changes in their value structures. In this process, the age groups have an important role, for upon them depends the passage from authority linked to the 'family' and seniority to that authority linked to the larger social group beyond the 'family'. For this reason, the aging crisis can become particularly significant in the contemporary Black-African context.

There is still another important aspect to be analyzed: the relationship of age dynamics with kinship ties. In theoretical terms, according to the model of S.N. Eisenstadt, age groups would have a linking function; it is up to them to extend family solidarity to the whole of society (Eisenstadt 1956: 50). Even so, this passage implies a transcendence of the restrictions that the family itself imposes, impeding the full development of its members until adulthood, which does not happen without conflict. The discourse that I have outlined, based on particular narratives, shows that in the Black-African case this function is exercised through the materialization of a social conscience, where age and family questions are only aspects of wider relationships between the world of the living and that of the dead. These questions show that generational position and seniority are manifestations of deeper links to the principle of ancestrality. This is a theoretical problem for which the discourse contained in the narratives offers us a quite consistent interpretation and which certainly expresses much of what those societies have accumulated in terms of knowledge about the life cycle.

I conclude, therefore, that in the Black-African societies seniority is part of the particularities of political and kinship structures. It is in this way that the elder is at the same time a representative of an age group, of a lineage, of seniority and of ancestry. He is multiple as the link in the chain of descendants and also as the link with the world of the ancestors.

Finally, it should be emphasized that this work is limited to narrative analysis and that more detailed field studies are still needed for a more complete understanding of the aging process. Thus, my contribution resides in the selection of material for amplifying the inventory that will allow the development of a further comparative knowledge of Bantu-speaking societies.

ACKNOWLEDGMENTS

Many thanks are due to Esther Jean Langdon and Ierecê Lucena Rosa for the translation of the text.

Notes

1. This work is part of my Ph.D. thesis entitled *Aldeias de jovens: a passagem do mundo do parentesco ao universo da política em sociedades banto-falantes* (Young boys' villages: the passage from the kinship world to the universe of politics in Bantu-speaking societies, Rifiotis 1994). An earlier version of this work can be found in Rifiotis (1998).

2. I specifically dealt with narratives produced by the Makonde (Mozambique), Mbala (Democratic Republic of Congo), Tumbuka-Kamanga (Malawi), Tshokwe (Angola) and Luba (Democratic Republic of Congo).

3. Guerreiro, Manuel Viegas. 1966. *Os Macondes de Moçambique. Sabedoria, língua, literatura e jogos.* vol.4. Lisboa: J.I.U., 249-252.

4. Mudindaambi, L. 1972. *Mange ces dents! Mythes mbala 1.* Bandundu: CEEBA Publications, 186-191.

5. Young, T.C. 1931. *Notes on the Customs and Folk-lore of the Tumbuka-Kamanga peoples.* Livingstonia: The Mission Press, 242-247.

6. Barbosa, A. 1973. *Folclore angolano. Cinqüenta contos quiocos.* Luanda: Instituto de Investigações Científicas de Angola, 144-145.

7. Kazadi, N. & Ifwanga, wa P. 1984. *Contes luba et kongo du Zaire.* Paris: Edicef, 144-189.

8. Bouveignes, O. de. 1938. *Entendu dans la brousse: contes congolais.* Paris: Librairie Orientaliste Paul Geuthner, 5.

9. In structural analysis, the 'cardinal function' corresponds to the narrative sequence that promotes the progression of the report. On the other hand, what is called a 'catalyst function' is a concentration of elements that allows movement in the narrative. For instance, in the 'Molenda' narrative the refusal by the youngsters to obey the elders and do the work that the latter demand is equivalent to a catalysis function, as it amplifies the youngsters' dissatisfaction with the life organized by the elders.

10. The only reference to the father occurs in the narratives of the Luba, a patrilineal ethnic group. The remaining narratives come from matrilineal societies, in which the maternal-uncle becomes the socially important figure.

11. This test functions as an enigma, i. e., the truth cannot be immediately revealed. As shown in Rifiotis (1994), the solution to the problem perhaps can be associated to the narrative of Oedipus.

12. Traditionally, for the Tshokwe, one of the qualities a chief must possess is to be a good hunter (Lima 1971); this quality is not shown by the chief of the young boys' village, for he is taken prisoner by the snake.

13. It is only in the Luba variant, in which the marriage of the chief is discussed, that another enigma is proposed - the request that the spring water be transported in a smoke basket as a condition for the marriage.

14. This kind of threat occurs in an even more generalized manner during succession, when a new lineage chief is chosen or a new village is formed. Age differentiation is amplified through the

contact with the ancestors and the knowledge of various 'remedies', the latter term meaning both 'medicine' and 'poison'.

15. In this sense I follow F. Leite's notion that elderliness possesses an ancestral dimension. (Leite 1982).

16. Regicide represents an attempt to socially control life and death, symbolized by control of the king's life. In symbolic terms, this equivalence may also be meaningful to the local chief or even to the elder, when the forms of social organization privilege the local power instead of the central power, as in the cases of the monarchic states (Rifiotis 1996).

17. This mythical narrative is associated to the narrative '*Kalala Ilunga*' and the foundation of Luba royalty. In this tradition, *Kalala Ilunga* kills his maternal-uncle, *Nkongolo*, a drunk and incestuous king, and introduces new principles for the king's succession associated to possession of the sacred drum.

18. A man would be responsible for producing a new village, and he would be a kind of pivot of the village; upon his death, the unity of the village could indeed be broken. According to J. Vansina, to the Lunda these villages were created by '[...] ambitious individuals who are surrounded by all sorts of relatives' (Vansina 1965: 24).

19. Oral communication by Professor Jacqueline Eberhardt-Roumeguère, Paris, 1991.

20. What we call 'appropriate' is tied to a founding gesture that will inspire the subsequent ones; this is the case of the *Nommo*, which removes all femininity from the men via circumcision. The removed foreskin will be transformed into an animal 'which is classified as snakes are' (Griaule 1966: 20).

21. This takes us to the complex symbolism of fertilization tied to the snake. According to J.Roumeguère-Erberhardt, the *Venda* (Trasvaal) have chosen it as the center of their cults. The *Domba* is a well-known initiation dance of the *Venda*, which simulates the great snake of creation. According to L. Heusch, a snake that vomits the creation is found among the Kuba. Among the *Venda* the snakes control the reproduction and the vital cycles, for they are tied to the discovery of sexuality and to the passage to puberty (Roumeguère-Eberhardt 1986).

22. As a symbol, the wise elder approaches the figure of the king, and is associated with the idea of renewal (Rifiotis 1996).

References

Barbosa, A. 1973. Fo*clore angolano. Cinqüenta contos quiocos.* Luanda: Instituto de Investigações Científicas de Angola.

Baumann, H. & D. Westermann. 1948. *Les peuples et les Civilisations de l'Afrique; suivi de Les Langues et l'Éducation.* Paris: Payot.

Bouveignes, O. 1938. *Entendu dans la brousse: contes congolais.* Paris: Librairie Orientaliste Paul Geuthner.

Calame-Griaule, G. 1965. *Ethnologie et langage. La parole chez les Dogons.* Paris: Gallimard.

Cicero. 1928. *Dialogue sur la viellesse.* Paris: Librairie Hachette.

Eisenstadt, S.N. 1956. *From Generation to Generation: Age Groups and Social Structure.* London: Routledge and Kegan Paul.

Erikson E.H. 1990. *El ciclo vital completado.* Buenos Aires and México: Editorial Paidos.

Griaule, M.1966. *Dieu d'Eau. Entretiens avec Ogotemmêli.* Paris: Fayard.

Guerreiro, M.V. 1966.*Os Macondes de Moçambique. Sabedoria, língua, literatura e jogos.* vol.4. Lisboa: J.I.U.

Heusch, L. de.1982. *Rois nés d'un coeur de vache.* Paris: Gallimard.

Hochegger, H. 1975. *Le Soleil ne se leva plus! Le conflit social dans les mythes buma.* Bandundu: CEEBA Publications.

Kazadi, N. & IFWANGA, wa P. 1984. *Contes luba et kongo du Zaire.* Paris: Edicef.

Leite, F. 1982. *A Questão Ancestral. Notas sobre ancestrais e intituições ancestrais em sociedades africanas: Ioruba, Agni e Senufo.* São Paulo: USP (Tese de Doutoramento).

Lima, M. 1971. *Fonction sociologique des figures de culte Hamba dans la société et dans la culture Tshokwé (Angola).* Luanda: Instituto de Investigação Científica de Angola.

Mead, M. 1979. Le Fossé des générations. Les nouvelles relations entre les générations dans les années 70. Paris: Denöel/Gonthier.

Mudindaambi, L. 1972. Mange ces dents! Mythes mbala 1. Bandundu: CEEBA Publications.

Paulme, D. & Seydou, Ch. 1972. 'Le conte des 'Alliés animaux', dans l'Ouest Africain', *Cahiers d'Études Africaines* 12: 76-108.

Rifiotis, T. 1994. *Aldeias de jovens: a passagem do mundo do parentesco ao universo da política em sociedades banto-falantes. Abordagem sócio-antropológica da dinâmica dos grupos etários através de estudo da literatura oral.* São Paulo: USP (Tese de Doutoramento).

————. 1995. 'Grupos etários e conflito de gerações: bases antropológicas para um diálogo interdisciplinar', *Revista Política & Trabalho* 11: 105-123.

————. 1996. 'Pourquoi le tuer? Uma revisão teórica do regicídio em sociedade negro-africanas', *África: Revista do Centro de Estudos Africanos da USP* 18-19: 213-229.

————. 1998. 'O Ciclo vital completado: a dinâmica dos sistemas etários em sociedades negro-africanas', In BARROS, M.M.L., ed., *Velhice ou terceira idade? Estudos antropológicos sobre identidade, memória e política*. Rio de Janeiro: Fundação Getúlio Vargas, 85-110.

Roumeguere-Erberhardt, J. 1986. 'La notion de vie, base de la structure sociale venda', in *Pensée et Société africaines: Essais sur une dialectique de complémentarité antagoniste chez les Bantu du Sud-Est*. Paris: Publisud.

Vansina, J. 1965. *Introduction à l'ethonographie du congo*. Kinshasa and Bruxelas: Éditions Universitaires du Congo.

Vincent, J.-F. 1976. 'Conception et déroulement du sacrifice chez les Moufu', in *Systèmes de pensée en Afrique Noire* (Le sacrifice I). Paris: CHRS.

Wagner, G. 1981. 'A organização política dos povos bantos', in Fortes, M. & Evans-Pritchard, E.E, *Sistemas políticos africanos*. Lisboa: Calouste Gulbenkian.

Young, T.C. 1931. *Notes on the Customs and Folk-lore of the Tumbuka-Kamanga Peoples*. Livingstonia: The Mission Press.

Zahan, D. 1960. Les sociétés d'initiation Bambara. Le N'Domo, Le Kore. Paris: Mouton.

Chapter 9

GENEALOGY AND THE ARTIST'S ARCHIVE: STRATEGIES OF AUTOBIOGRAPHY AND DOCUMENTATION IN THE WORK OF A SOUTH AFRICAN ARTIST

Jennifer A. Law

These are the soul's changes. I don't believe in aging. I believe in forever altering one's aspect to the sun. Hence my optimism.
-- Virginia Woolf. *The Diary of Virginia Woolf, vol. 4 (ed. by Anne O. Bell, 1982),* entry for 2 October 1932.

Every passion borders on the chaotic, but the collector's passion borders on the chaos of memories.
-- Walter Benjamin. 'Unpacking My Library: A Talk About Book Collecting', *Illuminations.* 1999 (first pub. 1955).

CHAOS THEORY

[T]here is in the life of the collector a dialectical tension between the poles of disorder and order. Naturally, his existence is tied to many other things as well: to a very mysterious relationship to ownership ...; also, to a relationship to objects which does not emphasize their functional, utilitarian value — that is, their usefulness — but studies and loves them as the scene, the stage, of their fate. The most profound enchantment for the collector is the locking of individual items within a magic circle in which they are fixed as the final thrill, the thrill of acquisition, passes over them. Everything remembered and thought, everything conscious, becomes the pedestal, the frame, the base, the lock of his property. The period, the region, the craftsmanship, the former ownership

— for a true collector the whole background of an item adds up to a magic encyclopedia whose quintessence is the fate of his object. In this circumscribed area, then, it may be surmised how the great physiognomists — and collectors are the physiognomists of the world of objects — turn into the interpreters of fate. One has only to watch a collector handle the objects in his glass case. As he holds them in his hands, he seems to be seeing through them into their distant past as though inspired. So much for the magical side of the collector — his old-age image, I might call it (Benjamin 1999: 62).

I distinctly remember the first time I entered the Johannesburg home of South African artist, Penny Siopis. It was the 22nd of February 1996. The exuberance of objects startled me. Every square inch emerges either occupied — or waiting to be so. As one enters, a table looms at the doorway, a make-shift mountain of accumulation, spilling photographs, slides, randomly assembled books and papers, the odd religious icon, a stray piece of jewelry... A glass-doored cabinet of idolatry stands loudly behind, spewing false gods — blazing heart Christs, multi-limbed Ganesh, the occasional virgin, cerulean Krishnas. A post-modern altar to religious hybridity. The walls are green, blue, pink, red, exhibiting a private, rotating gallery of the artist's work. Moving cautiously toward the living room, one hesitates over things extant, looming object-tricksters sneaking imperceptibly inwards. A Moroccan footstool conceals itself under a blanket of texts, while a halved gargantuan coconut shell languishes to the side, flashing its bearded bottom at the visitor-voyeur. Several severed seraph's heads, macabre souvenirs of the tomb, improvise an interim mausoleum on the floor. These fallen angels are accompanied by the odd stony limb, a proverbial lost sheep... The skeptic is easily converted to animism.

On the electric hearth, thirteen plaster sheep —each a faithful replica of the one before — graze the alloy surface. The fireplace itself is stuccoed with a profusion of plastic knickknacks gessoed white: synthetic flowers, sea-shells, diminutive dinosaurs and savannah beasts, cupie dolls, an intermittent troll... The child's treasure trove assembled by the artist and her young son, epoxied into a simulacraed heaven of ossified kitsch turned decor. To the left of the hearth towers a glass case in the style of a 19th Century museum cabinet. Pushing seven feet with no shelves, it displays a single box on its bottom surface, atop of which is perched a faded brown felt doll modeling a grass skirt — an ethnographic gift from the past. Once a complimentary mass-produced souvenir to 1930s cruise-liner passengers en route to Africa from Europe, she is now alone and land-bound in her glass-house: the commodity turned anomaly. She slumps to the side; a dead-ringer for Josephine Baker with pearly shell teeth and bona fide human hair, coifed in the preferred fashion of flappers. She has a beautiful smile.

There is a schizophrenic wall in the kitchen which sports several plaster guises — a fisherman, a geisha — while the fridge hosts magnet cutouts of Mandela and Michaelangelo's David respectively in their skivvies, their 2-D magnet wardrobes spread out around them. Next door, the azure bathroom triumphantly boasts a plaster inauguration notice for the new democratic president, ostentatiously pigmented and boldly proclaiming 'God bless South Africa'.

The things stretch out like object-tentacles, invading every space and surface. As Beckett might have said, everything oozes. Such is the artist's cabinet of curiosities. The home as intimate memorial; a private archive of desire coveting the anomaly and cheekily indulging the copy. Some, accustomed to the tamed domestic surfaces of modern commodity fetishism — every dutifully conscripted, polished center-piece catalogued, arranged and reverently dusted on pine counter-tops and white-washed walls — might shift nervously as they enter. There is no sequence here, no center, no place to anchor the gaze. The objects, undisciplined, boast clutter. They reek of havoc. Yet to the collector, the scene exudes a comforting and familiar chaos between 'the poles of disorder and order'. A chaos which stands as testament to a life still living. There is no segregation between art and its artifact. Penny's is a collection that is not exiled to the shelf, but is freed to the *tableau vivant*, released to the colloquial to be dwelled within. I have long been awed by the ease with which she slips through the material world as if it were an organic extension of her very limbs. Objects slip through fingers like nectar, sticking softly to skin in traces; pollen on furry bee-legs. A true lover of things, she is at ease as a keeper walking through a swarm. Things stray, scatter, teem; seeping from hairline cracks in the domestic veneer. Through the object trace, the artist's biography lies fragmented before us, waiting assembly. The room, the life, is practically bursting at the seams. She lives within the baroque texture of the vernacular laid bare.

I have since returned to Penny's home several times. I have even lived as a guest amongst these things for varying periods. Gifts, artifacts, heirlooms, curios, kitsch... Objects of fascination and necessity. All of necessity. I have witnessed them rotate, mutate, be replaced, conceal themselves and peak out from their respective perches. They don't rest. Like the artist, they seem constantly on the verge of flight. Some things are carefully hoarded, ostentatiously coveted and displayed, while others fade to the background in neglect. Some die. Several migrate, while others wither under dust. More than occasionally they disappear, or leave of their own accord. But few are thrown away. The still-life performance is indeed never still. Claustrophobia sneaks up from behind, and one feels under constant siege and threat of suffocation. So I hover, the anthropologist, Benjamin's physiognomist, at the corners — it is the only available space — struck by 'the most profound enchantment'.

PORTRAIT OF THE ARTIST AND HER OBJECTS

Penny Siopis is one of South Africa's foremost artists — and, it would seem to some, collectors. She has had a celebrated career. During the 1980s, she played a leading role as a so-called 'struggle' artist under Apartheid and continues to create work that addresses questions of race, sexuality, post-coloniality, and nationalism within the current democratic dispensation. Her significance as an artist is matched only by her importance as a teacher. A professor in the Department of Fine Art at the University of the Witwatersrand, her influence has been profound, perhaps most clearly felt in the work of a younger generation of artists (particularly women artists). Her work continues to inspire both secondary school art projects and university level research. In addition to making a significant contribution to South African contemporary art and criticism over the past two decades, she is rapidly gaining international acclaim within a global artistic community.

The main motivation for this chapter, however, is not to continue along the lines of conventional biography or anthropo-logical life history as such, but rather to explore the ways in which biography and autobiography may lend itself to a form of documentation which is 'counter'-, if not quite 'anti'-, chronological. That is, I wish to exploit a form of biographical journal-ism which operates like memory itself. In this, biography emerges as a process that necessarily resists an ordered telling neatly unfolding in uni-lineal sequence. I have long been suspicious of auto/biography for its sneaky inclination toward tidying and containing that which is by nature simultaneous, duplicitous, and messy. Memory does not unfold in neat sequence. It flashes, leaks, catches unaware. It hits, tears through, approaches softly and storms loudly. It comes in waves. It does not respect chronology. It is always triggered — a smell, a sound, a touch, an object — and as such its arrival remains necessarily unpredictable, haphazard even. One may go to retrace steps to the past, and find the route blocked, the 'key' lost. Indeed the route is rarely the same; the key always slippery. To the individual, life of coarse unfolds temporally — moment by moment. But a life is never recalled in its entirety. Complicate this a million fold with the collective remembrance. A million keys turning in a million locks. The lineal trace turns suddenly lateral.

In the artist's life, the personal memoir is complicated, if also complimented, by material history. The object surfaces as *aide-memoire*, provoking return, calling up the past, while alternately posing between artifact and *objet d'art*, between the pragmatic and the sentimental. The object, in this respect, has its own biography that plays itself out in relation to, yet mutually exclusive of, that of the collector, emerging from within a moral economy of which the possessor herself subscribes. Things circulate, are exchanged, move in and out of typologies, are auctioned, coveted, worshipped, discarded, replaced, excavated, rediscovered, and transformed. Those who survive, have quite a tale to tell — if one cares to listen.

Within this project of object-divination (which extends well beyond the bounds of this text), I knowingly, and somewhat uncomfortably, hover between the worlds of anthropology and art criticism. The object-methods of both make me wary. Anthropologists — acclaimed recorders of genealogies and celebrated illustrators of kinship diagrams — have long recognized the biographic potential of object-divining. Indeed, the ethnographic tradition of recording object genealogies stems at least as far back as 1910, when W. H. R. Rivers in his article, 'The genealogical method of anthropological inquiry' proposed compiling a biography of artifacts which traced object-lineage through ownership, and in so doing could be used to pursue the social structure through generational-time, and one would assume, space (see also Kopytoff 1986: 66). Certainly there have been some infamous documentors of the ethnographic object — Pitt Rivers, Franz Boas, Emil Torday, and Herbert Lang, some of the more distinguished among their ranks — who have bequeathed their collections to the posterity (and shelves) of the discipline. More recently, Arjun Appadurai and Igor Kopytoff have picked up where other great anthropological object-chroniclers have left off (refer to Appadurai 1986). In his invaluable essay 'The cultural biography of things: commoditization as process', Kopytoff argues that compiling a biography of an object is much like anthologizing one of the individual. He even sets out a set of guidelines for the novice approaching the object informant:

> In doing the biography of a thing, one would ask questions similar to those one asks about people: What sociologically, are the biographical possibilities inherent in its 'status' and in the period and culture, and how are these possibilities realized? Where does the thing come from and who made it? What has been its career so far, and what do people consider to be an ideal career for such things? What are the recognized 'ages' or periods in the things 'life', and what are the cultural markers for them? How does

the thing's use change with its age, and what happens
to it when it reaches the end of its usefulness? ...

Biographies of things can make salient what might
otherwise remain obscure (1986: 66-7).

What appears straight forward enough in theory, however,
becomes increasingly complex in practice — i.e. when one actually begins to 'interview' the thing. Objects afterall, as Martin
Hall has effectively noted, have an uncanny aptitude for polyva-
lency. That is, as Hall explains, the object's 'ability to mean different things to different people at the same time' (1998: 189). Add
to this the debates between art versus artifact, the ethnographic
versus the aesthetic, and it becomes increasingly difficult to tell
which of the object's ends is up.

Traditionally, anthropology has so often cast the object as
mere ethnographic prop to social action, the evidence of production, container, commodity, material culture, the raw substance
of thick description, the evidence-debris — if not exactly 'mirror'
— of social life, the threads of moral fabric. In contrast, the art
critic fetishes the object to the point of idolatry; the aesthetic
emerges for its 'own sake' and the object is introduced as protagonist. To the anthropologist, the object speaks through ventriloquism — it lies. To the art critic, the object evangelizes; it
speaks only Truth. I do not have to be converted to the cult of
the object; I am already a confirmed collector, a 'vase tickler',[1] a
diviner. What I desire as a researcher of the material world is to
find a means of speaking the experience — the affect — of the
object which does not reduce the material to mere 'container'
of meaning, yet neither does it succumb to an aesthetic which
elevates the object to the level of the transcendent. While I agree
with Alfred Gell that the anthropology of art 'ought to be about'
art-making itself [i.e. part of the process thereof] (1996: 37)
— I do not agree that the anthropologist need be an aesthetic
atheist in order to understand the object of her study. That is,
in Gell's words, 'without succumbing to the fascination which
all well-made art objects exert on the mind attuned to their
aesthetic properties' (1992: 42). Indeed, if we fail to succumb
to that curious fascination, that profound enchantment, we fail

to do little more than offer a 'thick description' of the object of our study. We fail, despite Gell's own caution in this regard, to cast the object as little more than social prop. The anthropologist who practices 'methodological atheism' in the study of religion, for analogous example, does little more than *describe* and 'unpick' the processes of worship and the 'rationality' of belief systems. This does little to represent, nay reproduce the experience of faith. It is that experience which I wish to speak to. It is not so much a project of conversion as a hermeneutic proposition. It is about seeking out that middle ground between utility and transcendence, for it is there that the artist is at home.

Thus, through revisiting the object-world of this influential South African artist, I aim to examine the complexity of a specific art practice both in its own terms and as part of a larger social framework. In this way, I hope to raise important questions concerning the relationship between art and civil society which include examining the shift from 'traditional' art media to installation and technology, raising questions around identity (race, gender, sexuality, ethnicity, age, etc.) and biography, and exploring the recording of collective and individual, public and private histories and memory within a culture of truth-seeking. Certainly, Penny's work over the past two decades may be seen as broadly paradigmatic of important moments or shifts in recent social history and the development of the visual arts in South Africa. As Kopytoff remarks in the tradition of Margaret Mead: 'one way to understand a culture is to see what sort of biography it regards as embodying a successful social career' (1986: 66).

Finally, and importantly as regards this volume, if 'age' may be understood as a means of marking time and the stages of transformation in an individual's life, then I am interested not only in the ways in which the artist's work over the past twenty years reflects changes within socio-political circumstance and ideology, but likewise aim to explore the ways in which the artist's collection of *objets trouvés,* the paradigmatic *aides memoire*, have transformed over the years. In reflecting upon the aging object, we may come to understand the ways in which such things may be used (post-Rivers) to trace a genealogy of desire. Indeed, Penny's recent practice has increasingly turned overtly and self-consciously toward strategies of autobiography and documentation via the object-trace as a means of recording (the self's) life history. In so doing, the artist engages and critiques private and public histories while simultaneously staking out originary claims of legitimacy and 'belonging' as a white South African.

PSYCHOSIS

In the wake of the Truth and Reconciliation Commission (TRC) hearings which began in 1996 and recently drew to a close at the end of 1998, there has emerged a public culture which encourages the individual to add personal testimony to historical chronicle and in so doing legitimize the subjective account. In the words of Emerson, biography is 'nothing less than the miniature paraphrase of the hundred volumes of the Universal History' (1995: 161). Through autobiography the intimate remembrances of vernacular experience may be simultaneously mourned and reclaimed, documented and written back into history. In the light of the TRC, autobiography may be viewed as a therapeutic means of healing. As Italo Calvino writes, 'biographical data, even those recorded in the public registers, are the most private things one has, and to declare them openly is rather like facing a psychoanalyst' (1997).

Since 1994, there has been a marked shift toward the autobiographical in South African art and literature which has prompted several observers to discuss this recent trend in relation to strategies of collective and personal healing and catharsis (refer to Nuttall and Coetzee 1998). Such a shift is evidenced by publications like Mandela's *Long Walk to Freedom* (1994), ex-warder James Gregory's *Goodbye Bafana: Nelson Mandela, My Prisoner, My Friend* (1995), Black Consciousness leader Stephen Biko's lover Mamphela Ramphele's *A Life* (1995), amongst others. In addition to these 'factual' autobiographies there are likewise a number of semi-fictionalized personal accounts recently published such as J.M. Coetzee's *Boyhood* (1997), Antjie Krog's *Country of My Skull* (1998), and Breyten Breytenbach's *Dog Heart* (1999). In all of these texts, the political is overtly underwritten by the personal. Visual art has similarly become increasingly autobiographical and candidly confessional. There is a level at which art and literature, of course, is always autobiographical. And yet there has been a discernible shift in South African art of late which witnesses a form of image-making which has settled more easily upon an indulgently reflective self.

I have discussed in depth elsewhere the ways in which a desire for (democratic) normalcy in South Africa has found expression in a form of auto/biography. Thus, in seeking to purge a sense of loss, it finds fulfillment in the mundane details of the everyday, thus marking a recovery of the 'ordinary' and the restitution of the individual in a society where personal desire was held hostage under Apartheid to political objectives and responsibility (Law, forthcoming). I wrote at that time that I was interested 'in exploring, through the work of two artists [one of whom was Penny], the ways in which the vernacular has moved from the periphery to the center of contemporary art practice, and how processes of restoration inevitably involve the reinstatement of the personal in the aim of recovering dignity or right' (*ibid.*). In this I noted that '[i]t is imperative to remember that recovery implies a return to an original site of loss' (*ibid.*). I am, of course, still interested in such an exploration, and for the purposes of this current project on auto/biography, I would like to pick up the investigation at that aforementioned point of loss. In this instance, I wish to concentrate on the dispossession of the 'fulfilled' self; a self that has matured within an ailing state, and in so evolving has come to imagine itself diseased.

MELANCHOLIA

During the states of Emergency in South Africa, in the mid- to late eighties, the protagonist of Penny's work emerged as the image of psychosis personified. That is, a representation of an embodied (generally psychic) disorder which comes to represent the impaired self. Lack, in this instance, surfaces as a diminished sense of feeling complete, whole, and/or 'normal'. Thus in 1986, at the height of civil unrest in South Africa, Penny painted a vision of colonialism in decline and called it *Melancholia*. The year was significant in that it saw the pass laws repealed, a nationwide state of emergency declared, the silencing of the media through censorship controls, the beginnings of violent conflict in

Kwa-Zulu Natal, and Anti-Apartheid legislation passed abroad. The scene that she has depicted invites us into a sumptuous and unmistakably European banquet hall, whose sharpened perspective stretches taut into the far distance. A feast has been laid out for our consumption, moments ago perhaps, but there are hints that it has been prepared for hours that it has been waiting for us indefinitely. Slices of exotic fruit sprawl out onto platters, spill over the edges of tables, threaten to erupt out of the boundaries of the frame. There is more than we can eat here. It is a feast for hundreds, thousands perhaps. The parameters of the room extend indefinitely. There are sweetmeats, melons, cassavas, bananas, nuts, crustaceans, candies, cakes and pastries. Gastronomical edibles intermingle with exotica (a monkey, an empty tortoise shell, porcupine needles, tropical flowers) and hedonistic statuary from classical antiquity and the European High Renaissance. These icons refer to a 'Golden Age', past eras of heroic civilization and the triumph of culture over nature. Statuary stand or recline in repose; their posture marks leisure. Labour is implicit, however, in the yielding of the produce on the tables, the laying out of the feast, and in the artist's assiduous layering of paint. But it is labor disguised. Any successful staging, however intricate and abstruse, grants the illusion of ease. In the right foreground, Michaelangelo's *Slave* sensuously peels back his garment, coyly and surreptitiously implying the erotics of oppression; the slave as object of desire. These are items that speak of luxury, surplus and excess. They insinuate flippant decadence and waste. Their acidic colour is that of full ripeness threatening decline. There is a suggestion of decay.

There is a slow urgency to this scene. An hourglass in the right foreground teeters precariously on the edge of a table, methodically dripping sand, grain by grain, marking progress (or descent). From the shadows we can discern that the light is one of late afternoon, dusk perhaps, a time of decline and setting, a moment of between: Twilight. Time and its passage are irreversible. Anticipation is tacit but indeterminate as to its object. The room is empty in its fullness. In this, in all its desire spread before us on the table, there is absence. Lack persists. As Ernst Bloch writes of utopia, there is melancholy in fulfillment (1993: 2).

Still life has remained a constant motif in Siopis' work from early on, often serving to juxtapose and unify objects of Africa with those of European association. This banquet scene, like much of her work, is baroque, heavily ornate, and extravagant. It is weighted down by profusion and bears the burden of the senses. Objects appear precariously crammed into the frame, balanced and leaning against one another, spilling out and gluttonously brimming over edges. All senses are invoked: the heavy odor of ripe, exotic fruit and flowers in full-bloom, the cacophony of a banquet and of celebration slowly silenced. Echoes linger in a long hall. The doubled weight and flocculent caress of heavy, velvet curtains frame the translucent skins of fruit and alabaster flesh. Ephemerality is pitted against permanence. The seduction of thick oil applied to canvas, decadent in its application, becomes a richly tactile surface demanding touch. Whether in painting or in her more recent installation work, objects are used in a corresponding way: to incite desire, to test the subtle boundary between object-comfort and aesthetic claustrophobia, and to seduce the senses while taunting saturation.

Inspired by Dutch seventeenth century still life paintings, such images celebrate the mundane. The domestic object of the everyday, of home, merges with the exotic curio of the foreign. Similarly and relatedly, the authenticity of the object is brought into question, as the real and illusion are blurred. Boundaries fold and confuse, moving in and through one another. These are scenes of contradiction, of instability and contestation. They hint at transcendence, yet they remain illusory and out of reach. There is a conscious connection to the *Vanitas* paintings of Calvinist Holland, heavily burdened by symbolism, where the meaning of precious objects 'piled up like so much rubbish' may be recognized by the viewer (Martin 1971: 136). They solicit contemplation. As John Rupert Martin explains of the Dutch Baroque:

> The secret of many a seventeenth-century still life painting lay in the fact that it offered the observer a stimulating and life-enriching illusion of reality, while at the same time inviting him — paradoxically — to reflect on the brevity of man's existence and the insubstantiality of all worldly things (*ibid.*: 134).

Thus, the artist-collector invites us to gorge ourselves on the 'vain trappings of worldly rank and power' (*ibid*: 136). She partakes in the feast herself. As was occasionally the convention of Dutch still-life painters, the artist positions herself in the far right-hand middle ground of the scene. This image may be a mirrored reflection, or a simulacrum in stone. Regardless there are other tenuous references to both her location in the present and to the tradition and inheritance of identity which grounds her, perhaps even freezes her for the moment, in her ancestral past. Penny, a third generation South African, is of Greek decent, and she stands amongst and blends in with the Greek classical statuary which surround her. There is recognition of complicity, but hers is an absent presence that personifies lack. In an interview I conducted with her in September 1996, Penny reflected upon her feelings of thwarted confidence which she maintains many South Africans felt in relation to making legitimate claims of 'belonging' and identity under Apartheid. This insecurity has subsequently translated into what is often articulated as a sense of loss and mourning in the present for something that remains unclear and indefinable. Penny explains:

> South Africans just feel a sense of loss. I think it's definitely because they haven't been able to have a sense of history before, because their sense of history was always marked as political and contested. And that in itself didn't allow people, or 'allow' is the wrong word, it didn't *facilitate* people to feel, in the sense of identity. Dispossession usually comes with a sense of either a loss of identity or of not ever being able to have had an identity. It is a sense of mourning for something that actually never was, but *should* have been (personal communication, 6 September 1996).

The senses here are expanded to include that which is often taken for granted — a sense of home, a security of knowing where one belongs and how one is defined. In *Melancholia*, Penny invents such an identity by surrounding herself with history through European monuments and material culture. But it remains an empty affiliation; an attachment maintained tentatively through inheritance. In this respect, hers is an identity inherited but not owned. There is a self-reflexive cynicism here and a critique of the then current Apartheid regime in decline. The past and present are evident, but the future hesitates at the edges, lurking in slow and uncertain anticipation. *Melancholia* pictures a moment of unsettled anticipation. There is the conviction of an inevitable ending, but uncertainty as to the precise moment and means of its arrival. While many people, including Penny's husband and fellow artist, Colin Richards, described a (past) knowledge that Apartheid 'would end but not in our lifetimes' (*ibid.*). Penny remained somewhat more optimistic. She was active in student resistance movements and following her university days took an operative stance against the regime through her image making. She reflects back on how she viewed the situation thus:

> I felt that there would be some sort of revolution, maybe because I was active in student politics... We had a revolutionary spirit about us. And although it might have just been student idealism, I certainly had the sense that the old government would be overthrown. I mean I absolutely had that sense about it. The thing is, however, the time period was another issue (*ibid.*).

In *Melancholia*, there are no guarantees or cure-all solutions, but hope continues to bide its time in a glimmer on the margins.

PATIENCE

Through the late 1980s, Penny continued to explore issues around heritage, memorialization, and identity. *Patience on a Monument — 'A History Painting'*, depicts a black woman, as loosely robed as a Greek statue, one breast exposed, perched serenely on top of a mountain of objects-in-refuse. She is the allegorical representation of Africa, based on the sculpture of Nubia in the Musee d'Orsay in Paris (Rankin 1992: 5). Scenes of colonization envelope her. Yet she sits stoically, almost obliviously, idly peeling a lemon, her fingers pressing into its sour, citric flesh. Her feet sink into the excess — objects of *Vanitas* discarded in the pile: a skull, a pair of spectacles, fruit peelings, books, an hourglass, the edge of a canvassed-frame blending with truncated figures, a squatting decapitated body, an organic heart torn from its cavity. There is a quiet violence about this assemblage. History accumulates around the monument-mountain extending infinitely into the distant landscape. The figures of this narrative seem to be moving in an embroiled chaotic procession, lacking order, superimposed on top of one another through repetitive facsimiles over-traced with paint. The baroque quality of Penny's earlier work is transfigured onto the landscape — the 'objects' have become bodies, but they continue to amass, over-spill, and press against each other and their frame. Interior surplus is here exteriorized. No figure, save for Patience herself, takes obvious precedence over any other — British soldiers, Zulu warriors, Bushman slaves, Voortrekker laagers, all fuse into a discordant pattern of events. It is a memorialization of all and therefore nothing. History becomes waste. Patience, personifying a calm endurance of hardship, provocation, pain and delay, withstands. She is heroic in her domesticity and composed in her perseverance. As an emblem of endurance, Patience *is* the monument, perched precariously on an accumulation threatening collapse. She seems to possess an extraordinary capacity for calm, self-possessed waiting.

This series of paintings, exemplified by works like *Patience On a Monument*, root themselves firmly in the art historical tradition of 'history painting'. Throughout the eighteenth and nineteenth centuries, such paintings were intended to be monumental in their breadth of subject matter, dealing with moments of heroic triumph and generally commissioned and/ or authorized by the state to celebrate and legitimize its governance. They grant the illusion of objectivity by fixing history in a permanent, frozen pictorial guise. The characters are generally arranged in a grand and heroic setting, and stand as evidence of history by their mere presence on the stage. Penny's series is built upon this narrative tradition, yet uses the very language of the state to invert and challenge its edified perspective. In such works, allegorical markers of colonial conquest and the triumph of civilization litter the canvas, overlapping and crowding one another, competing for space, slipping into decay like so much waste. So, while *Melancholia* comes to imitate historical waste through the accumulation of heavily applied paint to surface, later works begin to incorporate the material in a much more immediate way. By 1988, the surface itself succumbs to a more literal strategy of accumulation. Increasingly, practice comes to mimic content. In *Patience On a Monument*, for instance, images are gleaned from history books, photocopied, and pasted directly on the surface in layers to become the foundations, the ground, of the landscape imaginary. The detritus of simulacra overwhelms. Atop the mountain of debris sits the black female body, Patience in waiting, engrossed in the domestic, mundane task of peeling a lemon. The bitter fruit of history laid open. Tradition is used against itself. Penny explains:

> I work within the tradition of Western painting in ways which attempt to turn its own values against itself, to show that it is not only the representation of politics that is an issue, but the politics of representation as well (Williamson 1989: 22).

HYSTERIA

We have witnessed *Melancholia* give way to resigned *Patience* which in turn succumbs to *Hysteria*. In *Dora and the Other Woman*, also from 1998, Penny invites the historical biographies of two very different women to intermingle and become mutually implicated by one another. The reference to Dora is taken from Freud's studies on hysteria. The young Viennese woman, Ida Bauer (or Dora as she is more popularly known), was sent to Freud by her father after a suicide note was found in her possession. After conferring with the girl, Freud came to the conclusion that she was being used as a pawn between her father and the husband of her father's mistress — thus becoming an object of barter between the two men. She was diagnosed as suffering from 'hysteria', a condition defined by Freud as a wild, uncontrollable psycho-neurotic emotional response to a stressful set of circumstances which is triggered by a functional disturbance of the nervous system. As extreme psychological stress is endured, hysteria reveals itself in uncontrollable responses of the body— ticks, giggling, coughing, outbursts, and the like. The symptom becomes physical evidence of the psychic disease. Hysteria serves

as the psyche's defense, a means of both resistance and reconciliation. Freud writes:

> No one, I believe, can have had any true conception
> of the complexity of the psychological events in a case
> of hysteria — the juxtaposition of the most dissimilar
> tendencies, the mutual dependence of contrary ideas,
> the repressions and displacements, and so on (1990:
> 155).

It is an ailment manifest of contradictions, and in so being
becomes for Penny an allegory of the colonial encounter. The
term 'hysteria' that is etymologically derived from the Greek
hustera, or womb, has generally been associated with women as
the condition was originally thought to emanate from a disorder of the uterine functions. Recent feminist re-readings of the
case study have argued that hysteria may be seen as a resistance
to patriarchal domination. By drawing upon this dual-image
of resistance and reconciliation, the feminized native and the
patriarchal colonizer, Penny examines the ways in which politics
is quite literally embodied (Williamson 1989: 22). The body
sickens and rebels and yet, via the symptom, simultaneously and
paradoxically resigns the body to (live with) the disease.

In the heavily layered pastel drawing, Dora is black. Yet she
is drawn from the body of the artist. Her partially clothed body
endeavors to hide behind heavy drapery pinned with nineteenth
century images of Saartjie Baartman who was taken on tour
in Europe as ethnographic evidence of primitive sexuality. As
Sander Gilman (1985) points out, during the nineteenth century,
the African woman came to represent the prototype of 'primitive atavism', displaying an exaggerated, primal sexual appetite as
evidenced through her primitive genitalia [often referred to as
the Hottentot apron] (1985; see also McClintock 1995). Thus
was she crafted into a Victorian vessel of displaced desire. Following this, Saartjie Baartman has become *the* paradigm for the
oppressed female African body; displayed as an exhibit before a
voyeuristic nineteenth century European public, subjected to the
scrutinizing gaze of Western male medical science, autopsied and
dissected in death and placed in the Musee du L'Homme where

she still resides despite appeals for her repatriation and burial by the Griqua National Conference of South Africa and other lobbyist groups.

Heavy baroque velvet curtains frame the scene as a theater stage, abandoned shoes (the debris of Western dress and a metaphor of travel) are scattered across the foreground, and the images of Saartjie seem to extend back forever into the horizon. This is the object-trail which pins us to the past; a history of voyeurism. The images document the violence of the gaze; Dora hides her face from the viewer, and yet the images persist in clinging to her cloak, exposing her. The identities of Dora and Saartjie, merge and blur. They are brought together in resistance, clinging to one another, moving in and through each other's skin, becoming indistinguishable. They are united in an oppression that cuts across race, gender, time, and space. Indeed, in both cases such a superimposition serves to challenge the very idea of identity as 'singular' and self-contained. Theirs is a oneness that welcomes and absorbs duplicity. Their biographies repeat; they overlap.

'The other woman' in the title of the piece has generally been interpreted by commentators to be Saartjie, present through historical inference and the documentation of her exhibition(ism) pinned to Dora's attire (refer to Rankin 1992; Williamson 1989). Certainly, this appears obvious. Yet, if we understand Dora and Saartjie to have become one, the other woman may just as easily be read to be the artist herself. As the other woman, the artist is implicated in the scene through inference. She simultaneously stands both within the frame and without — waiting in the wings, constructing the stage upon which such a comparison is possible. She remains, however, on the periphery. As mentioned above, in Freud's original case study, Dora was seen as a commodity of exchange — a token of promise — between her father and his mistress' husband. A daughter in exchange for 'the other woman'. The other woman is present in testimony, forever in the background, implicated as the cause (or at least the 'inspiration') of anxiety and yet similarly a pawn in a patriarchal competition.

According to Penny, these images are intensely personalized. They are 'of' the artist, and yet she laments, most people persist in reading them as overtly (and straightforwardly) political, as if the two can be separated. She reflects, at length:

> I want to dwell for a moment on the relationship between the personal and the political, or put slightly differently, the private and the public. For it is not only that these relations remain integral to my practice, but they persist in discussions on South African art...
>
> In autobiography, the personal usually somehow precedes the political, the private conditions the public. Oppositions between these, story and history, subjective and objective, fiction and fact, still hold sway, whatever the recent challenges to what we know as 'the constitution of the subject'. In South Africa these oppositions have been both marked and blurred in culture. At least for my generation. As author André Brink has said in relation to South African literature 'the personal was the political'...
>
> Playwright Athol Fugard said of his work that 'the only safe place is inside a story'. One must wonder what precisely threatens that safety, and what precisely makes it necessary. At any rate Fugard's statement — Brink notes, 'demonstrates most eloquently how impossible it was — in those circumstances — to disentangle the personal from the public, or story from history'.
>
> Whilst I have always considered my works extremely personal I have also understood how the circumstances of which Brink speaks produced them as political, or rendered them available for political reading. This is something I have obviously consciously used. But what I want to ask now is whether changes in art practices, forms, readings simply follow changes in circumstances? Does, for example, developing national democracy automatically make a space for these micro-narratives which were hitherto arguably suppressed under the pressure of, for example, the all-encompassing 'grand narrative' of apartheid? Is it that the real possibility of liberty allows us now to

take liberties with until relatively recently politically trivial or in consequential content; now that our minds and imaginations are apparently decolonizing? And here I am not only speaking of making but also of reading (Picton and Law, forthcoming).

Are we, as Penny asks, simplistically and naively binarizing artistic practices into 'Struggle' work versus 'Post-Apartheid' work, where the former is considered political and collectively oriented while the latter is now interpreted as personal and individually motivated? Are we now succumbing to the temptation to read all post-election art as 'democratically inspired' simply because it is produced within a nation which now defines itself as such? Is our memory so short-term and do our visions change so rapidly and uncritically? Of course the personal as it exists in the mundane was never absent under Apartheid, and assuming that it was not only separates the individual from responsibility for politically inspired actions but naively places the Apartheid years outside of history by setting this period beyond the boundary of the everyday. And yet, as Penny herself attests, the personal, particularly during the struggle years, was so often cloaked in the language of the 'objective' as a conscious strategy of subversion. The personal harbored both hope and refuge for the ordinary person under Apartheid, and yet the de-subjectified political was where strength and courage in both resistance and oppression could be found. In many of Penny's images of struggle, the absent, partial-self is present, made whole, through the body of the other, not as an act of blind romanticism or displaced colonization, but as a conscious act of restoration, to reinstate that which has long been absent. Significantly, the reinstatement of the absent black other was seen in some way to require the erasure, however temporary, of the dominant white self.

DESCENT

Genealogy. An account of one's descent from an ancestor who did not particularly care to trace his own,

Ambrose Bierce. *The Devil's Dictionary* (1881 - 1906).

And so we commence our descent into the personal, familial past. As we have seen, Penny's early work belongs to a generation of 'struggle' art and has long been built upon the debris of the domestic. Increasingly in her work, however, more general allegories of racial conflict, sexual inequality, and bodily and psychic violence, have been superseded by more intimate and autobiographical narratives. The body of the artist has quite literally become the surface for (re)inscription, as in *Per Kind Permission (Fieldwork)* from 1994. In the video component of this installation, the unidentified white-gloved hand of her artist-husband, Colin Richards, primes her exposed back with white gesso, then proceeds to first draw the image of a 'traditional' African mask upon her skin in black ink, and then erase, re-prime and re-inscribe the surface with a portrait of the artist herself as a young girl. The latter is a representation of the objectified self, seen through the eyes and hand of an intimate other, and imposed upon one's own body. The ink seeps deeply into epidermal pores, leaving a trace even when erased. The consecutive priming and expunging with solvents draws blood, leaving the artist's skin visibly raw and irritated — sensitive, exposed and vulnerable to inscription. The video was then installed amongst various objects of 'traditional' African 'material culture' in the ethnographic section of the Gertrude Posel Gallery at Wits University. Subjectified 'Art' here commandeers objectified Anthropology. Personal narrative overlaps and at times overtakes collective remembrance.

No where is this more apparent then in Penny's recent autobiographical video, *My Lovely Day* (1997).[2] First screened at the Second Annual Johannesburg Biennale [October 1997 to January 1998] in the bowels of the Electric Workshop in the central Johannesburg market precinct, Penny constructed a miniature theater in which to screen her family history. *My Lovely Day* is, in effect, a collective endeavor: three generations of women collapsed into a moving narrative, three lifetimes folded into a single day. We are drawn into this Lilliputian playhouse through scarlet drapery curtaining a darkened incardine interior that recalls an earlier era of silent film making. This theater is a bantam facsimile of a cinema built in the 1930's by the artist's grandfather in Umtata. Its small darkness suggests intimacy. We feel as though we have entered into a private screening of another's mind remembering. Yet this claustrophobic space and the images which are projected remain somehow distantly familiar. The unclear visions clipped and reassembled from her mother's family film archive have the acidic line and color of memory. Subtitles have been gleaned and added to each frame from remembrances of stories her grandmother would recount to Penny and her siblings as children. These silent titles overlap and are subsumed by the melodic voice of a woman who sings the euphony of yesterday through the crackle of age and memory preserved in an old gramophone record. This is a voice from the past. We are only alerted to her identity as the artist's mother through a sub-titled hint to an opera career never realized. Testimony is often anonymous or told by others. As in a 'silent' film, it is the music that shouts the deafened tempo of the visual into sound. The film is a documentary of origins distending to a moment of advent. The narrative speaks of immigration, displacement and belonging; it interrogates arrival and seeks out a 'home'.

Towards the end of the film Penny's grandmother asks 'How did we end up here' in this 'Godforsaken place'? This is a question which frames the film, and as Penny explains 'brackets and deepens all her various statements and musings about identity and belonging (or not) to savage places like Greece or South Africa, about the savagery she felt in England because she married a Greek' (in Picton and Law, forthcoming). Settlement in South Africa is revealed to be 'an accident of history' (*ibid.*); hastened by the urgency of war and forced expatriation — a draw of the hat between two colonies, South Africa and America. Exile is a space of discomfort, of always being outside even when a return to an originary home is made possible. As the film progresses, the maternal voice which sings 'My Lovely Day' at the beginning eventually melts into various melodies of primordial belonging: Greek folk songs, dances from a distant island, rituals from an earlier time, only to return full-circle to the voice of the mother (the generational mediator between daughter and grandmother) at the end.

It is the artist's mother who holds the camera, who stands behind the lens on the peripheries of motion while her daughter, in the process of editing four decades later, positions the eye. Yet it is the grandmother who is perhaps most immediately 'visible', who lends word to image from the grave. She speaks to the artist as a child through subtitles borrowed from old postcards and remembered conversations; history inherited easily in the evenings as oral entertainment. Switching back and forth from the past to the present tense, she speaks of travel and blood ties. She speaks of what it is to 'become'. The viewer as historical witness is reminded that the 'age of globalization' has extended well into the previous century; that travel and upheaval and relocation have always been a part of tracing one's position in the present. The past is not static and in travel it is always the 'other' who appears foreign, even when at home. This, after all, is a foreign film.

At the time of writing in South Africa when personal history has become collective spectacle and 'truth-seeking' has become integral to the processes of nation-building, the artist has offered her audience a 'true' story to contemplate. The film, as social document, examines the ways in which knowledge is inherited and transferred from one generation to the next. The words of the author's grandmother, the overlay of music and the film itself are treated as 'found objects'; that is, artifacts which are already 'out there' in the world — 'survivals' — to be collected and reused. Found objects are, in this sense, akin to Durkheim's social facts (self-contained, independent, and exhibiting their own internal logic). Like a *memoire trouvee*, such social facts are at once whole and fragmentary, ancillary and autonomous. They transcend the individual, and yet are entirely dependent upon personal interpretation. Penny explains:

> Like family, certain memories precede us. Herein lies
> the significance of the film as a sort of 'found object',
> a 'ready-made' if you will. 'My Lovely Day' comprises
> sequences spliced from home-movie footage taken by
> my mother during the 1950s and 60s. She was an avid
> and sometimes quirkily indiscriminate documentor
> of family life. Inevitably, historical events figured
> in this avidly domestic documentation. I combined
> these cut sequences with each other and with texts
> — in the form of subtitles — really to produce a

story told by my maternal grandmother. So the film consists of images drawn from two generations of women whose relationship was at once close and distant from me (Picton and Law, forthcoming).

My Lovely Day documents personal, familial history against a backdrop of historical circumstance. In one frame the artist as a child dressed in the costume of an adult, dances with her siblings on the lawn of their home, while in a later frame we witness a scene of (anonymous) white children performing gymnastics in celebration of the 1961 Republic Festival. Frames flow smoothly from private to public and back again. There is no rupture. It involves every tedious, vernacular moment. History happens in the present, in every simultaneous second, enveloping individuals plural. In being grafted together from various documentary narratives, the chronology of the film is concealed as inherently artificial through the very illusion of its 'uninterrupted' construction. The fabrication of the film thus mimics the theatrical and selective manufacture of History (proper) itself..

Through memory, the film has the advantage of foreshadowing events already past. It is a space of projection; a space where events and lives seemingly foreign to one another find an opportunity for exchange. It reveals that destiny is always contingent upon chance. Penny reflects:

> At the film's end my grandmother answers a question 'How did we end up here?', a question which returns to her opening line about ending up in 'this Godforsaken place'. This brackets and deepens all her various statements and musings about identity and belonging (or not) to savage places like Greece or South Africa, about the savagery she felt in England because she married a Greek. It was indeed an accident of history that we ended up here, in South Africa. My maternal grandfather, a refugee with a sick asthmatic child, had to 'find a warmer place' to settle and so survive. Whilst I never met my maternal grandfather I knew him from the stories. On the other hand I also never met my paternal grandfather, but of him I knew nothing. He was a stranger to me. My father apparently had no qualms cutting ties with his parents, his country

— something to do with his 'Macedonian blood', if my grandmother is to be believed. She accuses him of never becoming 'a citizen of this country, never willing to settle'.

This being so it might be worth mentioning that at that time in South Africa a quota system limiting immigrants from 'non-scheduled' countries was in operation. These countries included Greece, Latvia, Lithuania, Poland, Russia, and Palestine. My father's arrival in South Africa was also an accident of history, notwithstanding quotas. He served in the Greek army for the Allied forces in Egypt in World War II and was injured. It was not injury but illness — coincidentally like my mother's family — in the form of contagious tuberculosis that found him aboard a ship bound for South Africa. So many accidents…

Through accident we lived, in my grandmother's jaundiced but not unkind words, a 'charmed life', 'wanting for nothing', 'spoiled rotten' with 'nothing to fear'.

Not all white children grew up this way. There were poor whites; low class children, 'gutter snipes' she called them, Afrikaners who did not wear shoes. Black people were closer, more dignified, sanctified by victimhood. And, at a safe distance.

'My Lovely Day' is her story, my story, a story not untrue for many others… (*ibid.*).

The question of 'How did we end up here?' begs for a re-tracing of antecedent steps and reveals a desire to account for a present restless moment. The question hints at discomfort, a dizzy confusion following a somersault of spiraling historical events. It echoes the embarrassed words of ex-Vlaakplas leader Dirk Coetzee as he gave his testimony before the Commission: 'Why could I have allowed myself into such a mess?', and in so doing invokes questions of responsibility and intentionality. We are asked to admit accident into historical incident, to seek out a balance between directed, foreshadowed action and blind misfortune, between individual choice and social destiny. The narrative speaks of what it is to be 'African' through the voice of a displaced British woman married to a Greek settler in the heart of the South African veld. It exposes us all as strangers. This is a space 'between': between Africa and Europe, between native and foreigner, between the real and the imagined. Through the ventriloquism of another's voice, the artist reveals herself as complicit to the spectacle of her history. Toward the end of the film, Penny is chided by her grandmother's sub-titled words: 'What do you know of massacre, disaster, catastrophe?' And with that remembrance, she is suddenly a child again, void of adult responsibility, robbed of legitimate experience, blind to the tragedy that surrounds her. The voice continues: 'But you play as if nothing is happening around you. Carrying on with your escapades. Up and down the garden. In the dust'.

INHERITANCE

> [I]nheritance is the soundest way of acquiring a collection. For a collector's attitude toward his possessions stems from an owner's feeling of responsibility toward his property. Thus it is, in the highest sense, the attitude of an heir, and the most distinguished trait of a collection will always be its transmissibility... But one thing should be noted: the phenomenon of collecting loses its meaning as it loses its personal owner. Even though public collections may be less objectionable socially and more useful academically than private collections, the objects get their due only in the latter... [A]s Hegel put it, only when it is dark does the owl of Minerva begin its flight. Only in extinction is the collector comprehended (Benjamin 1999: 68).

We turn at last to the object bequeathed; the object passed down through inheritance, revealing some small glimpse of what came before to future generations. In dispersion, the collection loses its meaning only as it existed as a whole; heirlooms whither only in losing their companions. Objects have the uncanny ability to alternately fracture and reassemble, to move in and out of circulation, forming new wholes and collections. In this way, things seem to collect collectors as much as collectors collect things. They thrive particularly as gifts, heirlooms, '*benofacts*', if you will, and are incredibly adept in the art of camouflage, needling their way into new collections, blending into their surrounds. While some may die or retreat in a loneliness provoked by separation and isolation from their fellows, many more prosper in renewal.

In turning to questions of inheritance, the transmissibility of memory and material culture, and personal and collective strategies of history making and recovery, Penny has recently been inspired to take inventory of her collection. Her object-world has found a home in the archive, which though (in this instance) private, nevertheless catalogues and embraces public heritage. Long has Penny sought after and acquired souvenirs of national history, anointing them into her intimate *trove*; collective heritage annotated to private remembrance. We have witnessed such mementos spread out before us in *Melancholia*, the painted portraits of relics, trophies and heirlooms; later to resurface materially in collage and installation. The two-dimensional object is slowly relinquished to the three-dimensional in a bid for heightened reality. As illusion becomes tangible, the space of the viewer is increasingly infringed upon. The suffocating accumulation expands forever outwards, demanding a greater stage.

Objects spanning from the nineteenth century through the Apartheid years — history textbooks and salvaged school projects, sepia photographs, family and documentary film footage, gramophone records, tear-gas canisters, instruments of torture and healing, body casts, mannequins, wire spectacles, Christian amulets, and army fatigues — have recently been joined by souvenirs of the 'new' South Africa: rugby paraphernalia, Madiba curios, rainbow kitsch. Within a climate of 'nation-building' in the new South Africa, Penny continues her on-going project of nation collecting. She gathers with some urgency, recovering the abandoned and discarded — the abject. She has spent two decades or more scouring the markets, museums, and archives of South Africa, Europe and elsewhere, drawing these things to her. Things that aid remembrance, and in so doing assist the collector in tracing a fragmented route to the present. Hers is an accumulation of 'triggers', slippery keys. Each object takes its place in succession, marking time from colonialism through to the late twentieth century. Yet while these things infer chronology in their very being, they persist in mingling indiscriminately, sometimes blurring together, deceiving the viewer and becoming confused. They compete for space. They are neither collected nor displayed in neat sequence. Relations between things are established in randomness.

In recent installations such as *Reconnaissance: 1900 — 1997*, objects from past works are assembled and revisited. Spread out on an extended surface, they perch like sacrifices on an altar. We have seen these things before, but the links remain tentative. Most have been resurrected from past works. Black face-casts, for example, reappear from *Per Kind Permission: Fieldwork*. A birthing model, plaster hand casts, mannequins, Angolan military relics and army fatigues, are similarly gleaned from *Mostly Women and Children* (1996) which was commissioned for the 1996 exhibition *Fault Lines: Inquiries Around Truth and Reconciliation*.[3] Some of these objects, such as the army gear, had also appeared in an earlier cibachrome series, including the work *Comrade Mother* (1994). In this piece, the artist and her young son pose in the camouflage fatigues worn by Penny's husband during the Angolan crisis, when he was conscripted into the army and taken to South-West Africa.[4] They embody an inherited and uncomfortable history passed down through generations via the object-trace. These things, assembled in photographs, were then incorporated into subsequent installation works including the *Fault Lines* piece. Thus the photograph itself becomes a souvenir of the souvenir. The objects circulate from 'active-context', to installation, to photographic 'document'.

Medical sphincters and glass vials that emerged in the cibachrome *South African Postcard* series (1995) are resurrected and neatly piled to the side of the *Reconnaissance* tableau. Baby booties used in Penny's turn of the century African studio portrait series, including *Boy with Ostrich Egg* (1996), are likewise carefully assembled. Indeed this *Boy* himself was once part of an aforementioned work, stripped of his booties, in *Comrade Child* (1994). Also laid out on the memory altar is the gargantuan coconut that we witnessed reclining on the floor of the artist's home. Here it becomes erotic fetish, its backside like buttocks — mimicking the black body casts that are also in evidence on the table. All is debris — that which countless unknown others have, for one reason or other, relinquished to the commodity circuit. Yet nothing goes to waste. Objects snatched from the vernacular take on a new life as art. They are recycled — there is no finished product, no completed work, which stands beyond the grasp of re-inscription. Most objects are 'directed towards' as much as they are projected behind, and in so being directed, foreshadow works to come. The backdrop photo of her grandfather's theater in Umtata, for example, served as partial inspiration for *My Lovely Day*, and the film collected in ordered reels on the table is the very footage which was later to be edited and projected in Penny's bantam theater.

Reconnaissance: 1900 — 1997 thus acts as both an archive of the artist's past work, and a repository of objects for works to come. It prompts the viewer to revisit key works, many of which are by now well known to the student of South African contemporary culture, through the display of remnants, object-keys. Several of the original works, particularly installations such as *Mostly Women and Children*, no longer exist except through the fragment. Designed for a limited time and defined site, they have since been disassembled and reconstituted into other work. They live and are renewed through metamorphosis. Some of these keys are not originals, but rather copies. They trigger remembrance through their likeness to past things and their proximity to previous events. Thus for example, although no object could be lifted directly from the painted surface of *Melancholia*, there are references to such inceptive aesthetic moments through the installation's very construction. *Reconnaissance* pays homage to early work through inference. As one commentator, Hazel Friedman notes of the *Reconnaissance* installation: 'In many respects it is a quieter, 3-D version of *Melancholia*" (*Mail & Guardian*, 21 February 1997).

HOLDINGS

Reconnaissance itself was only a temporary archive, a moment to pause and take inventory, an opportunity to regroup. Following the *Lift Off* exhibition at the Goodman Gallery in Johannesburg, for which the archive-work was originally commissioned, the tableau was dismantled and parts of it eventually remade into an installation for a show entitled *Holdings: Refiguring the Archive.* This new work was not an exact reconstruction of *Reconnaissance* by any means. Rather, it drew from the object-archive of its fore-bear; embellishing and subtracting from it, reconfiguring it into something, at first glance, quite novel — almost unrecognizable. *Reconnaissance* as it originally existed now endures as a whole only in the photographic record. It persists via the fragment as the object-trace.

Curated by Jane Taylor for the launch of the University of the Witwatersrand's Graduate School, the *Holdings* show aimed to reopen the archive to reflection and in so doing demonstrate that the repository of material history is neither fixed nor neutral. This project may be situated within a much broader national pre-occupation with truth, documentation, and historical revision-ism in South Africa. Indeed, the colonial history of Africa is a history of the archive; a chronicle of heritage-collecting which is ironically entangled with the long-enduring premise that Africa had no history (refer to Schildkrout and Keim 1998). Africa's colonial past leaves behind a complex legacy of accumulation and waste, of dispossession and desire. In South Africa under Apartheid, the archive was sealed. Documents mysteriously dis-appeared, files went missing. Boxes of photographs and records were painstakingly smuggled out of the country at great risk to their messengers, so that future generations would not forget. Many of these documents have only recently been returned to South Africa and special archives built to accommodate them, including the Mayibuye Centre at the University of the Western Cape. Interestingly, the word '*Mayibuye*', in the Nguni languages, means 'let it return'.

Traditionally, the archive makes neat that which is by nature chaotic. It orders objects into typologies, maps their genealogies, catalogues their history, their collection dates, and their benefactors. It assigns each a number that is then tattooed onto object-flesh. It packages them, files them, places them in drawers and cabinets and boxes on shelves. Temperatures are controlled and lights dimmed. The archive protects. It does not free memory, it contains it, forcing it to be still. Tragically, the archive so often acts as mausoleum; the place where things go to die. Or worse, are buried alive. And yet, filled as it is with object-traces, evidence of the past, the archive preserves and contains with the future in mind. In all its looking backwards, the archive emerges as a *trove* of national heirlooms carefully preserved for future generations. With this in mind, the walls of the South African archive have been enthusiastically scaled of late; its contents raided, dormant files awakened, and absences scrutinized.

The opening 'archival' theme of the Graduate School, imaged not only through the art exhibition but continuing through a series of workshops and seminars, stands as testament to this current historical, memory-bound fixation. The post-graduate research and coarse-directed curriculum on offer at the School are listed in their promotional material as including such themes as 'Creating, Curating, and Critiquing', 'Heritage Studies', 'Culture Studies', 'Pre-colonial Studies', and 'Rock Art Studies'. At first glance, such topics are overtly history-centric, and yet in a commentary in the *Mail & Guardian* by James Sey, the refigured archive in South Africa emerges as future-oriented, if not quite prophetic. Sey writes:

> As a documentary depository, an apparently objective and factual memory-record of a society or a specific part of a society, archives form the grounds on which knowledge, cultural heritage and a national or even individual sense of identity can be built.

> In South Africa, if we think only of the strange, sad and twisted histories and records that have emerged from the Truth and Reconciliation Commission's hearings, we can see how partial and ideologically charged the existence of the archive might be.

> Investigating the very concepts of cultural memory
> and recording at this point in our history is thus a
> forward-looking project rather than the historical
> one implied by the use of the archive idea. We need
> to begin sifting not only what has been recorded, but
> asking why certain things have been remembered or
> preserved and what forgotten or lost, how and by
> whom (7 August 1998).

For the *Holdings* show, Penny installed an accretion of entangled objects into three recessed windows. The objects in each of the respective rectangular window frames were grouped by color — khaki, red, and white — granting the impression of a multi-textured flag. The objects in collection act as opaque veils; we can no longer see through the accumulation. The past is indeed blinding. Each object nestled within has its own history traced through the artist's life's work. A monument of desire, the refigured artist's archive mingles objects of curiosity and myth with historical refuse and the mundane apparatus of domesticity. As Brenda Atkinson writes, 'the form, which questions the point of collapse between system and sentiment, becomes heraldic of personal history, a map of fetishes and testimony to memory, violence and loss' (*Mail & Guardian*, 7 August 1998).

Following its installation, Penny commissioned an assistant to catalogue every object on display, based upon what the observer *thought* she was seeing. The list spans several pages, and the object descriptions become more detailed with recognition and interest. Reproduced in (small) part the inventory reads:

Panel One [Khaki]: Left to Right, Top to Bottom

square sprinkbok cushion; beaded apron; wooden mask; army satchel; model ship; doll; leather strap; blonde hairpiece (plait); army bottle holder; oval silverware; silver sugar bowl; 2 x silver teapots; animal skull...; explosives container; wooden object; warthog?; skin; leather muzzle; dog ornament; hot water bottle with screw-in cap; army clothing bag; silver plated child's money box (train); springbok skin; dark brown hairpiece; wooden curio axe; silver miniature trophy; silver miniature trophy; silver miniature trophy (handle broken off); stuffed monkey...; Voortrekker artwork; doll (damaged)...; family photograph in wooden frame with gold stars...; Book: *Livingstone the Pathfinder* by Basil Matthews...

Panel Two [Red]: Left to Right, Top to Bottom

red velvet cloth; feather cap; flag; pink head wear; South African tourist bag; red towel; red soap holder (plastic); bag (red with black strap); Queen Elizabeth memorabilia; red fire escape rope; Bolero (Greek, male, dancing costume); child's swimming blow-up wings; picture frame fragments; old South African flag (Apartheid era); silk rose; rubber frog; picture frame fragments; dummy hand; knobkerrie (urban); Book: *Afrikaanse Kinderensiklopedie*; feathers (red); 3 x hand mirrors...; tourist doll (Scottish, no head, male)...; new South African flag; Christian holy kit...

Panel Three (White): Left to Right, Top to Bottom

quilt filling; canvas bag; sheep toy (headless); human skull (cranium); floral cloth; rubber mould; fluffy toy dog; white sheet; bamboo fan; dummy arm; canvas bag with green trim; Penny Siopis mask; Turkish shoe; plastic chicken; felt penguin; cotton wool; fish jaws; Christian icon; white dress (wedding type); beaded animal skin; Italian tourist doll; 'Stephana' (Greek marriage crown); 11 x dummy hands; embroidered cloth; beaded animal skin — South African; femur and other bones (model?); 6 x dummy hands; dummy baby with open mouth; 3 satin baby bibs with embroidery and lace trim...; Christ figurine...; wax votive offerings: 1 x leg, 1 x baby; 2 x Grecian figurines; plastic holy water bottle...; Elizabeth I coronation mug; President Mandela mug...

CHARMED LIVES

These are life's charms, both literally and figuratively. They are objects of fact and superstition, decay and resurrection — memory-amulets painstakingly knotted onto forward-facing windows. Alone these objects signal waste; many are broken, damaged, or violated in some way. Yet they take on new life in the collection through their relationships with one another; the juxtaposition of the new with the old, the ordinary alongside the extraordinary. They configure the future through the past; false guarantors of a destiny scarred by memory. Together they captivate and enchant.

In (re)assembly, the artist's work — the biographical archive — is always in process. To seek closure in her work is to miss the point, as the archive is a boundless project. The collection could accumulate indefinitely. The objects of biography are in constant anticipation, circulating through Penny's life's work. They periodically return to her home, to languish on shelves, in cabinets, in every available space. She lives both among them and through them. They have become her signature. Over the years, acquaintances (both intimate and professional) have requested various parts of her collection as gifts; heirlooms to be relinquished to the recipient when the artist no longer has a use for them. Penny's latest work in progress has been the compilation of these requests into an artist's will, a list of benefaction.

Much has been made of the 'gift' since Marcel Mauss' pivotal monograph *Essai sur le don, forme archaique de l'echange* was first published in 1925 (repub. trans. 1967). To Mauss, material and moral life is exemplified through gift-exchange, which as a system of binding reciprocity functions 'in a manner at once interested and obligatory' (1967: 3). Furthermore, as Mauss goes on to add, 'the obligation is expressed in myth and imagery, symbolically and collectively; it takes the form of interest in the objects exchanged; the objects are never completely separated from the men who exchange them; the communion and alliance they establish are well-nigh indissoluble' (*ibid.*). The thing given is not inert, but has a hold over the recipient, and is in this way personified.

In reflecting upon the 'spirit' of a thing, I am here reminded of one passage in particular in which Mauss speaks of the Maori belief in the *hau* of an object given. He explains:

> I shall tell you about *hau*. *Hau* is not the wind. Not at all. Suppose you have some particular object, *taonga*, and you give it to me; you give it to me without a price. We do not bargain over it. Now I give this thing to a third person who after a time decides to

give me something in repayment for it (*utu*), and he makes me a present of something (*taonga*). Now this *taonga* I received from him is the spirit (*hau*) of the *taonga* I received from you and which I passed on to him. The *taonga* which I receive on account of the *taonga* that came from you, I must return to you... I must give them to you since they are the *hau* of the *taonga* which you gave me... Such is *hau*, the *hau* of personal property, the *hau* of the *taonga*, the *hau* of the forest...

The obligation attached to a gift itself is not inert. Even when abandoned by the giver, it still forms a part of him. Through it he has a hold over the recipient, just as he had, while its owner, a hold over anyone who stole it. For the *taonga* is animated with the *hau* of its forest, its soil, its homeland, and the *hau* pursues him who holds it (1967: 8-9).

This complex web of circulation, exchange, and obligation stretches indefinitely outwards, linking a network of givers and recipients through the object. The spirit of the object persists, pursuing and binding the keeper to its benefactor. Even when abandoned, the object continues to form part of its giver. The gift is thus animated, remaining rooted through tentative threads to its originary owner and, as Mauss writes, to its homeland. As he explains, the gift's *hau* 'wants to return to the place of its birth' (*ibid*: 9). The thing awaits a return that is ultimately predicated upon a nascent moment. In this way, the possessor himself is possessed; the collector collected by the spirit of the thing embedded in the land and its history.

In anticipation of death, the promise of such possession and ascendancy over the living is indeed seductive. A gift *causa mortis* is generally one made by the benefactor on anticipation of death. But to draw up a will is not simply to foresee a life's ending, but to ensure a life's continuance through the ongoing biography of the heirloom. Such is the lure of resurrection, predicated not upon closure but perpetuity. The will is a natural extension of the archive in that it guarantees the continuation of the collection and the persistence of memory through an act of giving which forever promises return. The heirloom, after all, is most effective in its ability to haunt, to remind. But the donor in the act of benefaction is herself freed from memory; from these objects which through their very being embody the past. The will, in this instance, anticipates not so much death, as regeneration. It is perhaps this promise of renewal that attracts Penny both to the archive and its imminent bequest.

Inheritance in the new South Africa is linked with a mourning that is doubled against the expectation of restitution and repossession. As much as this is a cultured climate of remembrance, it is equally a time of strategic amnesia. As Ingrid de Kok writes:

> It is understandable for a country in a historical moment such as this to attempt to erase the fouler accretians of its past, the physical signs, totems, and fetishes. As the edifices of apartheid are being dismantled, papers are shredded, signs painted over, departments renamed. American collectors are buying the old 'whites only' signs that South Africans now repudiate. Those intent on promoting reconciliation at all costs see those who wish to preserve the history of the past as spoilers at best, revenge merchants at worst. But for the project of reconciliation to succeed, individuals and the nation require the physical evidence of our suffering and complicity to be displayed as part of a new pattern (1998: 71).

The need to remember is forever tempered against the desire to forget as a shortcut to forgiveness. Such desire manifests itself in erasure; the calculated destruction of the *aide memoire*. Yet the willing of objects is not an amnesiatic act of abandonment, and nor does it represent a 'clean break'. Giving, as we have seen, is indeed a messy enterprise that leaves a trail of a thousand threads billowing behind. To bequeath one's collection is to recognize the limits of its configuration in the hands of a single possessor. It is an act of 'contractual sacrifice'; a bid of forfeiture which ensures that the biographies of the collection's objects are renewed through inheritance and its ensuing set of contractual obligations which are integral to the preservation of memory and the continuation of tradition. It is the recognition that such objects, the 'physical evidence' of both suffering and celebration, need be passed on in order to be reinterpreted and reconfigured into 'the new patterns' which de Kok speaks of. As Albert Camus writes, 'it is normal to give away a little of one's life in order not to lose it all' (1963). In the process of giving away, the self is at last fulfilled. The biography of the artist continues through the biography of her objects, as life takes on new meaning as art. After all, in the words of Penny's grandmother, 'What is life if you can't make art of it?'

Notes

1. A term adopted from Tibor Fischer's insightful and incredibly entertaining autobiography of (at least what appears to be) a Sumerian bowl, *The Collector Collector* (1997).

2. The following account of *My Lovely Day* is reproduced in part in 'My Gosh, We're Normal!': 'Recovering the Ordinary in Post-Apartheid Art' (Jennifer Law, forthcoming); to appear in *Divisions and Diversions: The Visual Arts in Post-Apartheid South Africa*, John Picton and Jennifer Law, eds., London: Eastern Art Publishing.

3. The Fault Lines project, organized by Jane Taylor in 1996, was a series of cultural events that aimed to engage with current debates surrounding truth and reconciliation. The art exhibition which opened on the 16th June 1996 at the Castle of Good Hope in Cape Town (marking the twentieth anniversary of the Soweto uprisings), invited thirteen artists to take up a period of residency at the Mayibuye Archives housed at the University of the Western Cape.

4. For more information regarding Colin Richard's own resurrection of these objects, refer to 'Performing on a Fault Line: The Making(s) of a South African Spy Novel and Other Stories', by J. Law (in press), in *Para-sites: A Casebook Against Cynical Reason*, George Marcus, ed. Chicago: University of Chicago Press.

References

Appadurai, Arjun, ed. 1986. *The Social Life of Things: Commodities in Cultural Perspective*. Cambridge: Cambridge University Press.

Atkinson, Brenda. 1998. 'Archiving Art', *Mail & Guardian*, 7 August 1998.

Benjamin, Walter. 1999. 'Unpacking My Library', in *Illuminations*. London: Pimlico.

Bierce, Ambrose. *The Enlarged Devil's Dictionary*. 1967. London: Penguin.

Bloch, Ernst.1988. *The Utopian Function of Art and Literature: Selected Essays*, trans. by Jack Zipes and Frank Mecklenburg. Cambridge, Mass. and London: The MIT Press.

Breytenbach, Breyten. 1999. *Dog Heart*. Cape Town and London: Human & Rousseau.

Calvino, Italo. 1997. 'Grand Bazaar', in *The Literature Machine: Essays*, trans by Patrick Creagh. London: Vintage.

Camus, Albert. 1963. *Notebooks 1935 - 1942,* (entry for 22 November 1937). New York: Knopf.

Coetzee, J.M. 1997. *Boyhood*. London: Secker & Warburg.

De Kok, Ingrid. 1998. 'Cracked heirlooms: memory on exhibition', in *Negotiating the Past: The Making of Memory in South Africa*, Sarah Nuttall and Carli Coetzee, eds. Cape Town: Oxford University Press Southern Africa, 57-71.

Emerson, Ralph Waldo. 1995. 'Intellect, in *Essays and Poems*, C. Bigsby, ed. London: Everyman, 161.

Fischer, Tibor. 1997. *The Collector Collector*. London: Secker & Warburg.

Freud, Sigmund. 1990. *Case Histories I: Dora and Little Hans, Vol. 8.* London: Penguin.

Friedman, Hazel. 1997. 'Givon's Signs of the Times', in *Mail & Guardian*, 21 February 1997.

Gell, Alfred. 1992. 'The Technology of Enchantment and the Enchantment of Technology', in *Anthropology, Art and Aesthetics*, Jeremy Cootes and Anthony Shelton, eds. Oxford: Oxford University Press, 40-63.

Gell, Alfred. 1996. 'Vogel's Net: Traps as Artworks and Artworks as Traps', *Journal of Material Culture*, Vol. 1/1: 15-38.

Gilman, Sander. 1985. *Difference and Pathology: Stereotypes of Sexuality, Race and Madness*. Ithaca: Cornell University Press.

Gregory, James. 1995. *Goodbye Bafana: Nelson Mandela, My Prisoner, My Friend*. London: Headline.

Hall, Martin. 1998. 'Earth and stone: archaeology as memory', in *Negotiating the Past: The Making of Memory in South Africa*, Sarah Nuttall and Carli Coetzee, eds. Cape Town: Oxford University Press Southern Africa, 180-200.

Kopytoff, Igor. 1986. 'The Cultural Biography of Things: Commoditization as Process', in *The Social Life of Things: Commodities in Perspective*, Arjun Appadurai, ed. Cambridge: Cambridge University Press, 64-91.

Krog, Antjie. 1998. *Country of My Skull*. Johannesburg: Random House South Africa.

Law, Jennifer. In press. 'Performing on a Fault Line: The Making(s) of a South African Spy Novel and Other Stories', in *Para-Sites: A Casebook Against Cynical Reason*, George Marcus, ed. Chicago: The University of Chicago Press.

———. In press. 'My Gosh, We're Normal! Recovering the Ordinary in Post-Apartheid Art', in *Divisions and Diversions: The Visual Arts in Post-Apartheid South Africa*, John Picton and Jennifer Law, eds. London: Eastern Art Publishing Ltd.

Mandela, Nelson. 1994. *Long Walk to Freedom*. Randburg: Macdonald Purnell.

Martin, John Rupert. 1991. *Baroque: Style and Civilization*. London: Penguin.

Mauss, Marcel. 1967. *The Gift: Forms and Functions of Exchange in Archaic Societies*. New York: W. W. Norton & Company.

McClintock, Anne. 1995. *Imperial Leather: Race, Gender and Sexuality in the Colonial Contest*. New York and London: Routledge.

Nuttall, Sarah and Carli Coetzee, eds. *Negotiating the Past: The Making of Memory in South Africa*. Cape Town: Oxford University Press Southern Africa.

Ramphele, Mamphela. 1995. *A Life*. Cape Town: David Philip.

Rankin, Elizabeth. 1992. *The Baby and the Bathwater: Motif, Medium and Meaning in the Work of Penelope Siopis*. Johannesburg: Imprimatic.

Rivers, W.H.R. 1910. 'The Genealogical Method in Anthropological Inquiry', *Sociological Review* 3: 1-12.

Schildkrout, Enid and Curtis A. Keim. 1998. *The Scramble for Art in Central Africa*. Cambridge: Cambridge University Press.

Sey, James. 1998. 'New Forms for Cultural Memory', in *Mail & Guardian*, 7 August 1998.

Siopis, Penny. 1996. Unpublished paper. 'Shadow Casts – Mostly Women and Children'. Presented at Fault Lines Conference, 'Re: membering, Re:collecting, Re:constructing, A Rejoinder', 4th – 5th July 1996.

————. In press. 'Home Movie: A Document of a South African Life', in *Divisions and Diversions: The Visual Arts in Post-Apartheid South Africa*, John Picton and Jennifer Law, eds. London: Eastern Art Publishing.

Williamson, Sue. 1989. *Resistance Art in South Africa*. Cape Town: David Philip, Publisher (Pty) Ltd.

Woolf, Virginia. 1982. *The Diary of Virginia Woolf, vol. 4*, Anne O. Bell, ed. Harmondsworth: Penguin.

Chapter 10

ART, AGE AND COSMOLOGY: NARRATIVES OF SELF AND SOCIETY IN PAINTINGS BY CUTHY MEDE

Laurel Birch de Aguilar

Interpretation of art is at best a narrative, which approaches a truth, but never captures the entirety of the object. Interpretation, as in this chapter, renders the object into text, as well as the spoken words and written words about the art (Ricoeur 1979). Paintings are objects, which are bounded, but also unbounded, flat but also having depth, they exist on a canvas, but also exist beyond their physical self. Art is transcendent; art has spirit, or it is not art (Adorno 1984). Objects, artifacts, arts, now artworks, are interpreted in terms of their history, and the society in which they were made (Danto 1981, Vogel 1991). Interpretation of objects, artworks, art, is to 'piece together complex meanings through the analysis of language, myth and art' (Coote and Shelton 1992: 4). Myth, narrative and discourse as oral texts are useful in interpretation of society, and in this case, interpretation of art (Barber and de Moreas 1989).

All of these methods of interpretation, of understanding artwork, are present in this analysis of paintings by Cuthy Mede, an artist born and raised in central Africa. They are present, not only in my analysis and writing, but are all present in the artist's written words about his own paintings, and spoken words in reference to his paintings. Mede interprets his own work, expressing his idea of the spiritual, and infinity, that which is beyond the physical bounds of the canvas, assumed knowledge about people, society and historical events in Malawi, and the text of creation mythology in Malawi.

Therefore this analysis of Mede's artworks is greatly assisted by the cooperation of the artist himself, who conveyed his own interpretations of his work over a decade, in conversations, interviews, and his own written statements. In this interpretive work, the words of the artist are invoked over and again, both written and spoken, implied and stated, in reference to his paintings. There are many themes, streams of thought, ideas and experiences with which to frame these words and interpretations. For this particular chapter I have chosen the aspect of age, drawing out material related to age suggested by the artist over the years, including his own view of the life-cycle, passages in time and his own aging.

Various narratives evoke ideas about age and the artist, age in the life cycle and society, and age in the world interpreted through myth and cosmology. In each narrative, color and style are present, each following the same passages of change in the life course of the world, and the chronological life of the artist. Therefore, I interpret artworks by Cuthy Mede with the broad brush of age: his own personal age and aging over decades of work, and the concepts of age and aging in the social cosmology of local peoples in central and southern Malawi. The personal and the social are interwoven in the artworks. Passages in the personal life of the artist, the aging of the artist and the maturing of his work, elides with ideas about the life of the world as a whole, and the life-cycles of society in central Malawi.

Age and aging in this essay, are understood as cultural concepts (M. Aguilar 1998), as concepts which are creative and changing rather than static or simply a measurement of time. Age is perceived by individual persons and by society in different ways. In this interpretation age is involved in passing through stages, each stage or passage, with its own characteristics, its own creative energy and its own relation with the rest of world.

The paintings change: the styles, the colors, the use of line and space, the subjects, images and themes. Each painting is a reflection of change, one from another, reflecting back and forth, overlapping, intertwining, merging, the edge of one indistinct from another, yet a pattern, a *passage*, is framed. These passages in paintings over time form distinctive *styles*.

In the following narratives of four distinctive styles, I invoke the passive voice of the artist, referring to his work, his views, conversations, interviews, and insights, shared with me over more than a decade.

CUBISM: FOUR PASSAGES OF ART

While the work of Mede is rich and varied, I will focus on four styles of cubism, which have followed a progression of work over four decades. Cubism is the predominant style in Mede's paintings. Within the range of cubist works, four distinct styles emerge, which are described below. These styles are identified primarily by color: dark and white, monochromatic shades of red, multiple bright colors, and white and blue.

Darkness and White Transparencies

This early passage in Mede's work in cubism is characterized by deep, blackened colors covering the whole of the canvas, with transparent white triangular shapes emanating from a single point in the corner of the painting. Dark shapes outlined in layers of dark paint form faces, hands and figures. The faces are often fixed in emotional expressions described by Mede and his clients as agony, despair, struggle and awe.

Blackened deep green, blue and purple were common colors, with darker lines running through the canvas, separating color into separate shapes. As dark as the background was, the transparency overlying the painting was white in stark contrast. Mede claims his inspiration comes from the source of light, which is the single dot on the canvas. From this dot, white lines run freely over the whole of the dark painting. The blackened shapes and white shapes merge to form shapes of eyes, outlines of head and neck, forms of fisted hands, and suggestions of tight mouth and strained throat.

Mede sees the light as emanating from God, knowledge, goodness and love. This whiteness is the energy, which brings life itself, and relieves the paintings of their dark countenances. Energy from the light source flows in lines, forming cubist shapes, changing course, and merging with other lines. One line flows into another line into eternity, beyond the boundaries of the painting, overlying the whole of the darkened world. Like light waves and energy, the white lines are transparent, permeating all things, and extending beyond material objects.

Red Monochromatic Color

In the 1980's Mede entered another phase of cubist works. His work became bright, vibrant, and colorful, using reds, oranges, and yellows. He continued to work with pointillism in various colors, and with dark figures outlined with white shapes, but his new work was decidedly brighter. Figures appeared in shapes formed by a monochromatic range of reds.

Brighter paintings of orange-red, brilliant yellows and rich reds become light themselves. These brilliant canvases of red, orange and bright gold are described by Mede as the beginning of the world, of vibrant life, passions and chaos. He suggests that, as the world was formed with explosions and fire, so these paintings depict the beginnings, the chaos and fire that began new life. The entire canvas is filled with expanses of brilliant color. Figures are loosely outlined, in movement and dance, surrounded by blinding light. In the foreground a half-nude woman seems to stride across the canvas with a snake entwined in her arms in one painting, 'Power of Tradition'. Diamond-shaped masks rise in the background, all in the colors of flame. Mede suggests these images evoke the power of masks and female powers of sexuality and fertility.

These explosions in the early life of the world begin to cool, and Mede shifts from brilliance to monochromatic schemes of muted reds. This transition may be characterized by one painting in muted brown reds, with cubist shapes formed by layers of deepened red tones, emanating from the source of brighter yellow light in the right hand upper corner of the painting. The central figure is a woman with her back turned. This woman is wearing traditional clothing, a headdress known as a *duku* and a skirt known as *chitenji*. She is facing into the painting, holding an opened book, and before her are crowds of faces, suggested by the rounded lines and shapes. Rounded curves suggest a multitude of heads, and in the background rounded curves suggest hills.

According to Mede, this painting is about knowledge, wisdom, the teaching of the people. The source of light is again the source of inspiration for the painting, permeating the painting with its energy. The change in color suggests a world which is warming, no longer in deep darkness, but growing in warmer shades, earth shades and reddened shades. The lines of light are no longer stark white, but are muted tones of the same earth-reds, and the light is more than a dot, it is a sun of muted orange and yellow, and it is a rising sun, with the reddened light of dawn.

All Colors

Perhaps the best known work of Mede is his work in many colors, all colors, in cubist forms. In this period or passage, Mede explores all of life in a rainbow of bright and dark shades, one set against the other in contrast, and others blending into one another in layers of paint forming lines and shapes.

Mede sees the world as full of people and crowded with activity. These paintings depict life and the living, with the same energy flowing through the paintings, in red, blue and yellow. Figures are suggested in cubist shapes. Objects of life fill in corners. The space is crowded with people, movement, objects and shapes of color. No space is empty, since life itself is crowded. Pots, drums, horns, fish and plates of food merge with figures of people, limbs in motion, dancing, singing, and playing. Women carry pots on their heads and babies on their backs, in cubist outlines, shining yellow and brown.

In this range of color and light, Mede explores the passions of life. Greed is depicted in an unusual painting dominated by green, with blackened lines of light, and refugees with empty plates, drums lying untouched and figures limp beneath a covered dome, denying the light which shines from a yellow sun above. Cubist figures row a boat in thick white outlines over red and blue forms fleeing from oppression. Mechanical gears are contorted with hands, representing the loss of freedom in a mechanical age.

In a painting titled 'Wedding' Mede shows the light from a chalice, lifted high at the top of the canvas. A woman's face is shadowed several times, moving, a young woman and an old woman, a baby and a fertile breast, a man with raised knee dancing, drummers drumming, all jumbled together. All of life, all of age, happiness, youth and maturity, new life and birth, and the coming of old age and death, are shown in red and blues surprises of pastels, yellow and ochre, and muted lines of many colors overlapping forms and figures.

White and Blue Colors

In the 1990's Mede moved into another passage of work. The shift in color was dramatic, from deep contrasts and bright color to pastel, blue and white. The cubism remains, but the palette is entirely white and blue. The light, the orb from which light emanates, and all the lines and shapes and forms are in mixtures of blue and white paint. The blue ranges from medium shades to very pale white-blue. Whole spaces are empty and white. The canvas is not crowded with color; rather it presents the absence of color. Fewer figures appear, and fewer objects of life: pots, drums, instruments, food. Single images are more common.

In a painting titled 'Justice', a seated man is painted in red, but the white lines are so thick and cover so much of the canvas, that the painting is pale rose in color, a pink shade. The single figure dominates, with high forehead and large feet, which Mede describes as indicating intelligence, wisdom and balance.

In another painting, in the blue and white shades most common in this passage, there are no human figures. An ancestral mask appears in triangular forms, three forms in the center of the painting. There are two orbs, the moon and sun, the light and the dark, in blue and in white. White shapes and blue shapes blend in varying shades of these two colors. Higher in the painting, the white dominates, and the spaces on the edges are white.

In stark contrast to the previous passage, these paintings are empty. Mede describes this change as a seeking of the spiritual, and emptying of all that is material, of all activity, of all human passion, of food and movement. This spirituality is emphasized in the cooling of the earth, the cooling of passions and the cooling from the chaos of the explosive beginnings. He sees light blue as a spiritual color, and shiny white as the ultimate aim of endlessness and infinity, the closest to the ancestors, and to God.

NARRATIVES OF MYTH AND SOCIETY

These four passages are interpreted as stages in the life of the world itself. In the creation mythology of central Malawi (Schofeleers 1992) the world began as an empty, dry dark and barren place. Life began with a cataclysmic storm, with lightning racing across the skies. Dark clouds and lightning gathered, and rains began to fall. With these first rains came all life.

In this creation mythology, man played with fire, did not heed warnings, and set the world on fire. Animals ran away from humans in rage, and even God was forced to flee into the sky, away from the world. From that time onward, all life had to die to be reunited with God.

Schoffeleers (1985) interprets this myth as a charter for the seasons, and for the performance of masked dancers known as *Nyau*. There are two seasons; seasons of dryness and wetness. The rainy season begins in November and heralds the time of planting, new life and new growth. The dry season is a time of plants dying. At the end of the dry season the dried grasses are burned to make way for the new growth to come. Fires rage on hillsides, visible in the dark for miles around. Then the clouds thicken and darken in the skies, and thunder and lightning accompany the thickening clouds until the first rains begin to fall.

In another prominent myth from southern Malawi, *Mbona*, Schoffeleers (1992) re-tells narratives of the legend of rain making. Thunder and lightning bring both the desired rain, but also the lightning brings death. Filled with interpretations and images of the python snake, rainbow of color, heat and cold, red and white shiny bright light, this myth reveals social and cosmological associations with colors. The python snake is a symbol of renewed life, transformation, and the form of the spirit throughout the region. The python 'breathes' the rainbow, and the python snake dominates a multi-colored cubist painting by Mede.

Mede borrows from other ideas about the world as well, in his own interpretation of the beginnings of the world. For him, the world was dark and empty before the coming of God, who created all things, and as in the Bible, it was God who created light.

The first passage of darkness with white transparent lines across the whole of the canvas, is an interpretation of God's light coming in the world. For Mede, the tiny white dot on the painting is the source of all light, energy and life. The dot of light is the inspiration from which the rest of the painting takes shape, literally, in cubist forms. The stark contrasts of darkness and white lines is also a clear depiction of the darkness of the world at that time when life was being created in the sky in local creation mythology.

Dark clouds were laced with transparent, momentary bolts of jagged white light: lightning. The lightning and the dark clouds were the first signs of life coming to the empty world, as the lightning and dark clouds are the first signs of the coming rains to bring new life for the farmer's fields.

If the beginning of the world is the lightning streaking through the dark, then the second phase in the life of the world is the bright red of fire. Mede describes this passage of paintings in expanses of bright color as the 'Big Bang', the explosion of the world. Bridging myth and science, Mede interprets the early chaos of the world in explosive bright color.

Red is also associated with birth. After the darkness and the first light come the blood of birth, the blood of youth, the blood of menstruation and of young life. This redness is associated with women, and with women's power to give birth. Birth itself is painful and dangerous, sometimes causing death, as well as creating new life.

The young world, then, is an explosive one. Its energies are potentially dangerous, exciting, full of heat and fire, passionate and even destructive. The energies of youth are also the energies of sexuality, and the consequent life-giving energies of fertility and new birth. These are powers which, in local society, must be contained and directed to avoid destruction. Because these explosive passions are also life giving, creative and capable of renewing the world, they are potent, positive and full of hope as well as potentially destructive. Being both powers negative and positive, potent and pregnant, this fiery age of the world bears the characteristics of ambitious youth.

Youth, in local society, is associated with recklessness, physical power, and sexuality. When youth is directed by society, they will renew life, renew the earth and crops, renew the society, and renew connections with the spirits and all life. When youth rejects society, they veer toward danger, and may tear the society apart. Promiscuity, explosive anger, reckless actions, over-ambition, fighting and war could each lead to loss of life, loss of fertility, loss of crops and food, loss of political stability, loss of communion with the spirits and ultimately, as in war, the loss of the whole of the society.

This passage in the life of the world is a dangerous one, but also exciting in its potential to effect change. Positive change in society could be enacted by youthful power to re-create traditions, generating life, love and fertility, preparing the earth for crops, ambitions to improve society, carry on the work of elders, and using youthful power and strength to defend the society from enemies within and without. In short, youth brings new and renewed life, without which society would die.

This fiery age of monochromatic reds, oranges and yellows gradually gives way to the third passage of paintings. As the palette of explosive color cools, the world begins to age. Bright reds are reduced to dark embers, and blues are laced with red and yellow. This is perhaps Mede's most prolific period of work, and the passage of painting for which he is most renowned. The world is in its age of human endeavor, of activity, of wars and of successes. Political and social themes usher in the world past the chaos of its beginnings and youth, the world of adulthood. Society and people are in movement. There is celebration, and there is pain. The old and the young are present in the work, and society is revealed in its customs, dress, images, institutions and histories. The life in the world is crowded with births and deaths, and all that happens between. Happiness is tethered to wisdom as one cubist shape juxtaposes another. The danger of destruction is cooled, though it has not disappeared.

This passage of the world is an age of society, of people, of renewed life, of all that happens: the mundane and the remarkable. This is an age of *livingness*, of all that happens in a life. Birth, youth, and assumption of social responsibility, rising status, political position, chiefs and elders, seers and sorcerers, leaders and teachers are all present. The world is crowded with people, cities are created, towns rise and decay, land is developed for houses, farms and markets, but still there are the old images of well-being and life in the paintings. Continuity and change co-exist, filling every space on the canvas in every color; as active and varied as humanity itself.

This is the present age of the world, a mature age, but still growing; still destructive as in the red of the beginning, but also wise and cooled in the deep blues alongside the reds. This passage progresses from brighter, more clear and happier shades to muted colors and darker, thicker outlines. The world is aging now, and is past its youthfulness. Maturity and wisdom are also revealed as coming death and corruption. Corruption and greed are present now. But even worse are the paintings depicting the loss of soul and freedom, the plight of refugees from war, and the misuse of justice.

Mede moves from this passage of work, involving happiness and sadness, joy and frustration. The world moves from matu-rity to elderhood and from the crowded activities and passions of everyday life to contemplation and spirituality. In this most recent style of artwork, the world changes from the absorbing earth back to sky. From the sky, cloud and lightning, came the rains and all life; back to the sky, humans return as spirits, in death. In this passage of the life of the world, the colors are the colors of sky, white and blue, with larger spaces of light blue and white-blue, empty spaces as in the open spaces of sky. The world is no longer tied to the earth, but to the atmosphere around it. Air is the subject of Mede's paintings. Air, atmosphere, sky and the spiritual world. This period, which could be referred to as Mede's 'blue period', the life of the world has returned to preoc-cupation with the world above. Not in sadness, but in an intense spirituality.

In Malawian society, the elders are thought to be closest to the spirits, the graying of the hair and skin are signs of being closer to death. Elders are entrusted with the spiritual renewal of local societies. They are chosen and respected according to the wisdom and judgment they have shown throughout their lives. Elders are considered wise, and deserving of respect. Aged women and men are the teachers of local traditions, the overseers of local rituals and customs, and the keepers of local knowledge.

It is no accident that Mede has chosen older subjects in this phase of work. Cubist blue and white shapes form portraits of people Mede knew, but who have since died. The portrait of a woman smoking a pipe was a relative of Mede, living on Likoma Island. Her clothes are now old-fashioned, and her pipe is home made: signs of the past. Elders and the dead, the past re-created in the present, Mede's paintings in this period are memories, remembrances of the past. The past remembered in shades of sky are remembrances but also presences, as those who have died are now spirits and exist in the spiritual world.

In another painting the main subject is an ancestral mask, a diamond shaped mask reminiscent of the shapes of masks in earlier works in reds and multi-colors. Three masks are a kind of Trinity, with two orbs, sun and moon, above them. The range of blues are white and all light, but the darker shades are nearer the bottom of the painting, and the top corners are white. Spaces are looser, more open, larger shapes than in past paintings, and the canvas has open, empty whiteness.

Whiteness is the color considered closest to the spirit world. Mede, I suggest, uses this color and its attendant white-blue as representations of long-standing associations of this color, consciously or unconsciously. The whiteness refers to the spiritual world, as the redness refers to the bodily and earth-bound one. Whiteness best expresses what Mede describes as infinity, endlessness, empty expanses, which are also intense meditations on spirituality.

The life of the world, in these four phases are also passages of age. We begin in nothingness, the beginning of the world, and the darkness and promise of the pregnant womb. White light is life, and the early paintings bring that life which, as Mede says, comes from God. Following the beginnings of life, the world explodes in youthful exuberance, restlessness, recklessness and abandon. Fire rages out of control, and the Big Bang theory is depicted in the chaos of the world. Volcanoes erupting shape the contour of the land and seas, in the early age of this youthful age of the world. As the world cools, the world also ages. The heat and fire of the youthful past give way to a mature world, a world of every color in the rainbow, of yellows and greens and reds and blues. Pastels and darkness coexist, one beside the other, as the mature world embraces the continued renewal of life and the coming of death. The final passage of the world, to date, is the aging world. The fires are dimmed, and the world moves from the earth back to the sky. The atmosphere and air are the future, the spirit world is close, more present than before, and death becomes another renewal.

These passages, these ages of the world represented in Mede's stages of art, are also cultural representations of color. Darkness is the earth, the grave, death. Whiteness is life, health, spirits and God. Red is pain and red is passion. Birth and killing are both associated with blood red. Deeper colors are cooling, grays and muted colors are cooling, less dangerous. The muting gray mediates the heat and the coolness, and the world matures. All of humanity, all passions, emotions, actions are possible and present, as all colors are present. The colors dissipate, the vividness is whitened, as the world ages. Nearing death, color disappears, and only the whiteness, the spirituality remains. The closer to death, the less color is needed, and only the palest colors and sheer, shiny whiteness are sought.

This view of the aging world is inextricably linked to concepts of age and aging in society. Cultural representations of color, spatial representations of passages, and concepts of cosmology and spirits are woven into Mede's paintings. The age of the world is the aging of people, from the beginning of life to death. Youth is presented with its associations of dangerous power and passions, and maturity with its assumption of responsibilities as mothers and fathers, social leaders and teachers, crowd the paintings with images and movement. Elders are associated with the graying of color, the dampening of heat and passion with wisdom and spirituality. The cosmology of the people is in their keeping, and the elders are closest to the whiteness of the spirit world, empty of color, empty of activity, meditative and serene.

NARRATIVES OF THE ARTIST

Narratives of the paintings reveal ideas about the aging world and the life cycles of all humanity and society itself. Following are narratives about the artist, firstly his own background, secondly his interpretation of his own self, his body and the spirit which guides him, and thirdly a sequential review of his own life passages in his own words about the changes in his art.

Biographical Background

Cuthy Mede was born in 1943 in a miner's town in Zimbabwe, of Malawian parents. As a young boy, aged nine, his family returned to Malawi, to Likoma Island, surrounded by Lake Malawi. Mede's sister recalls her brother as a child, constantly drawing and creating images. If paper and pencil were not available, she once said to me, he would draw in the sands of the beaches around the island. Mede attended school on Likoma Island, and then went on to Malawi's only University at that time, Chancellor College in Zomba. Mede studied Fine Art, and later became a teacher of Fine Art in the same University. In the years following his graduation, Mede continued his work in painting and sculpting. His early work was in realism, but soon he developed his work in cubist and pointillist styles. Pointillism, Mede once said to me, reminded him of the island beaches, which were made of tiny pebbles in many shades of color, including red and green, as well as various yellows, golds, ochres and browns.

As Mede studied art, he became more familiar with modern artworks as well as classical artworks, and admired such artists as Pablo Picasso, Vincent Van Gogh, Salvador Dali, and Leonardo da Vinci. From the early 1970's, Mede began exhibiting his works in local venues. His work became widely known in Malawi, and he was offered international exhibitions, in Berlin, Canada, the United States and Britain. Mede has traveled widely since his days on Likoma Island, and his work has been sold round the world. He is, arguably, the best known artist in Malawi.

In 1985, Mede opened his own art gallery in the City Center of Lilongwe. Unlike other African artists, he chose not to emigrate but to remain in Malawi, where he encourages others to pursue their interests in arts. I met Cuthy Mede in 1984, at an exhibition of his work in the Capital Hotel of Lilongwe. Since then, I have been a frequent visitor to his gallery, and have documented certain paintings and periods of his work over more than a decade. While I was in Malawi in 1996, Mede offered extensive interviews, and showed me his older work as well as his most recent work.

MEDE: NARRATIVE OF ART, SELF AND AGING

As Mede writes about his work, 'My art is a revelation of my self, spirit and body. It is revelation of my soul. The spirit being the creator and the body being the recipient' (archival material 1996).

This relationship between the self, the body and the spirit recurs in his reflections about his work, and forms a kind of narrative, a self-reflexive review of thirty years of art work. Changes in thought over time coincide with changing perceptions of life passages, and both coincide with changing art.

Mede exposes his ideas about the spiritual versus the body. In interviews he refers to his body doing the will of the spirit, following the spirit. The body and the spirit are distinct, one in service to the other. 'I do not see things for myself only but also for other spirits and bodies- souls around my ambiance'. He adds, 'Everything is beautiful spiritually but bodily not.' (Mede doc.1)

According to Mede, the spirit, God, gods, and ancestors inspire his work through revelations. The body is the recipient of these revelations, and the self narrates the messages, significance and importance of the spirit in visual forms.

'Year by year my training has been to learn to understand God... I begin to understand myself better from inside myself and hence paint and sculpt to reveal things inside me. Year by year my spirit converses with ... Gods to provide the right approach to my works of art- to show to my body and the bodies of mankind' (Mede doc.1).

NARRATIVE OF PASSAGES, CHANGES AND AGES IN ART AND ARTIST

> 'Mede believes that important ideas in the human
> life-cycle should stand out in substantial works of
> art' (Matawere 1995).

As the above quote suggests, Mede's work expresses ideas about the life-cycle, from birth to death, from passage of age to passage of age, to larger themes of spiritual and social life-cycles which relate to the aging of Mede's own body. Mede re-interprets his work in new forms over time, in different ages. As the self is re-interpreted over passages of time, so the artworks change form, use of space, and color, associated with specific periods in the life cycle.

Mede describes his early work as follows: 'As a budding artist, before 1964, my scope of things around me was narrow, small, insignificant' (Mede doc.1).

It was only in 1964 (age 21) that he began to see the world as a cycle of life, and his first paintings beginning with the dot of light, with lines forming cubist shapes, reflect this change.

From his early twenties into his thirties Mede started perceiving his work within the human life cycle. Realism gave way to cubism and static pictures to images in motion. The dot of life, of light and energy was born in the beginning of Time, and he related this light of God to his own self, as the light of inspiration, and his own life, coming from God.

The subjects of his work come from many sources, all related to God. He writes, 'I work from myths and legends of Malawi-from time before my birth' (Mede doc.1).

As the myths of Malawi recur in his work, so do his dreams. In the 1980's as he entered his forties, Mede recounted a recurring dream about Jesus in a red robe. All around him were bright red colors, the whole world was red.

In 1985, at age 42, Mede opened his own Galerie Africaines to sell his paintings and sculpture, and a few works by selected artists. The range of his artworks to date, were all present, cubism, linear, pointillism realism. Matawere (1995) wrote about the Galeries Africaines, saying, '[it] attempts to show and sell the whole spectrum of African identity' ... 'the rain-maker, rustic women brewing *masese* beer, doctors operating in a hospital theater, traditional healing of hysteria, indigenous dancers and all about people in various human spheres'.

In answer to my question about themes in his work, Mede (doc 1) responded, 'Yes, the subject matter has indeed developed over the years.... [It] reflects changes in subject and thought. Some are political like *Pregnant Malawi*, some like *Chilembwe's Rising* and *Agonies of Nyasaland* are historical. Others are social events like *Moonlight Dancers* and the *Village Sanhedrin of Malawi*'.

He describes work in this period as a Linear style, 'making use of colored lines to form shapes of objects in space, ground or air. This style demands very thin multi colored lines set in any given direction as requested by the spirit' (Mede doc 1).

In interviews in 1996, Mede shifted from depictions of the emotional red world and images of political, historical and social life to yet another theme, another passage. Now in his fifties, Mede describes the themes of his work as spiritual, evoking eternity, endlessness, the turning to total spiritual forms, away from social and political themes. His recent paintings are now called *Mercy*, *Ancestors* and *Justice*.

Mede (doc 1) wrote, 'I have, especially now that I am over half a century old, have turned to spiritual and philosophical themes currently. I am interested in where I am going- that is life beyond the grave'.

In 1996 he began having a recurring dream. In this recurring dream, Jesus, (who wore red in the 1980's), now wears white, and the world around Jesus is white, and blue and shining (Mede doc 1).

This period, this passage, this age of his work in his fifties and now nearer sixties, to Mede, is the most important. In this period of blue and white work, he claims to perceive the future, and he suggests his work will enter yet another passage. This new passage, he predicts, will have different forms, 'My future work will be in circles and fluid forms to emphasize endlessness-infinity-. Art is endless. It flows like fluid and so art takes all forms and shapes and colors and it is also achromatic'.

Reflecting on his work in 1996, Mede (doc 1) recalls, 'as I grew year by year, God's revelation [became] wide, clear and is opened so I can see things beyond the grave...'. 'Yes, these styles offer me gradual changes towards what I pursue to do. Now, what, how and when the ending will be I do not know' (Mede doc 1).

Finally, we may interpret these passages in age through Cuthy Mede himself, and his body, and the aging of the world in life-cycles, the human world and the spirit world, as coming full circle, back to the beginning of the small dot of light. This return to the beginning is reflected in Mede's own words (doc 1),

'My most important works are those that are spiritual. Those that address the future. Those that address Love, Mercy, Peace, Tranquility, Eternity. Because they are close to the Beginning of Life Itself'.

NARRATIVE AND INTERPRETATION: A CONCLUSION

Age as a creative construction has been interpreted through the narrative of interviews with one artist, and the narrative of references to and interpretations of this artist's work. Interpretations of the artist's work are enhanced by social commentary, and research on local cosmologies. These interpretations, distilled from many discourses, publications, discussions, writings, field researches and artworks, are re-presented in this document as narratives about age.

The above descriptions of four passages in art styles have *become a narrative*, an interpreted text, a text, which is an interpretation. This narrative is partly biographical. It is about an individual and his own perceptions of age in his work and in the passage of years in his own life. These individual perceptions draw from the local social constructions of age, and from both the individual world-view and the local world-views. It is a narrative of four passages, four styles, of art, in three different dimensions, each reflecting upon the other.

The text about the paintings enlightens other discourses and other textual interpretations, apart from the actual paintings themselves. Without the visual image present, the artworks are rendered into interpretive text. Acknowledging this, the newly created text about paintings has a life of its own, and becomes a narrative of individual, social and cosmological discourses about age.

Each passage in the life cycle present in the artworks embodies ideas about time, the passing of time, the aging process from birth to death, but also the aging process from death back to the beginning of life again. These ideas about age and the human life cycle are interpreted by Mede, in color, in lines, in light, in space, in subject, theme, and image. His own ideas permeate social realms, and his own religious world view is echoed in parts by other world views within Mede's experience of his world. The spiritual, the chaotic, the beginning of time; conjure specific colors, as the multiplicity of maturity, the social, political and historical involvement with life, conjure multiple colors. And each is associated with the maturing passages of an artist's work, and coming to terms with one's own cycle of life.

ACKNOWLEDGMENT

Though I draw upon Mede's words, spoken and written, the responsibility for this interpretive analysis is solely my own. I am greatly indebted to Cuthy Mede for sharing his work over so many years, and for his friendship for which I remain grateful. The information about the artist is derived from discussions with Mede, his notes given to me, an interview with his sister, and documentation such as a list of exhibitions, and general background material.

References

Archival Materials

Hand-written notes by Cuthy Mede, archival document 1, 1996

Personal Interviews: 1984-86, 1988, 1992, and 1996.

Archived articles: Interviews, list of exhibitions, exhibit openings, news accounts

Cited: G. Matawere, 'Moving with a city on the move', *Daily Times* (Malawi) 23 October 1995, 10.

[Author not known] 'Preservation of African traditions' *Quest,* Malawi, second quarter, 1986, 22 and 42.

Chambala, Haxley Kalebe 'Cuthy Mede...the whole culture man' *This is Malawi,* September 1980.

Slides and photographs of paintings

Selected Paintings described in this chapter: *Justice, African Wedding, Power of Tradition, Chilembwe's Uprising, Death of Hands, Ancestral Masks, Money, Agonies of Nyasaland, Teacher, Pregnant Malawi, Village Scene, Python Snake,* and *Refugees.*

Books

Abiodun, Rowland, Henry J. Drewal and John Pemberton III, eds. 1994. *The Yoruba Artist: New Theoretical Perspectives on African Arts.* Washington, D.C.: Smithsonian Institution Press.

Adorno, Theodor W.1984. *Aesthetic Theory.* London: Routledge and Kegan Paul.

Aguilar, Laurel Birch. 1994a.'Mede: Catalyst for Change', *Southern African Art Journal* [Harare].

———. 1994b. 'Nyau Masks of the Chewa: An Oral Historical Introduction' *Society of Malawi Journal* 47 (2): 15-37.

———. 1996. *Inscribing the Mask: Interpretation of Nyau Masks and Ritual Performance among the Chewa of Central Malawi.* Fribourg: University of Fribourg Press.

———. 1998. 'Youth, Maturity, Aging and Ancestors in the Society of Masks', in Mario I. Aguilar, ed., *The Politics of Age and Gerontocracy in Africa: Ethnographies of the Past & Memories of the Present,* Trenton, NJ: Africa World Press, 151-176.

Aguilar, Mario I. 1998. *The Politics of Age and Gerontocracy in Africa: Ethnographies of the Past & Memories of the Present.* Trenton, NJ: Africa World Press.

Barber, Karin and P.F. de Moreas Farias, eds. 1989. *Discourse and its Disguises: The Interpretation of African Oral Texts,* Birmingham: University of Birmingham.

Coote, Jeremy and Anthony Shelton. Ed. 1992. *Anthropology, Art and Aesthetics* Oxford: Clarendon Press.

Danto, Arthur. 1981. *Transfiguration of the Commonplace* Cambridge. Mass. Harvard University Press.

DeLiss, Clementine *et al.* Ed. 1995. *Seven Stories about Modern Art in Africa.* Paris and New York: Whitechapel Art Gallery.

Fabian, Johannes. 1996. *Remembering the Present: Painting and Popular History in Zaire.* Berkeley and London: University of California Press.

Hackett, Rosalind. 1998. *Art and Religion in Africa.* London: Cassell.

Layton, Robert. 1992. 'Traditional and Contemporary Art of Aboriginal Australia: Two Case Studies,' in Jeremy Coote and Antony Shelton, eds., *Anthropology, Art and Aesthetics.* Oxford: Clarendon Press, 137-159.

Morphy, Howard. 1992. 'From Dull to Brilliant: the Aesthetics of Spiritual Power among the Yolngu,' in Jeremy Coote and Anthony Shelton, eds., *Anthropology, Art and Aesthetics.* Oxford: Clarendon Press, 209-244.

Ricoeur, Paul. 1981. *The Conflict of Interpretations: Essays in Hermeneutics.* Evanston: Northwestern University Press.

Schoffeleers, J. Matthew. 1992. *River of Blood: the Genesis of a Martyr Cult in Southern Malawi, AD 1600.* Madison: Wisconsin University Press.

Roscoe, A. 1985. *Land of Fire: Oral Literature from Malawi.* Lilongwe: Popular Publications.

Sieber, Roy and Roslyn Walker. 1989. *African Art in the Cycle of Life.* Washington, DC: Smithsonian Institution Press for the National Museum of African Art.

Vogel, Susan Mullin. 1991. *Africa Explores: 20th Century African Art.* New York: Center for African Art and Munich: Prestel.

Chapter 11

RETHINKING AGE AND THE CULTURE OF THE YOUNG PASTORALIST IN GARBA TULLA, KENYA

Mario I. Aguilar

Youth is what is young and what belongs to the future, and young people have repeatedly been associated with what is new in culture (Fornas 1995: 1)

Three strands concerning the ongoing anthropological study of age have been suggested by Paul Spencer:

1. The study of age systems.
2. The symbolic analysis of relations of aging, i.e. times of transition and interpretations of the life course.
3. The changing relations of power with age and by sex in terms of the rise and fall of systems of extended kinship, within processes of modernization (Spencer 1990:29-30).

Spencer's first strand has been traditionally associated with the study of age-sets in East and Central Africa (e.g. Bernardi 1985, Stewart 1977). Other recent post-colonial studies have also explored the life cycle process within localized communities as well as within the ritual and religious diversity of post-colonial Africa (e.g. Birch de Aguilar 1996, Kaspin 1993, Matory 1993). However, processes of aging in relation to processes of modernization have been less prominent in recent studies of an anthropological nature, particularly in the case of East Africa, and certainly in the case of pastoral societies (cf. Aguilar 1998a, Fratkin 1998: 52-65, Spencer 1988). In reality, it has been within those processes of modernization that particular social models of pastoral organization have been generationally contested, expanded, enriched, and diversified. It is within those processes of hybridity and post-colonialism that contestations of power, kinship, and gender relations within pastoralism call for contemporary processes of rethinking models of age, and their contemporary validity within pastoralism.

This chapter argues for an ongoing process of 'rethinking age', and constitutes a bridge between the essays already presented in this volume and those yet to come in future publications on the study of African youth, their challenging cultures, and their ongoing dialogical position within African societies and African nations. Thus, while I reiterate the importance of the study of age in all its aspects in order to understand East African pastoralism, in this chapter I focus on the ontological possibility of a changeable and unchangeable pastoral world, and a 'youth culture' within an African world of mixed temporalities.

In fact, the question already posed in the case of a possible African modernity, that is, 'how do we describe a set of dialectical processes between center and periphery, ruler and ruled, metropolis and margins, whose form is so broadly the same but whose content is often very different?' (Comaroff and Comaroff 1993: xiii) can also be asked in relation to social representations of the young and of the old. As a possible answer to such question I would suggest the use of a more diversified model of anthropological research, in order to continue rethinking pastoral societies. In such diversified model, I propose looking at the young rather than the old. From that perspective I further suggest that societal continuity is provided by the self-perception and appreciation of pastoralism as a cultural tradition and as a symbolic system. It follows that any ideas of a 'disappearing world of pastoralism', relate to a myth of cultural misunderstanding, connected to 'alienated forms of analytical thought' (Rigby 1996: 85), in which diversity and the Other do not have a place.

RETHINKING AGE AND GERONTOLOGY

Re-consideration of any localized social and cultural model of age, rather than solely age-systems, has to assume that while industrial societies conferred a low status position to the elderly, non-industrial societies are age-oriented. They are age-oriented, 'in the sense that much of their culture can be seen as geared towards the interest of the old rather than of the young' (Holy 1990: 181, cf. 167-168).

As already suggested the study of age has been primarily associated with those who have reached the final step of the process of human maturation and aging, i.e. the old. In fact, words such as gerontology and gerontocracy have dominated the literature on aging, particularly in societies where there are statistically larger numbers of old rather than young people (e.g. Britain or some particular districts within the United States). While the study of non-Western societies has in fact pointed to the prominent role of older members within society, Western industrialized societies, for example the United States, have given more and more cultural centrality to youthfulness, symbolized by hard work, sports, playfulness, and productivity. Thus, in the West, the old are not perceived as those who have survived a process of maturation (Spencer 1990) and as cultural heroes, but as a problem, as those who do not produce any longer, and on the contrary consume economic and public resources. As a result, and within a Westernized perception of youthfulness and work oriented perceptions of individual fulfillment, anthropological concerns for the whole process of maturation as a process of aging have failed to stimulate excitement and the so-called 'anthropological imagination'.

I would suggest that, cultural perceptions of aging are fundamental in order to understand societal perceptions related to the old and to the young. Universal perceptions of the old cannot be constructed on the basis of biological patterns associated with the life cycle, but need to be looked at from the relativist perspective of a multi-cultural and multi-dimensional social experience by the old and by the young themselves. From such culturally oriented perspective it is possible to argue that the young in Africa constitute an under-researched topic. This due to the fact that more emphasis has been given to a common African youth culture, rather than to the localized, diversified and contradictory images of the young in relation to the old.

Thus, African 'youth culture' corresponds in some ways to that 'culture' associated with other youngsters within a globalized world, however such 'youth culture' is culturally constructed, re-constructed and invented from their own perspective as well. Such perspective relates particular youngsters not to a whole world 'out there', but to their own contestation and relatedness with older members of their own societies, groups, networks, churches, places of work, and indeed their own families. If any universal social pattern could be suggested, it would relate to the fact that there are younger members of society who would like to re-think their own society and their surrounding realities in a different way than their older kin and relations but through a universal experience in itself.

Diachronically speaking, I would suggest that the young in colonial Africa were as the young today, and that contemporary youth in Africa share quite a lot with the young of yesterday. Both groups, the colonial youth and the post-colonial youth, had to find their own way into sociability, helped by others. Regardless of their own sense of egalitarianism, they remained younger than other older men. In the case of the Maasai, for example, 'shaved male' remains a terms for the 'novice *moran*', but at the same time can be used by a speaker to signify a younger person than himself. Thus, 'alluding to the fact that he can never catch up and relatively speaking will always remain a cub' (Spencer 1988: 79).

In fact, the young pastoralists can be described as those who have not married, or who have not assumed societal, political, religious or economic responsibilities, and have continued perceiving themselves as pastoralists, even when they have not been directly involved in the caring of herds within their home areas. However, they have portrayed their own cultural identity as different from that of their parents and grandparents, and have felt culturally closer to other young people within Kenya and indeed within Africa.

In the following sections, and by examining ways in which the Boorana pastoralists themselves have diversified their dealings with a nation-state such as Kenya, and within a larger phenomenon of globalization, I return to a basic parameter for the study of age. Namely that 'the very concept of old age is only intelligible in relation to youth and the lifelong experience of ageing' (Spencer 1990: 1). Thus, social changes and cultural continuities within pastoralism can only be understood by looking at the young as well as the old, within particular societies, and within the post-coloniality of contemporary African states.

THE POST-COLONIAL EXPERIENCE OF PASTORALISM

Constant changes have affected rural pastoral societies in East Africa, and those changes have been even more pronounced in cities, towns and urban centers in general. Such changes from the socially localized to the socially diversified have also been present within pastoralism, particularly in towns of Eastern Kenya, i.e. urban centers populated by kin extensions from the semi-nomadic pastoral communities of the arid and semi-arid areas of Kenya. Thus, towns such as Isiolo, Garba Tulla, Wajir, Garissa, or Moyale have become centers of migratory patterns associated with casual workers, famine recipients, converts to Christianity and Islam, recipients of scholarships for primary and secondary education, and pastoralists looking for better cattle and animal markets.

In comparison with colonial times, those migrations have increased within post-colonial times, due mainly to the existence of a certain freedom of movement within Kenya that was otherwise controlled and monitored closely before 1963. Therefore, economic migrations to administrative centers have increased due to the fact that urban centers tend to offer more opportunities, and in the word of the young pastoralists, 'they have life'. In fact, for those young pastoralists with some kind of education, particularly those who have attended secondary schools outside their localized peripheries, life in the pastoral settlements is considered boring. They are neither equipped with a certain experiential knowledge about herds, nor with the working capabilities associated with clerical jobs and steady incomes.

As it was already the case in the 1970s, not only town centres in northern Kenya, but also big cities such as Nairobi or Mombasa offer a special attraction to the young pastoralists. In those places and by using their extended kinship ties and network affiliation they model their future success on that of their migrant older kin. Therefore, even when systems of age are not in operation any longer, models of cultural gerontocracy are still present, as the young need their older kin and their already created networks in order to get jobs, sponsorship for education, and cash so as to start their married life.

In the case of the Boorana of northern Kenya, small migrations started to take place by the early 1970s, while other groups such as Maasai or Somali had already located themselves in Nairobi during the colonial period. Historically, Maasai and Somali were often employed by the colonial police and by European families as guards (*askari*). Boorana continued their moiety affiliation with other Boorana throughout northern Kenya and southern Ethiopia and were administratively confined to the Northern Frontier District (N.F.D.). In fact, any youth migration to urban centers was almost impossible during the colonial period, as pastoralists residing within the N.F.D. needed permits in order to cross their tribal areas and reside in other parts of the Kenya colony. The creation of a unified nation lifted those restrictions, creating a more fluid movement of pastoralists between the North and East into larger cities, particularly Nairobi. By the 1990s it was possible to suggest that most of the young Boorana pastoralists had moved at one point or another between their areas of grazing, their homes and the larger towns surrounding them, e.g. Marsabit, Moyale, Wajir, Isiolo, Meru, and Garba Tulla.

THE POST-COLONIALITY OF GARBA TULLA TOWN

The case of Garba Tulla is not different than any other town within East Africa. As an administrative center it represents a colonial creation that was taken over by the Kenyan administration. However, in relation to larger cities and more important towns such as Isiolo, it is still considered one of those many isolated administrative posts, spread throughout Africa, 'a town in the periphery' (Rea 1998:105). Even when it is a relatively small town pastoralists conduct business at the government offices, or at the Tuesday market, or live there in order to be closer to water, food, medical facilities and schools for their children. While nearly 5,000 people claim to have some roots there, it constitutes another example of the post-colonial mixed temporalities present in different clans, ages, kinship relations, diversified religious traditions, and also female headed households.

The town is perceived by Boorana and Somali as a Boorana town, due to the fact that mostly Boorana reside there. While it became an important market town and trade center during colonial times, the sad and violent events of the *shifta* war (1963-1967) made Garba Tulla a place associated with impoverished pastoralists, i.e. the Waso Boorana (Aguilar 1998a, Dahl 1979, Hogg 1981, 1986, 1990). At the time of Kenya's independence (1963), the Waso Boorana supported the Somali claim that stated that the N.F.D. should become another province of Somalia, due to the large numbers of ethnic Somali that resided there. As the N.F.D. became part of Kenya, a guerrilla war started, with roads being mined and government vehicles and functionaries attacked. The response by the Kenyatta government was firm, and the army restored peace by force, using strong punitive measures against the Boorana who remained in the district east of Isiolo (Aguilar 1996b).

As a result, the first experiences by Boorana pastoralists in a post-colonial era were devastating. By 1968 international relief was under way, and an increasing influx of aid and famine relief plus education opportunities provided by Christian churches and Islam had a tremendous impact on social relations within Boorana families and the town itself. In reality, while during colonial times the town existed because there was an administrative need to keep a presence in the area, after the 1970s Boorana were totally dependent on the town's existence for their subsistence.

It is within those parameters of social, economic, and political change, that constant patterns of cultural change have also emerged, and have influenced the perception of society and the world by young Boorana. Those cultural changes are related to changeable patterns of social organization and social classification that nevertheless create a pastoral continuity and some cultural diversity. Thus, people who have been raised within pastoral societies remain within such pastoral ideology, even when they locate themselves in urban areas and centers of commerce, populated by non-pastoralist peoples and peoples who speak Swahili or English. Such process of cultural imagination suggests that places of origin, dry lands, and religious rituals occupy a central place within constructions of pastoral identity, heavily influenced by social memories and pastoral memorials (Aguilar 1999).

I would suggest that the Boorana who reside within the Garba Tulla Division of Kenya can be considered pastoralists not because they have significant daily tasks related to herds, but because their cultural construction of life relates to their perception of self-identity in relation to herds and their management. As in the case of the Maasai, Boorana 'ethnic identity is fashioned –not given-' and therefore constitutes 'the very means of survival' (Waller 1993: 302).

BOORANA TRADITIONS REINVENTED

The most important memory for the old and for the young is the knowledge imparted and maintained within the Boorana *gada* system. A system of age-organization, understood by some as a political system, by other as a ritual and philosophical system, it induces memories associated with a better time long gone when *gada* was celebrated, and it also shapes contemporary perceptions of age within Boorana. While the older Waso Boorana departed from such system, the younger Boorana, who grew up after the *shifta* conflict have, like many other Oromo, found their identity in the memories of such system (Jalata 1998). In fact, for younger generations the *gada* system, that in the past provided a political and ritual cultural formation within Boorana society, has become an ideological metaphor for national cohesion and ethnic exclusion. However, the current ways of dealing with communal decisions, as described by Marco Bassi (Bassi 1996a, 1996b), suggests a re-invention of *gada* as a symbolic system of classification (Aguilar 1998c), somehow different than the classificatory model of political continuity argued by Legesse (1973).

Thus, while *gada* remains a marker of cultural identity for all Boorana, and particularly for Oromo nationalists, Baxter's symbolic and ritual interpretation of such system provides an important way of understanding the social location of the youth in Boorana. Within the complexity of any age-system, Baxter and Almagor have argued that 'age-systems attempt to create cognitive and structural order within and for a population by creating categories based on age and generation; as does a kinship system' (Baxter and Almagor 1978:5). In fact, the basic problem with the reliability and continuity of the *gada* system was the fact that the position of sons within such system depended on their fathers, and not on themselves. Therefore, there was no way of predicting when married men were to actually have children.

In such relation of a *gada* ideology, it is clear that young men boast of their solidarity, while old men (*gadamoji*) boast of past success as youngsters, some more than others (Baxter and Almagor 1978: 15). In fact, any current relations of Boorana youth with their elders does not necessarily imply a complete change in cultural outlook, but the challenge of youthfulness to those who are indeed controlling economic and cultural resources, namely older married men, some of them their own fathers.

Within those parameters of a young pastoralist who is rebellious till he acquires a more senior social and cultural parameter of existence, the young Boorana have different ways of embracing their social identity. I will describe those different, however complementary, ways of being young in the following sections. I take into account that while the *gada* system was a classificatory system where only men had a place, contemporary Boorana society offers different social identities and social roles to men and women within the same diversified social system.

THE YOUNG AND THE HERDS

The number of young Boorana men looking after herds, i.e. their more traditional role, is smaller than in the past. Three main reasons can be suggested for this fundamental pastoral activity,

1. There are less herds to be taken care of than forty years ago.
2. A significant number of youngsters have gone from Garba Tulla in order to search for employment in other parts of the Eastern and North-Eastern provinces of Kenya.
3. The insecurity created by bandits (*shifta*) during the late 1980s and 1990s has meant that older men, mainly married, are habitually looking after herds.

Those youngsters who look after herds spend considerable amount of time during the year away from Garba Tulla with the *fora* herd, that is kept between Garba Tulla and Kinna, and in other areas near Gafarsa. It is only during the dry season that more herds are brought back to Garba Tulla in order to water them at the wells. Many of those youngsters have not gone to school, or have decided to look after herds of older brothers, particularly those who have gone and have earned some cash, later to be invested in cattle, goats and sheep. Some of them have secured their future, in the midst of economic security, by marrying older women, who in turn have provided economic resources and herds.

In the case of Boorana young women, unmarried girls (*intal*) remain with their parents or kin in Garba Tulla. Some girls help by looking after the *hawicha* herd, those animals kept closer to the Boorana settlements (*manyatta*) in order to provide milk, or those animals that are sick and are unable to stay in the semi-desertic ecological niches (*deda*). Unmarried girls also help their mothers with the household chores, and some of them attend school during the day. However, the number of girls who attend school on a regular basis are much smaller than boys. Some girls marry young and develop new kin affiliations and demands, even when they only have children later on within their marriages. Therefore, a girl who has been promised in marriage to other family would stop attending school and would remain closer to other older women within her family.

Thus, I would suggest that within Boorana traditional roles and at an age when youngsters need the help of their parents and kin in order to move on, their activities and aspirations remain closer to the Boorana world. Such world is represented by animals in the case of the males, and by the house (*manyatta*) in the case of females. This becomes clear during Boorana weddings, when unmarried females sing their own songs, apart from the actual main celebrations, however, closer to the bride's home. Instead, young men mingle with other young males, friends of the bridegroom, listening to music, and keeping apart from females and older men (Aguilar 1998: 71-104).

While some Boorana youngsters have departed for other places in order to visit, fewer are those who at one point or another have not returned to Garba Tulla, or have moved with kin and relations to other Boorana towns and villages. However, some of the youngsters have moved outside their kin's realm of influence and are not part of a pastoral way of life any longer. That is the case of those who have received secondary, or college education, and have or are pursuing employment somewhere else. They constitute part of a youth culture that speaks of social rapture, globalization and modernity. However, small groups of elite youngsters remain part of a youth culture while single and unemployed. As products of the education system, they aim at doing well economically and socially and many do well indeed.

Nevertheless, when they marry or when they settle into jobs and business they turn once again to their home in the pastoral lands and they invest in animals, property, and land within arid pastoral areas. In fact, the initial process of national incorporation takes place at the secondary schools, however it stops with the next step of social maturation, i.e. marriage and the arrival of children. Schools create conditions of ordering that aim at the integration of youngsters into a wider world of prosperity, progress, and self-development.

WESTERN EDUCATION AND INDIGENOUS KNOWLEDGE

The education system in Kenya expects students from one area to attend school in other part of Kenya. Thus, students who have completed primary school education must apply to a centralized bureaucratic body, that after examining their primary school grades assign them to particular secondary schools. It is only privately funded schools that can accept students from the same area, and that in general keep the close connection, so common in Europe, between the family home and the local school. Apart from these exceptions, aimed at a Kenyan elite and to those many expatriates who live in Nairobi, the ideology behind the creation of secondary schools is to create good citizens (*wananchi*), young Kenyans who in the future will show more allegiance to the nation than to their ethnic group.

While recent events in Kenya have suggested that such ide-ology of nationhood has somehow failed, there has been some impact on the educated Boorana who have attended secondary school, and particularly on the few who have attended university. Some of the traits of youth culture within Boorana expresses the fact that they are aware of other youths within Kenya, and that their social values can be suggested as more universal than the localized customs and traditions of the Boorana (*ada Boorana*).

During my time in Garba Tulla there were only a couple of Boorana studying at the local Garba Tulla High School, while the majority of secondary school students were attending schools outside Garba Tulla district. Garba Tulla High School had been created and run by the Methodist Church during the 1970s, and during the 1990s it still had some expatriates teaching there. It was possible for those sponsoring bodies such as Christian churches or the Canadian Children Fund to request admission for a few Boorana within such secondary school. However, most Boorana youngsters experienced long journeys to schools as far as Meru, Embu, and Nairobi. In those situations they remained identified as Boorana, and they strengthen their ethnic identity through a daily social interaction with youngsters who spoke other lan-guages and had other customs in their homes somewhere else in Kenya (Aguilar 1996b).

In fact, Western education and the contemporary school system have accelerated changes within Boorana families and Boorana society in Garba Tulla. Those two phenomena have primarily affected a formerly unified cultural conception of two aspects of society, i.e. cultural knowledge and its centrality within the Boorana social process of maturation.

CONTESTATIONS OF 'OLD' AND 'YOUNG' KNOWLEDGE

One of the most common distinctions between the social realities of the young and of the old in contemporary Africa relates to the acquisition of knowledge. Members of society acquire and treasure different kinds of knowledge that allow them to deal with life and with social processes of maturation, adaptation, and change. In the past, and within Boorana society, the young, uninitiated and immature were instructed and had to pass through particular ways of social initiation in order to become adults and to be accepted as mature members within society. Knowledge allowed adults to operate and to participate properly in community activities and community decisions.

Most anthropological works related to African processes of social maturation and the life cycle have stressed the need to convey knowledge for the sake of society's survival and the toughness of such liminal processes of initiation. However, features related to the social contestation of acquired knowledge provide interesting insights into the evolving role of the young within Boorana society. Knowledge is contested in the public sphere, a sphere where the old traditionally exercise control over the young. Thus, knowledge and cultural wisdom are assumed as cumulative and growing with age. However, in the cases where there is a public contestation of the old by the young, the image of the old provided is not that of sympathetic elders who instruct the young. Their image is of 'calculating elders who withhold more than they teach and use claims on withheld knowledge to keep the young under their thumbs' (Murphy 1980:204).

While the traditional occasions where knowledge was imparted, i.e. the *gada* festivals, were never celebrated in the Waso area, several Sakuye who made a journey to Ethiopia in 1971 were invested with the care of Boorana knowledge by the Boorana sacred man, the *Kallu*. Those men and their sons exercised an absolute political and ritual mediation for twenty years, as they were highly regarded not only by the Boorana themselves, but also by religious leaders within the mosque and by the Kenya administration. While their fathers had converted to Islam and therefore abandoned their interest for proper Boorana knowledge, those older men of the 1990s had the last say in family and *manyatta* disputes. Their authority extended to daily negotiations with funding agencies and people involved in relief operations and development projects within Garba Tulla.

In the meantime a younger generation of educated males acquired a different kind of knowledge, i.e. Western education. Such younger generations started to become influenced by pan-Oromo discourses of a nationalistic nature, and by ideas of self-reliance and independence. In fact, those aspirations by the young were not that different from those of their grandparents during the colonial period, however they contested the absolute control of the older Muslim Boorana men and their families. Thus, during 1992, for example, older men wanted to talk to me about Islam and the massive Boorana conversion to Islam, while younger men and women wanted to talk and exchange information about Boorana traditions and ways of doing things. The young were particularly interested in their connections with other Boorana, and the fact that some Boorana were not Muslims. Such knowledge of other Boorana has shaped in them yet another kind of identity marker in a younger generation that feels more distant to Islam and closer to other Boorana. Such younger generation would like to acquire other kinds of knowledge in order to be 'masters of the future', i.e. Boorana 'real traditions', and the social skills required to do well within a modern world.

Some of those younger Boorana became educated professionals in Isiolo, Meru, Nairobi and other towns in Kenya. By the time that they had finished college, and one of them had gone on a professional visit to the United States, older men still treated them as youngsters. However, when they got married and when they acquired stock to be left in the Garba Tulla area, those young professionals started to have a voice within the Boorana assemblies. In some cases, they directed the assemblies, particularly at times when outsiders were present, and some of the conversations were conducted not only in the Boorana language, but also in Swahili and English.

I would suggest that some of those educated young people started to become influential within Boorana society not because they had received some education, some 'knowledge' that allowed the Boorana to converse with people from different 'worlds'. They became influential because they were perceived as mature by older Boorana, due to the fact that they had acquired a wife and herds within the Garba Tulla area. Most of those young men have remained Muslims, while practicing some of the ritual moments associated with all Boorana, such as the 'sacrifice of coffee-beans' (*buna qalla*), and the daily prayers. Thus, their perception of knowledge as a generation departs from that of older men, and those Boorana who settled into the Waso area in the 1930s.

There has been a constant ethnographic re-enactment of 'the problem of generations', as viewed by Mannheim, that has been used by scholars in order to understand the social roles of the young, as different from those of the old, and vice versa (Aguilar 1998a: 14-15, Spencer 1998: 232-233). As Mannheim (1952) argued, such problem is not only the fact that different generations create change within society, but they provide the possibility that the perception of society itself is created by groups of people, for example the old and the young. Those groups are to be considered 'generations' because they share the same perceptions and a common ethos, and they are not necessarily mutually aided because of their biological age. The challenge of such generational studies is to find the individual continuities, as well as the generational differences. To that effect, the passing of history remains a crucial factor, whereby older people 'are not viewed simply as a homogenous group, but rather as age cohorts moving through history, each with his or her distinct life experiences, influenced by the historical circumstances encountered earlier in life' (Hareven 1982: 2).

In the case of generations within Waso Boorana, there has been a constant re-interpretation of the past, and of the notions of Boorana identity. For many, the Waso Boorana are who they are because they are Muslims; for others, they are Boorana because they remain symbolically and ritually in relation to other Boorana and to their own places of origin in southern Ethiopia. Others speak of being Boorana as not being Somali, or Bantu, or European, etc. By using Mannheim's theoretical framework, many generations can be described. I would suggest that the young Waso Boorana are those who were born after the *shifta* emergency. They are nominal Muslims, they have very little knowledge of Islamic practices, and their daily lives are related to their extended family households (Aguilar 1998a: 18-19). They are nevertheless age-conscious, and they would like to have a larger say within Boorana society, outside the close social association between Boorana and the Islamic centers in Garba Tulla and the Waso area.

On the one hand that so called 'larger say' depends on their acquisition of different kinds of knowledge; on the other hand, such acquisition of knowledge remains linked with social processes of maturation, such as marriage, and their full social maturity, after having had children. Unmarried men or women constitute a social anomaly, and they are not given the chance to express their own opinions within Boorana. They remain as children, i.e. people who need to be told what to do, even when they have financial means outside the social and economic structures of family and kin. It is a contemporary reality that, in some cases, economic uncertainty does not allow youngsters, particularly orphans, to gather the necessary resources in order to marry. More and more, the unmarried can be associated with those who have had further education but have no money or animals, and have to postpone their marriages as a result. They move to towns in order to search for jobs or for employment. If such processes seem to be part of an impoverished contemporary pastoral reality, the habitual realities of the Maasai *murran* can also be compared with the contemporary Boorana situation. After all,

> The *murran* are suspended somewhere between boyhood and full adulthood and are placed in a limbo for an extended period of adolescence that stretches well into their twenties. They are trapped in a regime imposed by the elders and yet at the same time are a law to themselves, a society within a society (Spencer 1993: 141).

That process of symbolic (dis)-location between dependence on their parents and the independent formation of their households also extends to young Boorana females. A Boorana girl marries and acquires a house, and therefore her own domain, a completely different space than the public domain associated with men and their herds. Such female domain has also experienced changes, as types of houses have been diversified, and the realities of inter-marriage have become more frequent, particularly among educated Boorana girls.

UNMARRIED GIRLS, YOUNG WIVES AND YOUNG MOTHERS

The female sphere of control over a house only starts when the unmarried girls build the house before the actual wedding celebration. A girl marries, she acquires a house, and subsequently she becomes an adult by the procreation of children. If in the past such marriage required a longer process of negotiation between two families, the current situation of economic uncertainty has introduced other types and kinds of economic negotiations.

In fact, an impoverished pastoral situation affected the social and economic role of women within Boorana society, mainly because there were no animals to be given to females at birth, at marriage, or when they had children. In fact, insecurity and lack of resources affected the actual possibility of all young Boorana to marry whenever their families had reached a common agreement. Young males had to ask others to help them with the bridewealth needed in order to marry, and therefore in some cases they had to wait more than usual in order to get married. In the meantime some Boorana girls married soldiers or policemen stationed in the Waso area, instead of waiting for an uncertain future. In the past, parents would have certainly objected to such inter-ethnic marriages on account that those men, particularly Kikuyu, were not Muslims. Instead by the 1990s some parents welcomed such marriages as a relief to their economic situation and their parental worries. After all, those Kikuyu men had a job, a salary, and some stability to be offered to their daughters. Most young Boorana men could not offer such stability and their extended family could not offer it either.

However, in order to be considered really married and socially mature, those young married girls still need to procreate at least one child. Gudrun Dahl has pointed to the fact that 'it is the child who really provides [a married woman] with an anchorage in the husband's clan and gives her proper rights to milk cattle from the herd' (Dahl 1979: 119). Therefore, a girl (*intal*) remains as such till she has her first child. Thereafter she will be addressed as *nitti*. In such social context, the young need the recognition of others in order to continue their passing of age, and their process of biological and social maturation. In an impoverished situation, parents and their children make economic alliances with other non-Boorana in order to continue such maturation process. Social immaturity remains a cultural perception in cases where social processes have not been culturally recognized, a process that is certainly different than the youthfulness of those younger members who are still not ready for the next step of maturation, i.e. marriage and procreation.

THE POWER OF BLESSINGS AND GREETINGS

It is worth repeating here that all processes of maturation require the exchange and new allocation of cattle. Even today educated young Boorana need to secure a certain amount of cows in order to secure their marriage. If during colonial times cattle needed to be allocated by older men, the absence of large amounts of stocks within Boorana has meant that most cows needed for marriage are negotiated within the extended family, and in some cases through loans from others.

Abdullahi Bala, a young worker in the development office of Garba Tulla Catholic Mission recounted how in the late 1980s he did not have any cows, and he could not get them from his extended family. He bought cows with the cash he could get in order to secure the Boorana young lady he wanted to marry. Without such payment and the blessing of the older men he could not have married his wife. Economic exchanges and family agreements become firm only when older men have approved of them and they have, through a public gesture, bless those younger men.

The elders' blessings and the social recognition of the community play a more important role within Boorana society than the economic transactions associated with rituals of maturation. The economic part of these rituals can always be adjusted, while the conferring or denial of a blessing and community approval plays a crucial role not only in the marriage process, but also in all daily activities and moments within the aging process.

CONCLUSION: RETHINKING AGE IN AFRICA

It has been argued that 'we are all cultural producers in some way and some kind in our everyday lives', and thus' the absolute importance of trying to think in future oriented ways guided by tendencies already evident within current common culture' (Willis *et al.* 1990: 128). It follows from such statement that the young are not passive recipients of cultural traits, instead they are influenced by localized traditions, while re-inventing them in turn.

Such creativity is a universal and cultural phenomenon that could be termed 'youthfulness'. The young adapt and create common symbolic classifications in order to assert their own perception of society. While the contestation of the young and the old seems to be a universal phenomenon, youth culture cannot be perceived, described or suggested as universal. Instead youth cultures relate to localized social phenomena that depend as much on the past as on the social expectations for the future.

Therefore, I contest the universality of the young from the point of view of cultural studies, and further the total fragmentation of such social category, as argued by models related to individualism and post-modernism. The young, as a social category depend on a localized social construction as well as a self-definition in relative rather than universal terms of social differentiation, and indeed cultural ambiguity (Aguilar 1998b, Woods 1977).

Within such localized perception of age the study of the young in Boorana pastoralism provides clear parameters for social research. The social category of 'young' becomes a more fluid and less clear category. Such category does not depend solely on a measure of biological age, but in a societal perception of those who are not adults yet and are less socially mature. An attempt to culturally define the 'young' opens new avenues of investigation and provides more questions than answers. Some of those questions are: Are those considered young always to be associated with the unmarried? Are the unmarried young pastoralists to be considered as children, a category used many times by older people, teachers, and even politicians? Which social processes and cultural perceptions allow the young to be considered mature and older? Does economic stability and economic resources provide a differentiation in the age process? What is the localized relation between the educated young and community decisions or the political arena? Which social and religious rituals allow a public recognition of those cultural perceptions of youthfulness and cultural immaturity?

It must be recognized that the social parameters of continuity and discontinuity in a localized social setting become crucial in order to understand the social fabric and the (dis)-continuities that are continuously arising within Africa. In countries such as Kenya, where the young constitute the majority of the population, I would suggest that two social processes have become crucial for future generations of young people. On the one hand their contestation of the old and of current political processes will provide further social and cultural change. On the other hand, the failing multi-ethnic melting pot will make different groups into re-inventors of traditions. As a result, the past ethnic philosophies and localized political systems will be perceived as important markers of African ethnicity, and necessary markers for the future of African democracies, multi-ethnic states and cultural worlds of mixed temporalities.

Once again I would suggest that young Africans are caught in a generational problem. They want to assume a more globalized way of thinking and acting, while their contestation of current political developments makes them appreciate their own localized traditional backgrounds, the language they speak, and the differences they feel much more. The youth in Africa show different feelings than those shown by older politicians and leaders when they were young. Those older politicians grew up in the colonial and post-colonial struggle of international recognition and cultural in(dependence).

Modernity requires the invention and re-invention of tradition (Hobsbawm and Ranger 1983). However, tradition is understood not as a fossilised and never changing set of practices and rules, but portrayed 'as the expression of a meaningful life style to which pastoralists remain committed – a concept that yields guiding principles when men and women are faced with uncertainty' (Spencer 1998: 2). Thus, in the case of the Waso Boorana of Kenya, the uncertainty of an impoverished pastoralism made them reinvent their economic and symbolic pastoral world. Those who are older now were the younger Boorana who through community deliberations and their own habitual responses to national policies and the environment made it possible.

The 'problem of generations' for the researcher is not only how to understand different perceptions of social realities within a given 'ethnographic present', but also how to continue trying to understand social realities within changing parameters of generational social interaction. I would make a final suggestion. In order to understand changing social realities complementary studies should be undertaken. If most social studies concentrate on adults and their institutions, such studies of older people need a follow up related to the symbolic re-inventions of cultural understandings provided by younger members of particular societies, particular regions, or particular African countries. In that way, localized studies of age would connect directly with the open possibilities of comparative research, already outlined in the case of the older generations within the social parameters of social constructions and the politics of age and cultural gerontocracies (Aguilar 1998b, 1998c).

Nevertheless, those cultural perceptions of the young and of the old are indeed shaped by social institutions that can be studied with the help of history as well as through the challenges of subjectivism and the 'ethnographic present'. After all, youth is also a social category, framed by particular social institutions [...] directed towards age limits and coming of age, and social acts such as leaving home, forming a family, getting educated and finding a profession' (Fornas 1995: 3).

These are the social processes of identity construction and production that need to be researched and ethnographically assessed in future works related to the social construction of youthfulness in Africa and its localized mechanisms, cultural inventions and cultural adaptations.

ACKNOWLEDGEMENT

Fieldwork in Garba Tulla (Kenya) was conducted from 1987 to 1990, and during 1992. I acknowledge the support of the Society of the Divine Word (SVD), the staff of the Garba Tulla Catholic Mission, and the School of Oriental and African Studies (SOAS London), institution that gave me an Additional Fieldwork Award to help fieldwork during 1992.

References

Aguilar, Mario I. 1995. 'African Conversion from a World Religion: Religious Diversification by the Waso Boorana of Kenya', *Africa: Journal of the International African Institute* 64 (4): 525-544.

———. 1996a. 'Keeping the "Peace of the Waso Boorana": Becoming Oromo Through Religious Diversification', in P.T.W. Baxter, J. Hultin and A. Triulzi, eds., *Being and Becoming Oromo: Historical and Anthropological Enquiries*. Uppsala: Nordiska Afrikainstitutet and Lawrenceville, N.J.: The Red Sea Press.

———. 1996b. 'Writing Biographies of Boorana: Social Histories at the Time of Kenya's Independence', *History in Africa* 23: 351-367.

———. 1998a. *Being Oromo in Kenya*. Trenton, N.J.: Africa World Press.

———. 1998b. 'Introduction: Gerontocratic, Aesthetic and Political Models of Age', in Mario I. Aguilar, ed., *The Politics of Age and Gerontocracy in Africa: Ethnographies of the Past & Memories of the Present*. Trenton, N.J.: Africa World Press.

———. 1998c. 'Reinventing *Gada*: Generational Knowledge in Boorana', in Mario I. Aguilar, ed., *The Politics of Age and Gerontocracy in Africa: Ethnographies of the Past & Memories of the Present*. Trenton, N.J.: Africa World Press.

———. 1999a. 'Pastoral Memories, Memorials and Imaginations in the Postcoloniality of East Africa', *Anthropos* 94 (1-3): 149-161.

———. 1999b. 'Localised Kin and Globalised Friends: Religious Modernity and the 'Educated Self' in East Africa', in S. Bell and S. Coleman, eds., *The Anthropology of Friendship*. Oxford: Berg, 1999, pp. 169-184.

Bassi, Marco. 1996a. *I Borana: Una Societa Assembleare dell'Etiopia*. Milano: Franco Angeli.

———.1996b. 'Power's Ambiguity or the Political Significance of *Gada*', in P.T.W. Baxter, J. Hultin and A. Triulzi, eds., *Being and Becoming Oromo: Historical and Anthropological Enquiries*. Uppsala: Nordiska Afrikainstitutet and Lawrenceville, N.J.: The Red Sea Press.

Baxter, P.T.W. 1978. 'Boran Age-Sets and Generation-Sets: *Gada*, a Puzzle or a Maze?' in P.T.W. Baxter and U. Almagor, eds., *Age, Generation and Time: Some Features of East African Age Organisations*. London: C. Hurst & Co.

———— and U. Almagor. 1978. 'Introduction', in P.T.W. Baxter and U. Almagor, eds., *Age, Generation and Time: Some Features of East African Age Organisations*. London: C. Hurst & Co.

Bernardi, Bernardo. 1985. *Age Class Systems: Social Institutions and Polities Based on Age*. Cambridge: Cambridge University Press.

Birch de Aguilar, Laurel. 1996. *Inscribing the Mask: Interpretation of Nyau Masks and Ritual Performance among the Chewa of Central Malawi*. Fribourg: Fribourg University Press.

Comaroff, J. and J. Comaroff. 1993. 'Introduction', in J. and J. Comaroff, eds., *Modernity and Its Malcontents: Ritual and Power in Postcolonial Africa*. Chicago and London: The University of Chicago Press.

Dahl, Gudrun. 1979. *Suffering Grass: Subsistence and Society of Waso Borana*. Stockholm: Department of Social Anthropology, University of Stockholm.

Fornas, J. 1995. 'Youth, Culture and Modernity', in J. Fornas and G. Bolin, eds., *Youth Culture In Late Modernity*. London: Sage.

Fratkin, E. 1998. *Ariaal Pastoralists of Kenya: Surviving Drought and Development in Africa's Arid Lands*. London: Allyn and Bacon.

Hareven, T.K. 1982. 'The Life Course and Ageing in Historical Perspective', in T.K. Hareven and K.J. Adams (eds.), *Ageing and Life Course Transitions: An Interdisciplinary Perspective*. New York and London: The Guilford Press.

Hobsbawm, E. and T. Ranger. Eds. 1983. *The Invention of Tradition*. Cambridge: Cambridge University Press.

Hogg, Richard. 1981. 'The Social and Economic Organization of the Boran of Isiolo District, Kenya'. Unpublished Ph.D. Thesis, University of Manchester.

————. 1986. 'The New Pastoralism: Poverty and Dependency in Northern Kenya', *Africa: Journal of the International African Institute* 56: 319-333.

————. 1990. 'The Politics of Changing Property Rights among Isiolo Boran Pastoralists in Northern Kenya', in P.T.W. Baxter and R. Hogg, eds., *Poverty, Property and People: Changing Rights in Property and Problems of Pastoral Development*. Manchester: Department of Social Anthropology and International Development Centre.

Holy, Ladislav. 1990. 'Strategies of Old Age among the Berti of the Sudan', in Paul Spencer, ed., *Anthropology and the Riddle of the*

Sphinx: Paradoxes of Change in the Life Course. London and New York: Routledge.

Jalata, Asafa. Ed. 1998. *Oromo Nationalism and the Ethiopian Discourse: The Search for Freedom and Democracy.* Trenton, N.J.: Africa World Press.

Legesse, A. 1973. *Gada: Three Approaches to the Study of African Society.* New York: The Free Press.

Mannheim, Karl. 'The Problem of Generations', in P. Kecskemeti, ed., *Essays on the Sociology of Knowledge.* London: Routledge and Kegan Paul.

Murphy, W.P. 1980. 'Secret Knowledge as Property and Power in Kpelle Society: Elders versus Youth', *Africa: Journal of the International African Institute* 50 (2): 193-207.

Rea, W.R. 1998. 'Rationalising Culture: Youth, Elites and Masquerade Politics', *Africa: Journal of the International African Institute* 68 (1): 98-117.

Rigby, Peter. 1996. *African Images: Racism and the End of Anthropology.* Oxford: Berg.

Spencer, Paul. 1988. *The Maasai of Matapato: A Study of Rituals of Rebellion.* Manchester: University Press for the International African Institute.

———. 1990. 'The Riddled Course: Theories of Age and Its Transformations', in Paul Spencer, ed., *Anthropology and the Riddle of the Sphinx: Paradoxes of Change in the Life Course.* London and New York: Routledge.

———. 1993. 'Becoming Maasai, Being In Time', in T. Spear and R. Waller, eds., *Being Maasai: Ethnicity & Identity in East Africa.* London: James Currey.

———. 1998. *The Pastoral Continuum: The Marginalization of Tradition in East Africa.* Oxford: Clarendon Press.

Stewart, F.H. 1977. *Fundamentals of Age-Group Systems.* London: Academic Press.

Waller, R. 1993. 'Conclusions', in T. Spear and R. Waller, eds., *Being Maasai: Ethnicity & Identity in East Africa.* London: James Currey.

Woods, P. 1977. *Youth, Generations and Social Class.* Milton Keynes: The Open University Press.

NOTES ON CONTRIBUTORS

Mario I. Aguilar is Director of the Centre for the Study of Religion and Politics at the University of St. Andrews, Scotland. He is the author of several books including *Ministry to Social and Religious Outcasts in Africa* (1995), *Being Oromo in Kenya* (AWP 1998), *The Rwanda Genocide* (1998) and an edited collection *The Politics of Age and Gerontocracy in Africa* (1998).

Laurel Birch Aguilar is a Ph.D. graduate of the School of Oriental and African Studies (SOAS), University of London. She has been an Honorary Lecturer at the University of St. Andrews where she has taught the anthropology of art. She is the author of *Inscribing the Masks* (1996) and several articles. Her work is based on extensive field research in Malawi from 1984 to 1996. Currently she holds a full time position in the University of Edinburgh in development/trusts and foundations.

Thomas Burgess lectures in African history at Brigham Young University. He received his Ph.D. from Indiana University, with a dissertation titled 'Youth and the Revolution: Mobility and Discipline in Zanzibar, 1950-1980'.

Maria G. Cattell is co-author of *Old Age in Global Perspective: Cross-Cultural and National Views* (1994) and author of many articles and book chapters on ageing and the elderly in Kenya, South Africa and sub-Saharan Africa. She is also co-chair of the Commission on Ageing and the Aged of the International Union of Anthropological and Ethnological Sciences.

Julianne E. Freeman teaches courses in anthropology and women's studies at Fort Lewis College in Durango, Colorado. In addition to her research among older Bamana women of Mali she has conducted research on the experience of place and the meaning of home among older men and women in the United States.

Seyoum Y. Hameso is editor of *The Sidama Concern*. He is the author of several books including *Ethnicity and Nationalism in Africa* (Nova Science Publishers 1997), *Ethnicity in Africa: Towards a positive approach* (TSC, 1997), *State, Society and Development in Africa* (1997), and *Ethiopia: Conquest and quest for freedom and democracy* (co-ed. 1997). He has also contributed several book reviews and papers in different journals on post-colonial polity, language, culture, and freedom of information in Africa.

Stella Herzog is a Research Fellow at Brown University, Providence, RI. She completed her Ph.D. at the Department of Anthropology and African Studies Center, Boston University. She has published papers on the relation between traditional cultural symbols, structure and social organization and the promotion of new entrepreneurial activity, particularly the transport sector. Her current interests include religion in Africa, masquerades, women's societies, indigenous educational systems, work associations, unions and migration.

Jennifer Law completed her Ph.D. in Anthropology at the School of Oriental and African Studies (SOAS), University of London. Her research focuses on contemporary art in South Africa and the ways in which artists have responded to issues and debates surrounding democratic nation building and the Truth and Reconciliation hearings. She has published widely on contemporary art in South Africa, including a recent catalogue essay for *Liberated Voices: Contemporary Art from South Africa* (1999) exhibition at the Museum of African Art in New York.

She has co-edited *Divisions and Diversions: The Visual Arts in Post-Apartheid South Africa*.

Théophilos Rifiotis is a professor at the Department of Anthropology of the Federal University of Santa Catarina (Brazil), where he teaches and researches on the topic of domestic violence. He is also co-ordinator of the Laboratory of the Study of Violence (LEVIS) and of the Interdisciplinary Web of Research on Violence (RAIVA).

Bahira Sherif is a cultural anthropologist who conducted field research in Cairo, Egypt. She currently has a joint appointment in the Department of Individual and Family studies and the Department of Anthropology of Delaware University. She has recently published several articles on family issues with respect to Islam as well as the relationship between work and family among urban professional couples in Egypt.

Kathleen R. Smythe is an Assistant Professor of history at Xavier University, Cincinnati, Ohio. She completed her Ph.D. at the University of Wisconsin, and is currently researching and writing on African and missionary relations in southwestern Tanzania. Her recent publications include a chapter in *East African Expressions of Christianity* (1998) and a paper in the *Journal of Religious History* (1999).

INDEX